Wörterbuch der Materialwirtschaft
Dictionary of Materials Management

Deutsch – Englisch
Englisch – Deutsch

Alexandra Morana Lüders

Impressum

Wörterbuch der Materialwirtschaft
© Alexandra M. Lüders
Verlag: Konradin Verlag
Robert Kohlhammer GmbH, Leinfelden
Druck: Konradin Druck, Leinfelden
ISBN Nr. 3-920560-09-4, 2. überarbeitete
Auflage 1998

Danksagung

Das vorliegende Wörterbuch der Logistik sei den Mitarbeitern des Bundesverbandes Einkauf, Materialwirtschaft und Logistik e.V. gewidmet, die mich bei meiner Arbeit stets unterstützt haben. Besonderer Dank gilt Manfred Lensing, der mich zur Ausarbeitung dieses Wörterbuches ermutigt hat und immer bereit war, fachliche Fragen mit mir zu diskutieren. Weiterhin möchte ich Steve Drake für unermüdliche Hilfe beim Recherchieren und Selektieren in England danken.

Ganz besonders danke ich Michael Matthes für seine Kompetenz, Kreativität und Geduld beim Entwickeln und Programmieren der PC-Version des Wörterbuches.

Und meiner Mutter und meinem Vater – für alles.

Vorwort

„Purchasing and Materials Management going international" ist ein Konzept, das in den kommenden Jahren zweifellos weiter an Bedeutung zunehmen wird. In immer mehr Unternehmen wächst das Bewußtsein dafür, daß durch kluge Beschaffung in internationalen Märkten erhebliche Wettbewerbsvorteile erlangt werden können, die für die Sicherung von Unternehmenserfolgen ausschlaggebend sind.

Obwohl die Beschaffung in internationalen Märkten schon seit Jahren ein fester Bestandteil des Beschaffungsalltags ist, wird sie in Zukunft noch höhere Anforderungen an Einkäufer und Materialwirtschaftler stellen. Diese müssen sich deshalb noch mehr als zuvor darum bemühen, ihr Wissen auf den neuesten Stand zu bringen. Das Lesen internationaler Fachliteratur und Fachpresse ermöglicht nicht nur den direkten und schnellen Zugriff auf aktuelle Informationen über heimische

Acknowledgements

I would like to dedicate the present Dictionary of Materials Management to the head office of the German Association of Materials Management, Purchasing and Logistics in Frankfurt who have always supported my work. Special acknowledgements are due to Manfred Lensing who encouraged me to write the present dictionary in the first place and was never tired of discussing technical terms with me. Special thanks also to Steve Drake for helping me select and categorize the words and expressions for the dictionary during a long winter in England.

And very special thanks to Michael Matthes for his know-how, creativity and patience when developing and programming the PC version of the present dictionary.

And to my mother and father – for it all.

Preface

Purchasing and Materials Management has undergone dramatic changes in the last few decades, developing from a reactive, relatively limited activity to a strategic corporate function which contributes considerably to a company's competitive success. Moreover, corporate strategies have increasingly focused on international purchasing in recent years. "Purchasing and Materials Management going international" is therefore not only a slogan, it is a concept which helps companies to achieve the competitive advantages which can be gained in international markets.

Although international purchasing has long been part of the everyday routine of purchasers and materials managers, the skills and competences which were required by professionals in the past are not the same as those required today, nor will today's be sufficient in future. It is therefore vital that all those engaged in the field of Purchasing and

und ausländische Beschaffungsmärkte, Zulieferbetriebe und gesetzliche Bestimmungen, sondern bietet darüber hinaus auch die Möglichkeit des Vergleichs mit den Arbeitsweisen und Strategien ausländischer Firmen.

Vor allem aber der persönliche Kontakt zu Geschäftspartnern im Ausland sowie der Erfahrungsaustausch mit Kollegen bei internationalen Fachtagungen, Seminaren und Messen kann zu neuen Denkansätzen und Einsichten führen und Kooperation nachhaltig verbessern.

Dies erfordert jedoch, daß Einkäufer und Materialwirtschaftler auf internationalem Parkett sicher auftreten können und die Welthandelssprache Englisch in hohem Maße beherrschen. Allzuoft reichen allgemeine Englischkenntnisse nicht aus, um Sachverhalte erfolgreich diskutieren und Inhalte und Intentionen effektiv übermitteln zu können.

Das vorliegende *Wörterbuch der Materialwirtschaft* deckt einen großen Teil der einkaufsrelevanten Fachterminologie ab, die sowohl in der Theorie als auch in der Beschaffungspraxis gebraucht wird. Es kann zum Selbststudium als auch als Nachschlagewerk dienen, mit dessen Hilfe Einkäufer und Materialwirtschaftler sich relativ leicht und zeitsparend die für ihren Beruf wichtige englische Fachterminologie aneignen können.

Materials Management persistently try to increase their knowledge and expertise. International magazines and specialist publications provide up-to-date firsthand information on domestic and foreign markets, industries suppliers as well as new laws and regulations. At international conferences and trade fairs and in seminars professionals can discuss topics of mutual concern with colleagues and potential business partners from other countries. Apart from being an important source of information, these are excellent opportunities for establishing and developing business relationships. Foreign language skills are therefore vital in today's business environment.

Although English is the official language of the international business community, it can be very useful to speak another European language, be it Spanish, French or German. While the general English of your business partners is usually quite good, their knowledge of the technical vocabulary and special expressions used in your line of business might be limited. The same, however, applies to all those who have learned German at school and want to use it for business purposes now. Speaking the language of your business partners in Germany, Switzerland and Austria can bring you enormous advantages in negotiations and meetings.

The present *Dictionary of Materials Management* seeks to provide all those engaged in the corporate functions of purchsing, procurement, storing and distribution with the specialist German and English vocabulary and technical terms needed in this field.

Zum Wörterbuch

Das *Wörterbuch der Materialwirtschaft* ist komplett zweisprachig und kann somit nicht

The dictionary

The present dictionary is completely bilingual and can be used by both German and English

nur von deutschen Muttersprachlern, sondern auch von Einkäufern, Logistikern und Materialwirtschaftlern genutzt werden, die sich auf der Basis der englischen Sprache mit der materialwirtschaftlichen Fachterminologie in der deutschen Sprache vertraut machen wollen. In den Kapiteln, die sich mit dem gesprochenen Englisch, englischen Geschäftsbriefen und Definitionen englischer Fachbegriffe befassen, wurde besonderer Wert darauf gelegt, die englische Sprache möglichst so zu gebrauchen, wie ein Muttersprachler es tun würde. Benutzer dieses Wörterbuches werden deshalb feststellen, daß die englische Version eines Satzes bedeutend von der deutschen Version abweichen kann.

Das Wörterverzeichnis ist in einen deutsch-englischen und einen englisch-deutschen Teil unterteilt. Da eine ganze Reihe von Fachbegriffen der Materialwirtschaft aus dem Englischen eingedeutscht worden sind und nicht übersetzt werden, ist im Anhang A eine Auswahl dieser englischen Fachbegriffe erläutert. Die in Anhang B und C aufgeführten Beispielsätze und Musterbriefe sollen Einkäufern und Materialwirtschaftlern, die nicht täglich in englischer Sprache kommunizieren und korrespondieren müssen, in typischen Situationen des Beschaffungsalltags als Hilfestellung dienen. Die praxisnahen Beispiele eignen sich zum schnellen Nachschlagen und Auffrischen. Im Anhang D schießlich werden die Incoterms, gängige Abkürzungen des Wirtschaftsenglischen, sowie wichtige nationale und internationale Einkaufs- und Materialwirtschaftsvereinigungen aufgeführt.

speaking professionals who are interested in learning the specialist vocabulary in the field of Purchasing and Materials Management.

The dictionary includes general economic terms as well as a selection of the technical terms and expressions needed in purchasing, procurement, storing, distribution and recycling. When selecting and translating the technical terms for the present dictionary, the focus was on finding corresponding words and expressions in both languages and on using them in the way native speakers would actually use them.

The dictionary is divided into a German-English and an English-German part. As a number of technical terms in materials management are usually referred to in English and not translated into German, these terms are explained in Appendix A. The following parts, B and C, might be useful for all those purchasers and materials managers who do not regularly conduct business with German-speaking business people: a selection of phrases and letters which are often needed in the purchasing business can be used for self-studies or for refreshing your language skills. Appendix D lists the Incoterms and explains a number of common abbreviations in business English and German. Finally, you will find the addresses of important bodies and organisations in the field of Purchasing and Materials Management.

Inhaltsverzeichnis

Hinweise für den Benutzer

Wörterverzeichnis
A. Deutsch – Englisch
B. Englisch – Deutsch

Anhang
A. Definitionen
Englische Fachbegriffe der
Materialwirtschaft kurz definiert

B. Gesprochenes Englisch –
Hilfestellung im Geschäftsalltag

1. Am Telefon
▷ Einen Anruf machen
▷ Rückrufe
▷ Anrufe annehmen
▷ Nachricht hinterlassen
▷ Termine vereinbaren
▷ Erste Kontaktaufnahme mit neuen Geschäftspartnern
▷ Auskünfte einholen
▷ Treffen vereinbaren
▷ Besondere Vereinbarungen treffen
▷ Termine bestätigen
▷ Termine absagen

2. Konferenzen und Tagungen
▷ Konferenzen vorbereiten
▷ Unterkunft arrangieren

2.2 Verhandeln und diskutieren
▷ Hinweise
▷ Einwürfe
▷ Zweifel anmelden
▷ Verständnis zeigen
▷ Kompromiss vorschlagen
▷ Zu einer Übereinkunft kommen
▷ Ergebnisse zusammenfassen

Seite/Page

Contents

8   **Guide for the user**

11   **Vocabulary**
11   A. German – English
105   B. English – German

   Appendix
192   A. Definitions
192   A short definition of special terms in Purchasing and Materials Management

   B. Spoken Business German for everyday
197   use

197   1. On the phone
197   ▷ Making a phone call
197   ▷ Returning phone calls
197   ▷ Answering phone calls
197   ▷ Leaving a message
197   ▷ Making an appointment
198   ▷ Establishing the first contact with new business partners
198   ▷ Gathering information
198   ▷ Arranging to meet somebody
199   ▷ Special arrangements
199   ▷ Confirming appointments
200   ▷ Cancelling appointments

200   2. Conferences and meetings
200   ▷ Organizing meetings
201   ▷ Arranging for accomodation

201   2.2 Negotiating and discussing
201   ▷ Making a point
201   ▷ Interrupting politely
201   ▷ Disagreement and doubt
202   ▷ Considering other points of view
202   ▷ Suggesting a compromise
202   ▷ Reaching an agreement
202   ▷ Summarizing the results of a meeting

Seite/Page

3. Lieferung und Transport	203	**3. Delivery and transport**	
▷ Lieferung vereinbaren	203	▷ Arranging for delivery	
▷ Anfragen des Spediteurs	203	▷ Carrier asks for details	
▷ Lieferprobleme	204	▷ Delivery problems	
▷ Beschwerden	204	▷ Complaining about deliveries	
▷ Schlechte Qualität	204	▷ Poor quality	
▷ Lieferverspätung	205	▷ Delayed delivery	
▷ Auftragsstorno	205	▷ Cancelling orders	
4. Einkäufer auf einer Messe	205	**4. Purchasing at trade fairs**	
▷ Informationen im Vorfeld einer Messe	205	▷ Information about trade fairs	
▷ Geschäftskontakte knüpfen	205	▷ Establishing contacts	
5. Betriebsbesichtigungen	206	**5. Visitors at your premises**	
▷ Einführungen	206	▷ Making the introductions	
▷ Besichtigung	206	▷ A tour of the site	
C. Geschäftsbriefe	208	**C. Business letters**	
1. Anfragen	208	1. Enquiries	
2. Anfragen beantworten	209	2. Acknowledging enquiries	
3. Auftragserteilung	210	3. Placing orders	
4. Auftragsabwicklung	211	4. Dealing with orders	
5. Verpackung und Transport	212	5. Packing and transport	
6. Lieferbestätigung	212	6. Confirmation of delivery	
7. Beschwerden	213	7. Complaints	
D. Incoterms	215	**D. Incoterms**	
Incoterms und gängige Abkürzungen im Wirtschaftsenglischen	215	Incoterms and explanations of common abbreviations in business	
E. Kontakte	216	**E. Contacts**	
Nationale und internationale Einkaufs- und Materialwirtschaftsverbände	216	National and international associations of purchasing and materials management	

Hinweise für den Benutzer

1. Symbole

Durch einen Schrägstrich verbundene Wörter können synonym gebraucht werden.

In Klammern eingeschlossene können sein:
– die für einen Ausdruck gängige Abkürzung;
– die bei einem Wort oder Ausdruck zu verwendende Präposition;
– das Land, in dem das Wort oder der Ausdruck gebräuchlich sind;
– Worterläuterungen;
– Zusätze:
Beispiel: (first) instalment = sowohl *instalment* als auch *first instalment* heißt *Anzahlung*.
– ein **(s)** als Hinweis, daß der Plural verwendet werden kann.

Alle mit zwei Sternchen versehenen Ausdrücke sind eingedeutschte Fachbegriffe der Materialwirtschaft. Sie werden nicht übersetzt, sondern in Anhang A erläutert.

In Kursivschrift aufgeführte Wörter geben Hinweise auf den Kontext, in dem das jeweilige Wort in der angegebenen Bedeutung zu gebrauchen ist.

Guide for the User

1. Symbols

/ Words divided by a stroke or slash can be used as synonyms.

( ) Words or letters in brackets are either

– common abbreviations for an expression, or
– prepositions to be used with a word or
– explanations, or
– options:
Example: (first) instalment, i. e. *instalment* and *first instalment* both mean *Anzahlung*.

** All expressions marked with two stars are special terms in purchasing and materials management which are usually referred to in English and not translated into German; a definition of these terms is given in chapter C.

Aktien Words written in italics indicate the
Shares meaning of a word or expression in a certain context.

2. Oberbegriffe

Einer Reihe von Wörtern wurde eine Auswahl an gängigen Ausdrücken und Verbkonstruktionen zugeordnet, um dem Benutzer die Suche nach speziellen Ausdrücken zu erleichtern.

Beispiel:
Auftrag — order
– laufender Auftrag — current order, order on hand
– mündlich erteilter Auftrag — oral order
– einen Auftrag bestätigen — to confirm an order
– einen Auftrag einholen — to book an order, to secure an order

2. Word constructions

As a word's meaning often changes substanially according to the context in which it is used, a number of words in the present dictionary are followed by a list of expressions and word constructions which indicate how the word in question is used.

Example:
account — Konto; Einkaufsrechnung
– accounts receivable — Kundenforderungen
– to settle accounts — eine Rechnung begleichen

Wörterverzeichnis
Vocabulary

A.
Deutsch – Englisch
German – English

A

Abarbeitungsfolge	sequence of operations, operating sequence, routing
Abbau	cut, reduction
Abbildungen	illustrations
ABC-Analyse	ABC evaluation analysis
ABC-Klassifikation	ABC classification
Abfall	waste
Abfallmaterial	waste material
Abladen	off-loading
Ablauf	procedure
Ablaufdiagramm	process chart, flow chart
Ablaufplan	schedule
Ablaufplankontrolle	schedule control
Ablaufplanung	sequencing, operation scheduling, process planning
Ablaufterminierung	scheduling sequence
ablehnen	to reject, to refuse
ableiten	to derive, to deduct
Ableitung	derivation
▷ Ableitung von Kostenkurven	derivation of cost curves
Abmahnung	reprimand
Abmessungen	dimensions, measurements
Abnahme	inspection
Abnahmekriterien	acceptance criteria
Abnehmer	customer, consumer; buyer
▷ Abnehmer-Lieferanten-Beziehungen	consumer-supplier relationship
Abordnung	assignment
Abrechnung des Einkaufskommissionärs	account purchases
Abrüstzeit	dismantling time
Abruflieferung	delivery on call
abrufen	to call off
▷ eine Lieferung abrufen	to call off a delivery
Abrufzeiten	call off times
Absatz	sale
▷ Absatz finden	to find a market (for a product)
▷ den Absatz eines Produktes fördern	to promote the sale of a product
▷ befriedigenden Absatz erzielen	to achieve satisfactory sales; to sell well

Abweichung A

Absatz- und Produktionsplan	sales und production plan
Absatzaussichten	prospects for the sale (of a product)
absatzfähig	marketable; saleable
Absatzmarkt	market; outlet
Absatzorganisation	sales organisation
Absatzplanung	sales planning
Absatzprognosen	sales forecast
abschätzen	to estimate, to evaluate
abschicken	to send (off), to dispatch
Abschlagszahlung	progress payment
Abschlußtermin	date closed
abschreiben	write off, to
Abschreibung	depreciation
▷ leistungsbezogene Abschreibung	production unit basis method of depreciation; production method of depreciation; service-output method of depreciation
▷ Abschreibung auf Wiederbeschaffung	replacement method of depreciation
Abschreibungsrate	rate of depreciation
Abschreibungsrechnung	calculation for depreciation
absenden	to dispatch
Absender	consignor
Absendung	dispatch
absetzen	to sell
▷ Leistungen absetzen	to sell goods and services
Absichtserklärung; ggf. gesetzlich bindende schriftliche Verpflichtung, Waren zu einem bestimmten Zeitpunkt abzunehmen	letter of intent (LOI)
Abstimmung	adjustment; agreement
Abteilung	department, division
▷ Organisation einer Abteilung	departamental organisation
Abteilungskosten	departamental expenses
Abteilungstätigkeit	functional activities
abteilungsübergreifend	cross-sectional; interfunctional;
▷ abteilungsübergreifende Teams	interfunctional teams, cross-sectional teams
Abweichung	variance, deviation
▷ genehmigte Abweichung	authorized deviation
▷ von der veranschlagten Materialmenge	material usage variance
▷ mittlere absolute Abweichung	mean absolute derivation (MAD)

A Abweichungsanalyse

Abweichungsanalyse	cost variance analysis
Abwertung	devalutation, depreciation
abwickeln	to handle
Abwicklung	handling, processing
Abwicklungskosten	handling costs, processing costs; cost of transactions
Abwicklungszeit	oder processing times
abziehen	to deduct; to discount
Additive	additives
Änderung	change
▷ technische Änderung	technical alteration, engineering change
Änderungsantrag	engineering change application
Änderungsgeschichte	engineering change history, alteration history, product history data (eines Produktes)
Änderungsmitteilung	engineering change notice, alteration notice
Änderungsverfahren	updating procedure
AGBs	general terms and conditons
Akkordarbeit	piece work
Akkordsatz	piece rate
Akkreditiv	Letter of Credit (L/C)
akkumilieren	to accumulate
Aktie	share
Aktiengesellschaft (allg.)	share company
▷ Aktiengesellschaft (BRD/GB)	public limited company (Plc.)
▷ Aktiengesellschaft (USA)	incorporated company (Inc.)
Aktieninhaber/Aktionär	share holder
Aktiva und Passiva	assets and liabilities
Alleinimporteur	sole distributor
Alleinvertreter	sole agent
Amerikanischer Standardkode für den Informationsaustausch (ASCII)	American Standard Code for Information Exchange (ASCII)
Analyse	analysis
Analysewerkzeug	tools of analysis
anbieten	to offer
Anbieter	offeror, supplier
▷ einziger Anbieter	sole source supplier
Andlersche Losgrößenformel	Andler's batchsize formula

Annahme A

Anfahren	start-up, commissioning
Anfahrmannschaft	commissioning team
Anfang	start
Anfangstermin	start date
Anforderung(en)	requirements
Anforderungsbeschreibung	requirements description
Anfrage	enquiry, inquiry; request
Anfrageverfahren	enquiring procedure
Angebot	offer, tender
▷ angefordertes Angebot	quotation
▷ freibleibendes Angebot	offer subject to confirmation
▷ verbindliches Angebot	firm offer
▷ Angebot bei Ausschreibungen	bid
▷ ein Angebot eingehend prüfen	to study an offer
▷ ein Angebot machen/unterbreiten	to quote; to submit an offer; to tender (for)
Angebotsausschreibung	request for proposal (RFP); request for quote (RFQ)
Angebotsauswertung	quotation evaluation
Angebotsempfänger	offeree
Angestellte (Plr.)	staff, personnel, employees
Angestellter (Singl.)	employee
▷ leitender Angestellter	executive
Ankunft	arrival
Ankunftstag	arrival date
Ankunftszeit	time of arrival
▷ planmäßige Ankunftszeit	scheduled time of arrival
Anlage	facility, plant; attachment, enclosure
▷ als Anlage	enclosed, attached
Anlageertrag	return on investment
Anlagen	plants, facilities, installations
Anlagenbau	plant construction; plant erection
Anlagenwirtschaft	facilities management
Anlagevermögen	fixed assets
Anlaufkosten (eines Unternehmens)	cost of launching a new venture
Anlaufphase (eines Projekts)	start-up phase of a project
Anlaufserie	pilot lot; test series
Anlieferung	delivery
Annahme	acceptance
▷ die Annahme von Waren verweigern	to refuse to take delivery of goods; to refuse acceptance of goods

annehmen

annehmen	to accept; *Haltung:* to adopt
Annahmeverzug	delayed acceptance
annoncieren	to advertise
Anordnung, Anwesung	oder
Anordnung, funktionelle	functional layout
Anstrengungen	efforts
Anteil	share
▷ Anteil der Materialkosten	share of materials costs
Antwort	answer, response
Antwortzeit	response time
Anwender	user
Anzahlung	down payment, (first) instalment
Arbeit	work, labour
Arbeiter	worker
▷ angelernter Arbeiter	semi-skilled worker
▷ gelernter Arbeiter	skilled worker
▷ ungelernter Arbeiter	unskilled worker
Arbeitgeber	employer
Arbeitgeberpolitik	management policies
Arbeitnehmer	employee
Arbeitsablaufsteuerung	process control
Arbeitsanweisung	instruction; instruction sheet
Arbeitseinstellung	stoppage
Arbeitsgang	routing, operation
▷ alternativer Arbeitsgang	alternate routing, alternate operation
arbeitsintensiv	labour-intensive
Arbeitskräfte	labour, manpower
Arbeitskräftebedarf	manpower requirements
Arbeitskräftemangel	labour shortages
Arbeitnehmerüberlassung	manpower provision, hiring of personnel
Arbeitsanweisungen	work instruction
Arbeitsauslastung	work load
Arbeitserlaubnis	work permit
Arbeitskleidung	work clothing
Arbeitsplan	process sheet
Arbeitsplatzbeschreibung	job description
Arbeitsteilung	division of labour
Artikel	article
▷ Artikel der höheren Dispositionsstufe	parent item

Auftragserfüllung

▷ ein Artikel geht aus	to run out of an article
Artikelnummer	article/item/product/stock number
Artikeltyp	part type
Aufgabe	task
▷ arbeitsintensive Arbeiten ausführen	to carry out labour-intensive tasks
▷ Aufgaben verteilen	to delegate duties
Aufgabenverteilung	allocation/delegation of work responsibilities
aufheben	to lift, to remove
▷ Einschränkungen aufheben	to lift restrictions
Aufhebungsvertrag	cancellation contract
Auflisten	listing
Aufschläge	additional charges
Aufsichtsrat	supervisory board
Aufstellung	list, plan; schedule
Auftrag	order
▷ in Arbeit befindlicher Auftrag	work in process (WIP)
▷ ausgelieferter Auftrag	shipped order
▷ laufender Auftrag	current order, order on hand
▷ mündlich erteilter Auftrag	oral order
▷ einen Auftrag bestätigen	to confirm an order
▷ einen Auftrag einholen	to book an order; to secure an order
▷ einen Auftrag ausführen	to carry out/to execute/to enter an order, to fill/to meet an order
▷ einen Auftrag außer Haus geben	to subcontract
▷ einen Auftrag stornieren	to cancel an order
Auftrag mit Pauschalfestpreis	contract
Auftragsabwicklung	project execution, project handling
Auftragabwicklungszeit	contract period
Auftragsbearbeitungszeit	order processing time
Auftragsbestätigung	acknowledgement/confirmation of order
Auftragsbestand	orders in hand, order backlog
▷ eingefrorener Auftragsbestand	frozen order stock
auftragsbezogene Fertigung	production to order
auftragsbezogenes QS-Handbuch	contract-specific QA manual
Auftragsbuch	order book, order register
Auftragsdurchlaufzeiten	order processing times
Auftragseingang	incoming orders
Auftragseinplanung	Order Scheduling
▷ Auftragseinplanung je Maschine	shop planning
Auftragserfüllung	execution of an order

A Auftragserteilung

Auftragserteilung	placing of orders, order placement
▷ Auftragserteilung in konstanten Intervallen	periodic ordering
Auftragsfertigung	job order production
Auftragskoordinator	projector coordinator
Auftragskostenermittlung	job costing; job order costing
Auftragsmenge	order quantity
▷ Auftragsmenge in festen Intervallen	periodic order quantity
▷ wirtschaftliche Auftragsmenge	optimum order quantity
Auftragsnetz	order network
Auftragsnummer	order number; Order No.
Auftragsorganisationsplan	project organization chart
Auftragsplanung	order planning
Auftragspufferzeit	order slack
Auftragsrückstand	backlog of orders, back orders
Auftragsstornierung	cancellation of orders
Auftragsstrukturplan	work break-down structure
Auftragssystem	order system
▷ periodisches Auftragssystem	periodic order(ing) system
Auftragsteam	project team
Auftragsüberhang	backlog of orders, back orders
Auftragsverbund	joint order
Auftragsvergabe	placing of orders
Auftragswelle	flow of new orders; rush of orders
Auftragszentren	order centers (centres)
Auftragszustand	job status
Aufwand	cost, expense, expenditures
▷ betrieblicher Aufwand	operating costs
Aufwandskonten	expense accounts
Aufwendungen	costs, expenditures
▷ außerordentliche Aufwendungen	extraordinary expenditures
aufzeichnen	to record
Aufzeichnungen	records
Ausbeute	yield
ausbilden	to train
Ausbildung	training; education
▷ am Arbeitsplatz	on the job training
Ausbildungsleiter	training manager
Ausfall	downtime
Ausfallanalyse	failure analysis

Ausweicharbeitsgang

Ausfallkosten	downtime costs
Ausfallzeit	downtime
ausführen	to export; *Arbeiten:* to execute; to implement
▷ Arbeiten ausführen	to carry out/ to implement work
▷ Aufträge ausführen	to fulfil oders
Ausführung	implementation
Ausfuhr	export
Ausfuhrauflagen	export restrictions
Ausgangsstückliste	master bill of material
ausgebildet	qualified, trained
ausgleichen	to balance, to settle
aushandeln	to negotiate
Aushilfspersonal	replacement staff
Ausland, im	in foreign countries; abroad
▷ ausländische Handelszonen	foreign trade zones
▷ ausländische Zulieferer	foreign suppliers
Auslagerung von Prozessen	outsourcing
Auslastung	loading
Auslastungsfaktor	loading factor
Auslastungsgrad	loading rate
Auslieferung	shipping; delivery
Auslieferungsort	shipping point
Ausmaß	extent, scale, scope, volume
Ausrüstung	equipment
Ausrüstungsgüter	equipment (goods)
Ausschreibung	call for tenders
Ausschreibungsfrist	deadline for tenders
Außenhandel	external trade, foreign trade
außertariflich	non-tarif
Außenstände	outstanding accounts
Ausstattung	equipment; fittings
Ausstellung	exhibition
Ausstellungszentrum	exhibition centre
Austauschmaterial	replacement
Ausverkauf	sales
Auswahl	range; assortment; selection
▷ Auswahl einer geeigneten Bezugsquelle	selection of a suitable source of supply
Ausweicharbeitsgang	alternate routing, alternate operation

A Ausweichmaschine

Ausweichmaschine	alternate machine
Ausweichmaterialien	alternative materials
autorisierter Händler	authorised dealer
automatisiert	automatized, automated
▷ komplett automatisiertes Werk	fully automatized plant
▷ automatisiertes Lagerhaltungssystem	automated storage/retrieval system (AS/RS)
Automatisierung	automation

B

Bahnstation	railway station
▷ frei Bahnstation	free (franco) railway station
Bahnversand	dispatch by rail
Balkencode	bar code
▷ Balkencode erkennen	bar coding
Ballen	bale(s)
▷ in Ballen packen	to bale
Band	strap; tape
Bandbreite	range; spectrum
Bankerfüllungsgarantie	guarantee
Bankgarantien	bonds
bar	cash
▷ in bar zahlen	to pay in cash
Bargeld	cash
Bareinkäufe	cash purchases
Barzahlung	cash payment
Basisbestand	base inventory level
Basisindex	base index
Bauarbeiten	civil works
Bauelement	modul, component
▷ elektronisches Bauelement	component
bauen	to build, to construct
Baugruppe	component; subassembly
Baukastenstückliste	one-level bill of material; single-level explosion
Baukonstruktion	civil engineering
Bauliste	assembly list, parts list

Bedarfsabschätzung B

Baureihe	model; series
Baustein	module
Bausteinsystem	building-block system
▷ modulares Bausteinsystem	modular building-block system
Baustelle	job site
Bauteil	component; part
Bau und Montage	construction and erection
Bauwirtschaft	building trade, construction industry
Baukastenprinzip	concept of modular assembly; modular concept; modularity
Bayes'sche Analyse	Bayesian analysis
bearbeiten	to process
Bearbeitung	processing; machining
Bearbeitungsreihenfolge	machining sequence
Bearbeitungsverfahren	processing procedure
▷ Bearbeitungsverfahren in der Fertigung	machining procedure
Bearbeitungsvorschrift	work instruction
Bearbeitungszeit	processing time; lead time, operation time, process time
▷ Bearbeitungszeit an einer Maschine	running time
▷ Bearbeitungszeit für ein Stück pro Arbeitsgang	unit lead time
Bedarf	demand, requirements, need
▷ aktueller Bedarf	current requirements, imminent requirements
▷ alltäglicher Bedarf	day-to-day needs
▷ auftragsbezogener Bedarf	pegged requirements
▷ disponierter Bedarf	planned requirements
▷ dringender Bedarf	urgent need
▷ echter Bedarf	effective demand
▷ gemeinschaftlicher Bedarf	joint demand
▷ mittelbar entstandener Bedarf	dependent demand
▷ möglicher Bedarf	potential demand
▷ täglicher Bedarf	everyday consumption
▷ voraussichtlicher Bedarf	anticipated demand/requirements
▷ zurückgestellter Bedarf	deferred demand
▷ Bedarf an liquiden Mitteln	cash requirements
▷ Bedarf der eigenen Werke	interplant demand
▷ einen Bedarf decken	to cover a demand, to meet a requirement, to satify a need
▷ einen Bedarf befriedigen	to fill a need
▷ einen Bedarf neu ausschreiben	to rebid a requirement
Bedarfsabschätzung	estimation
▷ durch die Geschäftsführung	management estimation

Bedarfsänderung

Bedarfsänderung	requirements alteration; alteration planning
Bedarfsanalyse	demand analysis, need identification
Bedarfsartikel	requisits; necessaries
Bedarfsauslösung	creation of a demand
Bedarfsbefriedigung	satisfaction of demands/ requirements
Bedarfsbeschreibung	requirements definition, requirements specification
Bedarfsbestimmung	demand determination
Bedarfsbündelung	to coordinate/to synchronize demands
Bedarfsdeckung	meeting of requirements, supply of needs, need satisfaction
▷ kostenoptimale Bedarfsdeckung	cost-optimal coverage of demands
Bedarfsdeckungswirtschaft	subsistence economy
Bedarfsentstehung	emergence of a demand
Bedarfsentwicklung	demand trend
Bedarfsermittlung	determination/assessment of a demand
Bedarfsforschung	demand research
Bedarfsgegenstand	commodities, necessaries
bedarfsgerecht	tailored to suit the needs of the market
bedarfsgesteuerte Materialdisposition	material requirements planning (MRP)
Bedarfsgüter	basic commodities, consumer goods, necessaries
Bedarfslücke	demand gap
Bedarfsmaterial	material for a particular order; materials purchased to fill a particular order
Bedarfsmengenkontrolle	requirements control
Bedarfsmengenplanung	materials budgeting; requirements planning, planning of demand volumes
▷ bedarfsgebundene Bedarfsmengenplanung	consumption-fixed planning of demand; usage-based materials budgeting
▷ kurzfristige Bedarfsmengenplanung	short-term demand planning
▷ langfristige Bedarfsmengenplanung	long-term demand planning
▷ qualitative Bedarfsmengenplanung	qualitative demand planning
▷ quantitative Bedarfsmengenplanung	quantitative demand planning

bedarfsorientiert	demand-oriented
▷ bedarfsorientierte Fertigung	demand-oriented production
▷ bedarfsorientierter Material-transport	demand pull
▷ bedarfsorientiertes System	push system
Bedarfsplanung	requirements planning
Bedarfsprognose	demand forecast
Bedarfsrate	demand rate
Bedarfsrechnung	assessment of demands
Bedarfsstruktur	demand structure; preference system
Bedarfstermin	date by which something is required
Bedarfsträger	consumer, customer; user group(s)
▷ firmeninterne Bedarfsträger	in-house user groups
Bedarfsverlagerung	shift in demand
Bedarfswirtschaft	subsistence economy
Bedarfszeitreihe	requirements time series
Bedarfszeitpunkt	need date
Bedarfsziel	demand-covering objective
bedienen	to handle, to operate
Bedienungsanleitung	operation manual
Bedingungen	conditions, terms
▷ Bedingungen ändern	to alter conditions
▷ sich an Bedingungen halten	to adhere to conditions
▷ Bedingungen zustimmen	to agree to conditions
Befähigung	qualification
befördern	to transport, to carry, to convey, to forward
▷ auf dem Landweg befördern	to transport by land
▷ auf dem Luftweg befördern	to transport by air
▷ auf dem Seeweg befördern	to transport by sea
Beförderung	transport, carriage, conveyance
Beförderungseinrichtungen	transport(ation) facilities
befugt	authorized
begleichen	to settle
▷ eine Rechnung begleichen	to settle an account/invoice
begrenzen	to limit, to restrict
Behälter	bin
Behälterkennzeichnung	bin tag
behalten	to keep
Behandlung	treatment
beherrschen	to dominate
beigefügt, beigelegt	enclosed, attached; accompanying

B beilegen

beilegen	to add; to enclose; to settle
▷ eine Beschwerde beilegen	to settle a complaint
▷ Informationsmaterial beilegen	to enclose descriptive literature; to attach information material
Beilegung	settlement
▷ Beilegung einer Beschwerde	settlement/adjustment of complaint
beistellen	to provide materials and/or equipment (usually at customer's cost and expense)
Beistellung	provisioning of materials and/or equipment
Beitrag	contribution
▷ Beiträge leisten	to make contributions
Beiwerk	attachment
Belastung	load (Gewicht); debit (Konten)
▷ finanzielle Belastung	financial burden
▷ Belastung von Maschinen	loading
▷ abgeglichene Belastung von Maschinen	balanced loading
Belastungsausgleich	load leveling
▷ Belastungsausgleich am Montageband	line balancing
Belastungseinheit	work station, work centre
Belastungsgruppe	load centre, machine centre
Belastungshochrechnung	load projection
Belastungsübersicht	load report, load chart
Belegschaft	staff
Belegungsplan	loading plan, layout plan
▷ Belegungsplan von Kapazitäten	loading plan
▷ Belegungsplan von Fläche	layout plan
beliefern	to provide, to supply
▷ Kunden mit Waren beliefern	to supply customers with goods
▷ einen Markt beliefern	to supply a market
Bemühungen	efforts
▷ Bemühungen auf etwas konzentrieren	to focus efforts (on)
Benachrichtigung	notification
Benchmarking**	Benchmarking**
benutzerfreundlich	user friendly
berechnen	to calculate; to charge
berechtigt sein	entitled, to be entitled to
Bereich	area, field
bereitstellen	to provide, to supply; to make ready for use

Beschaffungsgruppe B

▷ bereitgestelltes Material | staged material
Bereitstelliste | picking list; staging list
Bereitstellung | provision(ing), supply
▷ Bereitstellung in der Logistik | kitting
Bereitstellungskosten | material overheads; expenses for maintaining inventory levels
Bericht | report
▷ Bericht über Über-, Unter- oder beschädigte Lieferung | over, short, or damaged report (OS & D report)
▷ Bericht über Verzögerung | delay report
Berichtswesen | reporting
▷ Berichtswesen zur Auftragsabarbeitung | order reporting
beschäftigen | to employ
beschaffen | to buy, to purchase, to procure, to acquire
Beschaffenheit | condition; quality, nature
▷ Beschaffenheit von Waren | nature of goods
Beschaffenheitsangabe | quality description
Beschaffenheitssicherung | quality protection
Beschaffenheitszeugnis | certificate of inspection
Beschaffer | purchaser, purchasing agent, buyer
Beschaffung | procurement, purchasing, acquisition; resourcing

▷ internationale Beschaffung | international purchasing/procurement
▷ klassische Beschaffung | traditional purchasing
▷ strategische Beschaffung | strategical purchasing
▷ Beschaffung bei mehreren Zulieferquellen | multiple source buying
▷ Beschaffung für die lagerlose Fertigung | just-in-time purchasing
▷ Beschaffung für die lagerlose Fertigung bei Sofortbedarf | hand-to-mouth purchasing/buying
Beschaffungsaufgabe | buying task
Beschaffungsbegleitkarte | purchase traveller
Beschaffungsbudget | procurement budget
Beschaffungseinrichtung | procurement facility; purchasing organisation
Beschaffungsermächtigung | procurement authorization
Beschaffungsforschung | procurement research
Beschaffungsfunktion | procurement function
Beschaffungsgruppe | buying centre

B Beschaffungsgüter

Beschaffungsgüter	supply goods
Beschaffungskartell	buying cartel
Beschaffungskosten	cost of acquisition/supplies, procurement costs
Beschaffungskredit	buyer credit
Beschaffungsmanagement	purchasing management
Beschaffungsmarketing	procurement marketing
Beschaffungsmarkt	input market, supply market
Beschaffungsmarktforschung	sourcing, supply market research
Beschaffungsmethoden	purchasing techniques
Beschaffungsnebenkosten	incidental procurement expenses
Beschaffungsplan	buying programme; procurement budget
Beschaffungspolitik	procurement/purchasing policy
Beschaffungspreis	cost price
Beschaffungsproblem	procurement problem
Beschaffungsquelle	buying resource
Beschaffungsstatistik	procurement statistics
Beschaffungsvertrag	procurement contract
Beschaffungsvollzugsplan	detailed procurement planning
Beschaffungsweg	procurement channel
Beschaffungswert	acquisition value
Beschaffungszeit	lead time, purchasing time
▷ Material mit langen Beschaffungszeiten	long lead-time material
Beschaffungszeitpunkt	order point
beschleunigen	to expedite, to accelerate
Beschwerde	complaint
▷ berechtigte Beschwerde	justified complaint
▷ unbegründete Beschwerde	unfounded complaint
▷ eine Beschwerde abwickeln	to handle a complaint
Beschwerdebeilegung	adjustment/settlement of complaint
beseitigen	to dispose (of)
besorgen	to buy, to purchase
Besorgung	acquisition, purchase
besprechen	to negotiate, to discuss
bestätigen	to confirm
Bestätigung	confirmation
▷ schriftliche Bestätigung eines mündlich erteilten Auftrages	written confirmation of an oral order
▷ Bestätigung der Vertragserfüllung	certificate of compliance

Bestellung B

Bestand	stock, store; supplies
▷ spekulativer Bestand	market hedge; option overplanning
▷ überhöhter Bestand	surplus stock
▷ Bestand an unfertigen Erzeugnissen (im Laufe der Produktion)	process stocks
▷ Bestand zum Bestellzeitpunkt	order point stock level
Bestandsabgleich	netting, balancing
Bestandsabwertung	inventory write-off
Bestandsaufwertung	inventory write-up
Bestandsbildung	stocking
▷ spekulative Bestandsbildung	hedging
Bestandskontrolle	stock control
Bestandsmaterial	stock-in-trade
Bestandspolitik	stock policy
Bestandteil	part, component
Bestandsüberwacher	stock analyst
Bestandsveränderung	stock movements, inventory change
bestellen	to order
Bestelldurchlaufzeit	purchasing lead time
Bestellformular	order sheet
Bestellkosten	ordering cost
Bestellmenge	order quantity
▷ feste Bestellmenge	fixed order quantity
▷ wirtschaftliche Bestellmenge	Economic Order Quantity (EOQ)
▷ zusammengefaßte Bestellmenge	batch
Bestellmengenrechnung	order quantity calculation
Bestellpunkt	order point
▷ gleitender Bestellpunkt	floating order point
▷ terminabhängiger Bestellpunkt	time-phased order point (TPOP)
Bestellschein	oder form; purchase requisition
▷ innerhalb eines Unternehmens (Bedarfsträger an Einkauf)	travelling requisition
Bestellschlüssel	ordering key
▷ A-Teile Bestellschlüssel	A-part ordering key
▷ B-Teile Bestellschlüssel	B-part ordering key
▷ C-Teile Bestellschlüssel	C-part ordering key
Bestellschreiben	order letter
Bestellsystem	ordering system
▷ bedarfsorientiertes Bestellsystem	push-type ordering system
▷ verbrauchsorientiertes Bestellsystem	pull-type ordering system
Bestellung	order
▷ frühzeitige Bestellung	early order
▷ Bestellung zur Lagerergänzung	fill-in order

B Bestellzeitpunkt

▷ Bestellung in festen Zeitintervallen | fixed period ordering, fixed interval reorder system

Bestellzeitpunkt | order point
▷ Bestand zum Bestellzeitpunkt | order point stock level
▷ spätester Bestellzeitpunkt | "must order by" date, deadline for placement of order

Bestimmungen | regulations, reglementations, rules
▷ neue Bestimmungen verhängen | to impose new regulations
▷ rechtliche Bestimmungen | legal regulations

Bestimmungsfaktoren | determinants

Bestimmungshafen | port of destination

Bestimmungsland | country of destination

Bestimmungsort | place/point of destination

bestreiten | to deny; to meet
▷ Kosten bestreiten | to meet costs

Beteiligung | share, stake
▷ eine zehnprozentige Beteiligung haben | to have a 10 % stake in a company

Betrag | amount
▷ geschuldeter Betrag | the amount owing
▷ offenstehender Betrag | outstanding amount

Betrieb | company; enterprise; firm; operation
▷ großer Betrieb | large company
▷ kleiner Betrieb | small company
▷ mittelständischer Betrieb | medium-sized company
▷ in Betrieb nehmen | to commission
▷ in Betrieb sein | to be in operation

betrieblich | operational, operating, managerial, corporate
▷ auf betrieblicher Ebene | at operational level
▷ betriebliche Teilaufgabe | (corporate) function

Betriebs- | corporate

Betriebsablauf | operational procedure

Betriebsaktivitäten | operational activities

Betriebsanalyse | operation(al) analysis

Betriebsanforderungen | operating requirements

Betriebsanlage | plant, facility, equipment

Betriebsanlagenwerte | plant assets

Betriebsaufbau | business structure

Betriebsauftrag | production order, shop order, job order, manufacturing order

Betriebsaufwand | operating cost(s)/expenditures; working expenses

Betriebsausrüstung, -ausstattung	industrial equipment
Betriebsdaten	operating data
Betriebsdatenerfassung	operating data collection
Betriebseinheit, industrielle	industrial unit
Betriebsergebnis	operational result(s); corporate/ trading profit
▷ das Betriebsergebnis steigern	to lift earnings
▷ geplantes Betriebsergebnis	targeted (net) income
betriebsfähig	in operative condition
▷ voll betriebsfähig	in fully operative condition
Betriebsführung	industrial management
Betriebsgewinn	operating result; trading profits
Betriebshandbuch	operating manual
Betriebskapital	operating/ working/ circulating capital
Betriebsklima	working environment
Betriebskosten	operating costs/expense/ expenditures; running costs
▷ Betriebskosten pro Einheit	unit working costs
Betriebskostenrechnung	operations costing
Betriebskreislauf	operations cycle
Betriebsleistung	business performance
Betriebsleiter	production manager, head of production
Betriebsmaterial	stock-in-trade; plant supplies; factory supplies
Betriebsmittel	working/circulating capital; operating funds/resources; stock; production equipment and facilities
Betriebsmittelbedarf	resource requirements; working capital requirements
Betriebsoptimum	minimum of average total costs; optimum cost; optimal output
Betriebsordnung	works regulation
Betriebspersonal	operating staff
Betriebsquote	profit ratio
Betriebsrat	works council
Betriebsrendite	return on assets
Betriebsstörung	break in production; breakdown of machinery
Betriebsstoffe	auxiliary material

Betriebsstruktur

Betriebsstruktur
▷ beschaffungsorientierte Betriebsstruktur
▷ produktionsorientierte Betriebsstruktur
▷ vertriebsorientierte Betriebsstruktur

Betriebssystem
Betriebsvereinbarung
beurteilen
Beurteilung von Unterlieferanten
bevollmächtigen
bevorraten

Bevorratung

Bevorratungsquoten
bewerten
Bewertung
bezahlen
beziehen
Beziehungen
▷ innerbetriebliche Beziehungen
Beziehungszahlen

bezüglich
Bezug
▷ Bezug beim Hersteller
Bezugsquelle
▷ Auswahl einer geeigneten Bezugsquelle
▷ einzige Bezugsquelle
Bezugsquellenforschung
▷ strategische Bezugsquellenforschung

billig
Billigimporte
Binnenhandel
Bitte
Blaupause
boomender Markt
Branche
▷ eine Branche beherrschen

corporate structure
supply-oriented corporate structure

manufacturing-oriented corporate structure
distribution-oriented corporate structure

operating system
company agreement
to estimate, to assess
assessment of sub-contractors
to empower/ to authorize a person
to store, to stockpile; to build up stocks

storing, stockpiling; building up of stocks

storage quotas
to evaluate, to assess
evaluation, assessment
to pay; to settle an account
to buy; to get; to obtain
relations, relationship
internal relations
ratios, relatives; relative numbers; index numbers

with reference to, referring to
purchase; *von Aktien:* subscription
direct purchasing
buying resource
selection of a suitable source of supply
sole source
sourcing**
strategic sourcing

cheap
cheap imports
domestic trade
request
blue print
buoyant market
(industrial) sector, sector of industry
to dominate a sector

computergestützt

branchenüblich	something normal/usual in a sector
Brennpunkt	focus
Bringprinzip	push principle
Broschüre	catalogue, leaflet
Brutto	gross
Bruttobedarf	gross requirements
Bruttobedarfsermittlung	gross requirements calculation
Bruttogewicht	gross weight
Bruttogewinn	profit before tax
Bruttonationalprodukt	gross national product (GNP)
Bruttosozialprodukt	gross domestic product (GDP)
Buchhaltungs- und Finanzwesen	accounting
Buchhaltungsrichtlinien, allgemeine	generally accepted accounting principles
Buchwert einer Firma	book value of a company's brand
Budget	budget
Budgetgrenze	budget limit, budget line
Budgetierung	budgeting, i. e. operational planning and financial planning
Budgetrahmen	budget lines
Bummelstreik	go-slow
Business Logistics**	business logistics**
Business Reengineering**	business reengineering**

C

Checkliste	check list
Chefeinkäufer	head of purchasing department; purchasing manager, chief buyer
Chefetage	executive floor, boardroom
Chefkonstrukteur	chief designer; head of construction
Chemieindustrie	chemical industry
circa	approximately, about
Computer	computer
computergesteuert	computer-controlled
computergestützt	computer-aided
▷ computergestützte Fertigung	computer-aided manufacturing (CAM)

C Computerprotokoll

▷ computergestützte Prozeßplanung | computer-aided process planning (CAPP)
▷ computergestützte Qualitätskontrolle | computer-aided inspection and testing
▷ computergestützte technische Entwicklung | computer-aided engineering
Computerprotokoll bei automatisierter Produktion | Manufacturing Automation Protocol (MAP)
Container | container
Containerschiff | containership
Controlling** | controlling**
C-Teile Bestellschlüssel | C-part order key

D

Darlehen | loan, credit
Darstellung | chart, illustration
Datei | file
Daten | data, information, figures
▷ ungenaue Daten | inaccurate data
Datenaustausch | data communication
Datenbank | data base
Dateneingabe | (data) input
▷ Daten in ein System eingeben | to input data into a system
Datenfluß | data flow
Datenflußplan (eines Systems) | system flow chart
Datenübertragung | data transfer
▷ papierlose Datenübertragung | electronic data interchange (EDI)
Datenverarbeitung | data processing
▷ elektronische Datenverarbeitung (EDV) | electronic data processing (EDP)
Dauerauftrag | standing order
decken | to cover
Deckung | cover
Deckungsbeitrag | contribution margin; profit margin
Deckungsbeitragsrechnung | contribution margin costing
Deckungsbestätigung | cover note
Deckungskauf | cancelation of order (in case of non-delivery) and subsequent acquisition

	of goods from another source, with supplier having to pay for additional costs and expenses
delegieren	to delegate
Delkredere	del credere
Design-to-Cost**	design to cost**
Designvorgaben	design input
Devisen	foreign currency, foreign exchange
Dienste, Dienstleistungen	services
▷ Dienstleistungen anbieten	to render services
▷ Dienstleistungen beschaffen	to purchase services
▷ reibungslose Dienste leisten	to render smooth services
▷ auf die Bedürfnisse der Kunden zugeschnittene Dienste leisten	to render services tailored to customers' needs
Dienstleistungsbeurteilung	service rating
Dienstleistungseinkauf	purchasing of services
Diplomingenieur	graduate engineer
Direktor	director
▷ geschäftsführender Direktor	managing director
Diskont	discount
diskontieren	to discount
Disposition	production control, materials planning, material requirements planning
▷ bedarfsgesteuerte Disposition	demand-controlled materials planning
▷ prognosegesteuerte Disposition	forecast-based materials planning
▷ verbrauchsgesteuerte Disposition	material planning by order point technique
Dispositionsstufe	level of explosion; level of product structure
▷ Artikel der höheren Dispositionsstufe	parent item
Dispositionsstufen-Code	explosion level code
Dispositionsüberwachung	materials planning control
Distribution	distribution
Distributionsplanung und -steuerung	distribution planning and management
Distributionsstufen	distribution stages
Dokument	document
Dokumentenakkreditiv	documentary credits
Dokumenteninkasso	documentary collection
Doppelbestellpunktsystem	double order point system

D — Dual Sourcing

Dual Sourcing	dual sourcing
Dumpingpreis	dumping price
Durchsetzen von vertraglichen Ansprüchen bei Nichterfüllung	claim management
Durchführbarkeit	feasibility
▷ Durchführbarkeit von Lösungen	feasibility of solutions
Durchführbarkeitsstudie	feasibility study
durchführen	to implement, to realize; to execute, to perform
Durchführung	implementation, realization; execution
▷ Durchführung von Einkaufszielen	implementation of purchasing objectives
Durchlaufterminierung	manufacturing lead time scheduling
Durchlaufüberwachung	flow control
Durchlaufwirtschaft	throughput economy
Durchlaufzeit	processing time, lead time, throughput time
▷ kumulative Durchlaufzeit	composite lead time
▷ Durchlaufzeit für Wiederbeschaffung	reorder cycle
Durchlaufzeitbestand	lead-time inventory
Durchschnitt, durchschnittlich	average
▷ im Durchschnitt	on average
▷ durchschnittliche Fehlermenge	average outgoing quality level (AOQL)
▷ durchschnittliche Fertigungsqualität	process average
Durchschnittskosten	average costs

E

Ebene	level
▷ dispositive Ebene	tactical level
▷ operative Ebene	operational level
Ecktermin	effective date
Eckwerte	key data, benchmark figures, reference figures
effektiv	effective
▷ effektive Zeit	actual time
effizient	efficient
Effizienz	efficiency

Einkauf E

Effizienzsteigerung	efficiency gains
Eichung	calibration
Eigenkapital	equity capital
Eigentumsnachweis	document of title
Eigentumsübergang	transfer of ownership
Eignung	qualification
Eilauftrag	rush order
Einarbeitungszeit	familiarization time
Einbau	fittings, installation
einbauen	to install, to fit, to build in
einbaufertig	ready for assembly/fitting/installation
Eindeckzeit	coverage time
einfacher Mittelwert	simple mean
einführen	to import
Einführungsrabatt	introductory discount
Einfuhr	import
Einfuhrauflagen	import restrictions
Einfuhrkontingente	import quotas
Eingabe	input
Eingabe-/Ausgabesteuerung	input/output control
Eingang, Eingangsbestätigung	receipt
Eingang-Ausgang-Steuerung	Input-Output Control
Eingangsbericht	receiving report
eingefroren	frozen
Eingruppierung	classification
Einkäufer	(trade) buyer, purchaser; purchasing staff
▷ Einkäufer für die Industrie	industrial buyer
▷ Einkäufer mit Entscheidungskompetenz	purchasing manager, senior buyer
▷ im Ausland ansäßiger Einkäufer	non-resident buyer
▷ ortsansäßiger Einkäufer	resident buyer
▷ Sachbearbeiter im Einkauf	purchasing assistant, junior buyer
Einkäuferkennzeichen	buyer code
Einkäuferschlüssel	buyer code
Einkauf	purchasing, procurement; purchase
▷ Einkauf auf Anzahlung/Raten	hire purchase
▷ dezentralisierter Einkauf	decentralized purchasing
▷ en-gros Einkauf	wholesale purchasing
▷ internationaler Einkauf	international purchasing
▷ klassischer Einkauf	traditional purchasing

E einkaufen

▷ streng zentralisierter Einkauf	rigidly centralized purchasing
▷ strategischer Einkauf	strategical purchasing
▷ unternehmerischer Einkauf	entrepreneurial purchasing
▷ zentralisierter Einkauf	centralized purchasing
▷ Einkauf über den Handel	indirect purchasing
einkaufen	to buy, to purchase, to acquire
Einkaufsabteilung	purchasing/buying department
Einkaufsabweichung	purchase variance
Einkaufsakkreditiv	buying letter of credit
Einkaufsanforderung	purchase requisition
Einkaufsanforderungsschein	purchase requisition form
Einkaufsangebot	purchase tender
Einkaufsauftrag	indent, purchase order (form)
Einkaufsbedingungen	purchasing terms and conditions
Einkaufsbuch	purchase book/journal
Einkaufsdarlehen	loan to finance purchases
Einkaufsermächtigung	purchasing permit
Einkaufsgenehmigung	purchasing authorization, (buying) docket
Einkaufsgesellschaft	purchasing agency
Einkaufsgremium (eines Unternehmens)	buying centre
Einkaufshandbuch	purchasing manual
Einkaufskommissionär	commission buyer
Einkaufskontingent	buying/purchase quota
Einkaufskonto	purchasing account
Einkaufskontrolle	purchasing control
Einkaufskonzentration	concentration of purchasing power
Einkaufsleiter	head of chief buyer, purchasing manager
Einkaufsniederlassung	purchasing branch; purchasing office
Einkaufspersonal	purchasing staff
Einkaufsplanung	purchase planning
Einkaufspreis	first cost; input/original/purchase price, cost price
▷ gezahlter Einkaufspreis	purchase price paid (PPP)
▷ tatsächlicher Einkaufspreis	actual cost price
▷ unter Einkaufspreis beschaffen	to buy below purchase price
▷ zum Einkaufspreis beschaffen	to buy at purchase price
Einkaufspreisvariable	purchase price variance
Einkaufsprovision	buying commission, commission on purchase

Einzelteil E

Einkaufsrabatt	purchase discount
Einkaufsrechnung	account
Einkaufsrechnungspreis	invoice price; invoiced purchase price
Einkaufssachbearbeiter	purchasing agent
Einkaufssteuer	purchase tax
einkaufssteuerfrei	purchase tax free
Einkaufstechniken	purchasing techniques
Einkaufs- und Verkaufsabteilung	buying and sales department
Einkaufsverband	purchasing association, purchasing cooperation
Einkaufsvertreter	buyer, purchaser, purchasing agent
Einkaufsvolumen	purchasing volume
Einkaufswerkzeug	purchasing tools
Einkauf und Materialwirtschaft	purchasing and materials management
Einkommen	income; earnings
Einkommenssteuer	income tax
Einkommensverteilung	income distribution
Einkommenszuwachs	increase in earnings
Einkünfte	income; earnings, revenue
Einmalfertigung	non-repetitive production
Einmalgeschäft	one-off deal
Einrichtezuschlag	set-up allowance
Einrichtung	facility, equipment; installation
Einschränkungen	restrictions
▷ Einschränkungen aufheben	to lift restrictions
Einsickern von Seewasser	seawater seepage
Einstandspreise	purchase/input price
Einstandswert	acquisition cost; cost price
einstellen	to employ; to stop
▷ Produktion einstellen	to stop production
Einstiegspreis	price point
einstufig	single level
Ein- und Verkauf	buying and selling; purchase and sales
Einzelfertigung	job production
Einzelhändler	retailer
Einzelhandel	retail trade
Einzelteil	single part

E Einzelteil-Fälligkeitstermin

Einzelteil-Fälligkeitstermin	single-part due date
Einzelverarbeitung	single processing
Eisenbahn	railway
Eisenbahnverkehr	railway traffic
eisenschaffende Industrie	iron and steel industry
Elektrizitätswirtschaft	electricity industry
elektronisch	electronic
▷ elektronischer Datenaustausch	electronic data interchange (EDI)
▷ elektronischer Transfer von Geldmitteln	electronic funds transfer (EFT)
Elektrotechnik	electronic/electrical engineering
Empfänger	consignee
Empfangsbestätigung	arrival notice
Empfangsschein	counterfoil (of delivery costs)
Endabnahme	final inspection and acceptance
Endbearbeitungszeit	finish lead time
Endmontage	final construction, final assembly
Endmontageplan	final assembly schedule (FAS)
Endverbraucher	final customer
Endprodukt	finished goods; finished product
Energie	power, energy
Energietechnik	power engineering
Energiewirtschaft	power industry
Engpaß	bottleneck
▷ infrastruktureller Engpaß	infrastructural bottleneck
▷ Engpaß-Arbeitsgang	limiting operation
Entlastungsauftrag	subcontracting order
Entnahme	withdrawal
Entnahmedatum	picking date
Entnahmeschein	stock requisition; stores requisition form
Entscheidung	decision
▷ Entscheidung ob Eigenfertigung oder Fremdbezug	make-or-buy decision
Entscheidungsfindungsprozeß	decision-making process
Entscheidungskompetenz	authorization
entscheidungsbefugt sein	to be authorized to make a deal
entsorgen	to dispose of waste; to cleanse
Entsorgung	waste disposal
entwerfen	draft, to

Ersatzteil E

entwickeln	to develop
Entwicklung	development
▷ technische Entwicklung	engineering
▷ computergestützte technische Entwicklung	computer-aided engineering
▷ teamorientierte technische Entwicklung	team design, team engineering
Entwicklungsauftrag	engineering order, design and construction order
Entwicklungsingenieur	design engineer
Entwicklungs- und Konstruktionsabteilung	development and construction function
Entwurf	draft
▷ Zeichnungsentwurf	draft of a drawing
▷ Vertragsentwurf	contract draft
Erfolg	success
Erfolgsfaktoren	success factors
▷ wichtige Erfolgsfaktoren	critical success factors
Erfolgsorientierung	profit orientation
Erfolgsplanung	performance/profit planning
erfordern	to demand, to require
▷ erfordert, erforderlich	required
erfüllen	to execute, to fill, to perform
Ergebnis	result, outcome
Ergiebigkeit	productivity
erhöhen	to increase, to improve
ermächtigen	to empower
Ernährungsindustrie	food processing industry
erreichen	to achieve
errichten	to build, to construct
Ersatz	replacement; substitution
▷ ersatzweise	in substitution, alternate
Ersatzarbeitsplatz	alternate work centre
Ersatzauftrag	replacement order
Ersatzbearbeitungszeit	alternate processing time
Ersatzbelegungszeit	alternate loading time, alternate occupation time
Ersatzmaterialien	alternative material(s)
Ersatzteil	spare part, replacements; service part
▷ Ersatzteilbedarf	spare parts demand
▷ Ersatzteilversorgungsgarantie	guarantee for availability of spare parts

E

Ersatzvornahme	indemnification
erschließen	to develop
ersetzen	to substitute, to replace; to supersede
Erstbestellung	first/initial order; pilot order
Ertrag	yield; output; proceeds, returns; revenue
▷ außerordentliche Erträge	extraordinary revenue
Ertragskraft	earning capacity
Ertragswert	capitalized value
Erzeuger	producer
Erzeugerpreis	producer's price
Erzeugnis	product
erzielen	to achieve
▷ ein Ziel erreichen	to achieve a goal
Export	export
exportieren	to export

F

Fabrik	factory
Fach	area; field; department; subject
Fachkenntnis	professional skills, expertise
Fachkompetenz	competence
fakturieren	to invoice
fällig	due
▷ überfällig	overdue
Fälligkeitsdatum	arrival date, due date
▷ aktuelles Fälligkeitsdatum	current due date
Fallstudien	business case studies
Faltblatt	leaflet
Fehler	mistake, fault
fehlerhaft	faulty, defective
▷ sich als fehlerhaft erweisen	to prove defective
Fehlerliste	fault report
Fehlgewicht	shortage in weight
Fehlmenge	shortage, stockout
▷ durchschnittliche Fehlmenge	average outgoing quality level (AOQL)

Fertigungsplan

Fehlmengenkosten	shortage cost
Feinplanung	finite planning, short-term planning
Feinterminierung	finite scheduling
Fertigerzeugnisse	finished goods/products
Fertigstellungsmenge	completed quantity
▷ gebuchte Fertigstellungsmenge	completed accounting quantity
Fertigteile	finished parts; purchased parts, bought-out components
Fertigung	manufacturing, production
▷ auftragsbezogene Fertigung	production-to-order
▷ bedarfsorientierte Fertigung	demand-oriented production
▷ computergestütze Fertigung	computer-aided manufacturing (CAM)
▷ lagerlose Fertigung	stockless production
▷ maschinelle Fertigung	mechanical production, mechanical manufacture
▷ produktorientierte Fertigung	dedicated production
▷ Fertigung von Teilefamilien	Group Technology, production of part families
Fertigung, Fabrikation	fabrication
Fertigungsablauf	production procedure, operations path
Fertigungsablaufplan	operation chart
Fertigungsanleitung	manufacturing instruction
Fertigungsauftrag	order/job manufacturing; order/job production, production order; shop order
Fertigungsauftragsberichtswesen	manufacturing order reporting; production reporting and status control
Fertigungsbericht	production report
Fertigungsdurchlaufzeit	lead time
Fertigungseinrichtung	production facility
▷ zur Herstellung verschiedener Produkte	blocked operations facility
Fertigungsfeinplanung	finite production planning
Fertigungsfreigabe	production release
Fertigungsgruppe, produktorientierte	Group Technology
Fertigungslos	production batch, production lot
Fertigungsmittel	means of production, production equipment
Fertigungsnest	machining cell
Fertigungsplan	manufacturing data sheet, routing sheet, production sheet

F Fertigungsrückstand

Fertigungsrückstand	backlog of work
Fertigungsschlüssel	production key
Fertigungsspektrum	production range
Fertigungssteuerung	manufacturing control; production control, flow control, production activity control (PAC)
▷ maschinelle Fertigungssteuerung	computerized production control
▷ simultane Fertigungssteuerung	simultaneous production control
▷ zyklische Fertigungssteuerung	cyclical production control
Fertigungssteuerungssystem	production control system
Fertigungsstraße (für Endprodukt)	dedicated production line
Fertigungsstückliste	production bill of material
Fertigungssystem	production system
▷ Fertigungssystem mit zentralem Montageband	single line system
Fertigungstiefe	depth of production; vertical range of manufacture
Fertigungsunterlagen	production documents, production papers
Fertigungsverfahren (Methode)	production method
Fertigungsverfahren (Prozeß)	production process
Fertigungszeit	manufacturing time
▷ kumulative Fertigungszeit	composite manufacturing lead time
Fertigwaren	finished goods, manufactured goods
Fertigwarenlager	stock of finished goods
Festangebot	firm offer
festsetzen	to fix, to evaluate
Finanz-, finanziell	financial
Finanzanlagen	financial assets
Finanzen	finance
finanzieren	to finance
Finanzwesen	finance
finanzwirtschaftliche Kennzahlen	accounting ratios
Firma	company, business; enterprise; firm
▷ im Handelsverzeichnis eingetragene Firma	registered company
▷ renommierte Firma	a reputed/renowned company
firmenintern	in-house
▷ firmeninterne Bedarfsträger	in-house user groups
▷ firmeninterne Parteien	in-house parties
Firmenübernahme	take-over
Firmenzusammenschluß	merger

Frachtbrief **F**

Fischgrätendiagramm	Ishikawa diagram
Fixpreis	fixed price
Flachwagencontainer (Bahn/Lkw)	container on rail/road flatcars (COFC)
Fließband	assemby line
Fließbandarbeit	assembly line work
Fließbandarbeiter	assembly line worker
Fließfertigung, -produktion	flow-line production; flow shop production, assembly line production; continuous production, flow/serial/standardized/ repetitive process production
Fließ- und Prozeßfertigung	continuous process production
Fließverfahren	flow process
Flußdiagramm	block diagram
Flußrate	flow rate
Flußschaubild	flow chart
fördern	to promote; to support
▷ Erdöl fördern	to produce crude oil
Folgeauftrag	follow-up contract/order
Folgekosten	consequential damages
▷ Folgekosten anmelden	to claim consequential damages
fordern	to demand, to call, to claim
Forderung	demand, call, claim
Forderungen	debts, claims
Form	shape; form
▷ Form-folgt-Funktion	form-fit-function
Formalität	formality
Forschung	research
Forschungs- und Entwicklungsabteilung (F + E)	research and development department (R + D)
Fortschreibung	updating
Fortschritt	progress
▷ technischer Fortschritt	technical progress
Fortschrittsbericht	progress report
Fracht	freight
▷ vereinheitlichte Fracht	unitized freight
▷ frachtfrei, Fracht bezahlt	carriage/freight paid
▷ frachtunfrei, Fracht bezahlt Empfänger	carriage forward, freight forward
Frachtbrief	*GB:* consignment note, letter of consignment, *Intern:* bill of lading

F Frachtführer

Frachtführer	carrier
▷ frei Frachtführer	free carrier (FCR)
Frachtgebühren	carriage charges, shipping charges
Frachtkosten	cost of transport(ation); freight cost
Frachttarif	tariff
Frachtvertrag	contract of carriage
frei	free; franco
▷ frei Schiff	free on board (F.O.B)
▷ frei Waggon	free on rail (F.O.R.)
▷ freier Platz (Warteschlange)	slot
▷ freier Werkstattbestand	floor stock
Freihafen	free port
Fremdfertigung	subcontracting; outsourcing
Fremdleistungen	subcontracted supplies and services
Fremdleistungskosten	costs for subcontracted supplies and services
Freihandelszone	free trade zone
Frühdisposition	early ordering
Frühdispositionskredit	early order discount
Führung	leadership; management; conduct
▷ unter der Führung von ...	headed by, lead by
▷ Führung nach Zielvorgaben	management by objectives
Führungsebene, auf	on management level; on managerial level
Führungsgesellschaft	head company
Führungskräfte	manager, managerial staff, executive personnel, executives
funktionell	functional
▷ funktionelle Anordnung	functional layout
Funktionsbudget	functional budget
Funktionsgliederung	functional departamentation
Funktionsorganisation	function-oriented structure
funktionsspezifische Leistung	function-related service
Fusion	merger, amalgamation
fusionieren	to merge; to amalgamate
Fuß (Maßeinheit)	foot (')

G

Garantie	guarantee
▷ Bankgarantie	bank guarantee, bond
▷ Vertragserfüllungsgarantie	guarantee for fulfillment of contract
garantieren	to guarantee
Gebiet	area, field, territory
Gebrauchsgüter	(durable) consumer goods
Gebühr	fee
gefährlich	dangerous, hazardous
Gefahr	danger, hazard
▷ mögliche Gefahren beobachten	to monitor possible threats
Gefahrenübergang	transfer of risk
Gefahrgut	hazardous materials
▷ Umgang mit Gefahrgut	hazardous materials handling
gefroren (nicht mehr änderbar)	frozen
▷ gefrorener Auftrag	frozen order
Gegenangebot	counter-offer
Gegenmaßnahmen	countermeasures
Gehalt	salary
Geheimhaltungsvereinbarungen	secrecy agreement
Geldinvestitionen	capital investment
Geldmittel	funds; money
Gemeinkosten	overheads; overhead costs, general costs
▷ intensive Gemeinkosten	costly overheads
▷ Gemeinkosten pro Produktgruppe	overhead pool
gemeinnützig	not-for-profit, non-profit (making)
▷ gemeinnütziges Unternehmen	not-for-profit organisation; non-profit organisation
Gemeinschaftsunternehmen	joint venture
Genehmigung	permission; authorization
▷ Genehmigung erhalten	to obtain permission/authorization
Generaldirektor	managing director
Generalvertreter	distributor
Gesamt-, gesamt	total
Gesamtbeschaffungskosten	total acquisition cost (TAC)
Gesamteinkommen	total revenue
Gesamthaftung	liability
Gesamtkosten	total cost
▷ kleinste Gesamtkosten	least total cost

G Gesamteinkünfte

Gesamteinkünfte	total revenue
Gesamtmaterialaufwand	total input cost
Gesamtproduktionsplanung	manufacturing resource planing (MRPII)
Gesamtprofit	total profits
Gesamtwirtschaftsanalyse	total value analysis
Geschäft	business, business enterprise; shop
▷ ein Geschäft führen	to conduct/to operate a business
▷ ein Geschäft leiten	to manage a business
Geschäftsabschlüsse	business transactions
Geschäftsbedingungen	terms and conditions of sale
▷ Allgemeine Geschäftsbedingungen (AGB)	general terms and conditions of sale
Geschäftsbericht	business report
Geschäftseinheit	business unit; section; corporate function
geschäftseinheitsspezifisch	section specific
Geschäftsfrau	business woman
Geschäftsführer	manager, managing director
Geschäftsführung	management, management board, board of directors
Geschäftsgebahren	business conduct
Geschäftsgewinn	business profits
▷ Geschäftsgewinne verbessern	to improve/to optimize business profits
Geschäftsjahr	business/financial/fiscal year; accounting/trading year
Geschäftsleitung	management
Geschäftspartner	(business) partner; associate
Geschäftsperson	business person
Geschäftspraxis	business practice
Geschäftsprozesse	business procedures/transactions
Geschäftsreise	business trip
Geschäftsruf	business reputation
Geschäftsumfeld	business environment, business context
Geschäftsvorgang	business operation
▷ einen gesamten Geschäftsvorgang außer Haus geben	to subcontract an entire business operation, to outsource
geschätzt	estimated
Gesellschaft	company, corporation; society
▷ Holdinggesellschaft	holding company

Großhandel

▷ Gesellschaft mit beschränkter Haftung (GmbH)	private limited company under German law
Gesetz(e)	law(s)
gesetzliche Vorschriften	statutory regulations, legal regulations
Gestehungskosten und Gewinnspanne	cost-plus
gesteigert	increased
getaktet	time phased
gewähren	to grant
gewährleisten	warrant, to
Gewährleistung	warranty
Gewährleistungszeit	warranty time
▷ eine Gewährleistungszeit von drei Jahren	a warranty time of three years
Gewalt	force, power
▷ höhere Gewalt	force majeure **; Act of God
Gewerkschaft	trade union
Gewinn	benefit; profit
▷ Gewinne verzeichnen	to record profits, to be in the black
Gewinnrücklage	revenue reserves
Gewinnschwelle	minimum of average total costs; optimum cost; optimal output; break-even point
Gewinnspanne	profit margin
Gewinn- und Verlustrechnung	profit and loss account
Gewinn vor Steuer	pre-tax profits
Girokonto	current account
Gläubiger	creditor
gleitend	floating
▷ gleitende wirtschaftliche Losgröße	least unit cost batchsize
▷ gleitender Bestellpunkt	floating order point
Gliederungszahlen	classification numbers
Global Sourcing	global sourcing
Grobdarstellung	outline
Grobplanung	rough-cut planning; rough planning
gros, en	in bulk
Größe	size, extension; bulk
Großabnehmer	bulk purchaser; large-scale user
Großbestellung	bulk order
Großfertigung	bulk production
Großhändler	distributor, merchant, wholesaler
Großhandel	wholesale

G Großhandelspreis

Großhandelspreis	wholesale price
Großlager	bulk storage
Großlieferant	contractor, main supplier
Großrechner	high-capacity computer(s)
Großserienproduktion	large-scale production, bulk production
Großunternehmen	large enterprise
Grund	reason
▷ aus Gründen, auf die wir keinen Einfluß haben	for reasons beyond our control
Grundbestand	basic stock
Grundkapital	capital stock
Grundstoffe	basic goods/materials; primary products
Grundstoffindustrie	basic goods industry
Gruppenfertigung	team production, group production
Gruppenklassifizierungscode	group classification code
Gültigkeit haben, Anwendung finden	subject, to be subject to
▷ Für diesen Auftrag gelten unsere umseitigen Einkaufsbedingungen	This order is subject to our purchasing terms and conditions overleaf
Güteklasse	quality; product grade
Gütesiegel	cachet
Güterabfertigung	dispatching
▷ zentralisierte Güterabfertigung	centralized dispatching
Gütertarif	goods tariff
Güterumlauf	circulation of goods
Gut, Güter	goods, merchandise
▷ auf dem Transportweg befindliches Gut	goods in transit
▷ beschädigtes Gut	damaged goods
▷ gelagertes Gut	goods in stock
▷ materielles Gut	physical asset
▷ sperriges Gut	bulky goods
▷ verderbliches Gut	perishable goods
▷ versandbereites Gut	goods ready for dispatch
▷ zerbrechliches Gut	fragile goods
Guthaben	credit
Gutschrift	credit note

H

Haben	credit, assets
Händler	dealer, agent, merchant
Händlerrabatt	trade discount
Haftung	liability
▷ Haftung des Frachtführers	carrier's liability
Halbfabrikate/Halbfertig-erzeugnisse/Halbfertigwaren	semi-fabricated/semi-finished products; goods in process
Halbzeug	pre-material
halten	to hold, to keep
Handbuch	manual
▷ für innerbetriebliche Abläufe	procedure manual
Handel	commerce, tarde; merchant
Handelsartikel	commodity
Handelsgesellschaft, offene (USA)	joint-stock company
Handelsgut	merchandise
Handelsmarke	trade mark
Handelsmesse	trade fair, trade show; exhibition
Handelsunternehmen	trading enterprise, commercial enterprise
Handelsvertreter	commercial agent
Handelsware	merchandise
Handhabung	handling, commissioning
Hauptproduktionsplan	mater production schedule (MPS)
Hauptvertragsnehmer	main contractor
Hauptverwaltung	head office, main office; headquarters
Hauptzielgruppe	main target group
Havarie	damage
Havariezertifikat	survey report
herrschen	to dominate
herstellen	to manufacture, to produce
Hersteller	manufacturer, producer
▷ Herstellerbestand beim Kunden	consigned stock
Herstellung	manufacture, manufacturing, production
Herstellungskosten	factory cost, production costs
Heutelinie	today's status line

H Hilfs- und Betriebsstoffe

Hilfs- und Betriebsstoffe	auxiliaries, materials and supplies; auxiliary material, indirect material
Hilfsmittel	general stores
Hochrechnung	projection
Höchstgrenze	ceiling
Holding Gesellschaft	holding company
Holprinzip	pull principle

I

Import	import
Importeur	importer
importieren	to import
Importauflagen	import restrictions
Importkontingent	import quota
Inbetriebnahme einer Maschine	putting a machine into operation
Indexzahlen	index numbers
indirekt	indirect
Indossament	endorsement
indossieren	to endorse
Industrie	industry
▷ eisenschaffende Industrie	iron and steel industry
▷ eisenverarbeitende Industrie	ironworking industry
▷ verarbeitende Industrie	manufacturing (industry), process industry
Industrieerzeugnisse	industrial products
Industriegebiet	industrial zone
Industriegelände	industrial properties
industriell	industrial
▷ industrielle Betriebseinheit	industrial unit
Industrienorm	standard industrial classification (SIC)
Industrieunternehmen	industrial enterprise
Industriezweig	sector/segment of industry; industry
▷ arbeitsintensive Industriezweige	labour-intensive industries
▷ materialintensive Industriezweige	materials intensive industries
▷ überholte Industriezweige	old-type industries; obsolete industries

Information(en)	information
Informationswege	information channels
Inkrafttreten (eines Vertrages)	effective date (of a contract)
Inland	at home; domestic
▷ im In- und Ausland	at home and abroad
Inlandsabsatz	domestic sales
Inlandsmarkt	home market, domestic market
innerbetrieblich	internal; in-company; in-plant
▷ innerbetriebliche Verbraucher	internal customers
Inselfertigung	group technology
inserieren	to advertise
Installation	installation
installieren	to install, to fit, to build in
Instandhaltung	maintenance
Instandsetzung bei Ausfall	breakdown maintenance
integrieren	to integrate
▷ integrierte Materialwirtschaft	integrated materials management
▷ integriertes Fertigungssteuerungssystem	integrated production control system
Integration	integration
Interdependenz	interdependence
interdisziplinär	multi-disciplinary; multi-functional
▷ interdisziplinäre Teams	multi-disciplinary teams
intern	internal
▷ interne Transportkosten	internal handling cost
▷ interne Rüstzeit	internal setup time
international	international
▷ internationale Beschaffung	international purchasing
▷ internationale Märkte	international markets
Inventur	to take stock
investieren	to invest
Investitionen	investment
Investitionsgüter	capital goods
Investitionsgüterindustrie	capital goods industry
Investitionskosten	capital cost
Investor	investor
Ist-Bestand	actual stock(s) on hand
Ist-Gemeinkosten	current overheads
Ist-Kapazität	actual capacity
Ist-Kosten	actual cost (s)
Ist-Kostenkalkulation	actual cost calculation

Ist-Kostenrechnung

Ist-Kostenrechnung	actual cost system
Ist-Leistung	actual performance
Ist-Wert	actual value
Ist-Zeit	actual time

J

jährlich	annual
Jahresbedarf	annual requirements
Jahresbericht	annual report
Jahresfehlbetrag	loss for year
Jahresprüfung	annual review
Jahresüberschuß	profit for year
Jahresverbrauch	usage per year
▷ voraussichtlicher Jahresverbrauch	projected usage per year
Just-in-Time-Prinzip**	Just-in-Time** principle

K

Kai	quay
▷ ab Kai	ex quay
Kaiübernahmebescheinigung	dock receipt
Kalkulation	calculation
Kapazität	capacity
▷ geschätzte Kapazität	estimated capacity
▷ unbegrenzte Kapazität	infinite capacity
▷ verfügbare Kapazität	available capacity
Kapazitätsabgleich	capacity alignment, capacity levelling
Kapazitätsbedarf	capacity required
Kapazitätsbedarfsrechnung	capacity requirement planning/plan (CRP)
Kapazitätsbelastung	capacity loading
Kapazitätsbelastungsrechnung	capacity load calculation

Kennzeichen K

Kapazitätsfeinplanung	finite capacity planning
Kapazitätsterminierung	capacity scheduling
Kapazitätsverwendungsnachweis	capacity where-used list
Kapital	capital, funds, means
▷ gebundenes Kapital	tied-up funds, tied capital
▷ Kapital beschaffen	to procure capital
▷ Kapital binden	to tie up capital
Kapitalausstattung	capital resources
Kapitalbedarfsrechnung	capital budgeting
Kapitalbeschaffung	procurement of capital
Kapitalbeschaffungskosten	capital procurement costs
Kapitalbindung	capital lockup; capital tie-up
Kapitalfluß	cash flow
Kapitalgesellschaft (GB)	joint-stock company
kapitalintensiv	requiring a large amount of working capital
Kapitalkosten	cost of capital
Kapitalrücklage	capital reserves
Kapitalumschlag	capital turnover; assets turnover
Kapitalwerte	assets
kaputt	broken; broken down
Kassakonto	cash account
Katalog	catalogue
Käufer	buyer, purchaser
▷ auf Rechnung und Gefahr des Käufers	at buyer's risk and expense
Käufermarkt	buyer's market
Kauf	purchase, acquisition
kaufen	to buy, to purchase, to acquire
Kaufkraft	purchasing power, buying capacity
Kaufteil	purchased part
Kaufvertrag	contract of sale
Kennzahlen	ratios, benchmarking figures; variables, benchmarks
▷ betriebswirtschaftliche Kennzahlen	management ratios/benchmarks
▷ finanzwirtschaftliche Kennzahlen	accounting ratios
▷ materialwirtschaftliche Kennzahlen	key data/benchmarks in materials management
Kennzahlenvergleich	key data benchmarking
Kennzeichen	code
▷ Kennzeichen der niedrigsten Dispositionsstufe	low-level code

K Kernarbeitszeit

Kernarbeitszeit	core time
Kernkompetenz	core competence
▷ sich auf seine Kompetenz konzentrieren	to concentrate on one's core competence
Kettenlaufzeit	cumulative lead time; manufacturing lead time, production lead time
Klassifikation, Klassifizierung	classification
klassifizieren	to classify
Kleinbetrieb	small company/enterprise; small-scale operation
Konditionen	terms and conditions
Konkurrenz	competition
▷ starke Konkurrenz	keen/stiff competition
▷ starker Konkurrenz ausgesetzt sein	to face keen competition
Konkurrenzanalyse	competitor analysis
konkurrenzfähig	competitive
Konkurrenzkampf	competition
konkurrieren	to compete
konkurrierend	competitive, competing
Konnossement	bill of lading
▷ reines Bordkonnossement	clean-on-board bill of lading
Konsignationslager	consigned stocks, consigment stock
Konstruktion	design
▷ rechnergestützte Konstruktion	Computer-Aided Design (CAD)
Konstruktionsbüro	design and constructive office
Konstruktionsgemeinkosten	design and constructivion overheads
Konstruktionsstückliste	construction bill of materials
Konsum	consumption
Konsument	consumer, customer
Konsumgüter	consumer goods
Konsumentenverhalten	consumer behaviour
konsumieren	to consume
Kontingent	quota
Konto	account
Kontoauszug	balance sheet, statement
Kontoverkäufe	account sales
Kontrolle	control, audit
▷ effektive Kontrolle von Lieferquellen erzielen	to achieve effective control of supply sources
▷ optimale Materialkontrolle erzielen	to achieve optimum control of materials

Kostenmanagement **K**

Konzepte	concepts
▷ logistische Konzepte	logistical concepts
Konzern	large enterprise; group
Kosten	cost(s); expense(s); charges
▷ beträchtliche Kosten	substantial costs
▷ fixe Kosten	fixed charges/costs
▷ laufende Kosten	running costs
▷ variable Kosten	variable costs
▷ veranschlagte Kosten	projected costs
▷ Kosten je Einheit	cost per piece, cost per unit, unit cost
▷ momentane Kosten je Einheit	current unit cost
▷ Kosten nach Abzug der Steuern	after-tax charges
▷ Kosten abschreiben	to write off costs
▷ für Kosten aufkommen	to meet costs; to pay
▷ Kosten fallen an	costs incur
▷ Kosten so niedrig wie möglich kalkulieren	to cut costs to the bone
▷ Kosten reduzieren	to cut back costs, to reduce costs
▷ Kosten, noch zu erwartende	costs still expected
▷ Kosten, unvorhergesehene	costs, unforseen
▷ Kosten, zu erstattende	costs, reimbursable
▷ Kosten zuordnen	to allocate costs
▷ Kosten einzeln auflisten	to break down prices, to break down costs
kosten	to cost
Kostenangleichung	cost adjustment
Kostenart	type of costs
Kostenaufwand	expenditures
kostenbewußt	cost-conscious
Kostenblock	pool of costs
Kostendämpfung	cost abatement
kostendeckend	cost-covering
Kostendeckungsplan	cost-ratio plan
Kostendeckungspunkt	break-even point
Kostenelastizität, geringe	low cash flow
Kostenengineering	cost engineering
Kostengefüge	cost structure
Kostenkalkulation	calculation of costs
Kostenkurve	cost curve
▷ durchschnittliche Kostenkurven	average cost curves
▷ kurzfristige Kostenkurven	short-run cost curves
▷ langfristige Kostenkurven	long-run cost curves
Kostenmanagement	cost management

K Kosten-Nutzen-Verhältnis

Kosten-Nutzen-Verhältnis	the benefit-cost ratio
Kostenoptimierung	cost improvement
Kostenoptimierungsmethoden	cost improvement techniques
Kostenplanung	cost engineering
Kostenrechnung	cost accounting
Kostenstelle	cost centre
Kostenstruktur	cost structure
Kostenträger	cost unit
▷ Kostenträger Produkt	product unit
Kostenvoranschlag	estimate; quote
Kostenvorgaben	target standard costs
kostenwirksam	cost effective
kostspielig	costly, expensive
Kraft	power, effect
▷ in Kraft treten	to take effect, to come into effect
Kredit	credit, loan
▷ kurzfristiger Kredit	short-term credit
▷ langfristiger Kredit	long-term credit
▷ mittelfristiger Kredit	medium-term credit
▷ unbeschränkter Kredit	unlimited credit
Kreditbrief	credit letter
Kreditgrenze, Kreditlinie	line of credit
Kreislauf	cycle; circular flow
▷ Kreislauf der Wirtschaft	trade cycle
Kreislaufmaterial	recycled auxiliary material
Kreislaufwirtschaft	circular-flow economy
Kriterien (Plr.)	criteria (pr.)
Kriterium (Sing.)	criterion (sing.)
kritisch	critical
▷ Kritischer-Pfad-Methode	Critical Path Method (CPM)
Kühlhaus	cold store
kürzen	to cut back, to reduce
kürzeste Operationszeit Regel (KOZ)	least processing time rule
Kürzung	cut, cut back, reduction
kumulativ, kumuliert	cumulative
kumulieren	to accumulate
Kunde	customer
▷ möglicher Kunde	potential/prospective customer
▷ Kunden anziehen	to attract customers
▷ einem Kunden entgegenkommen	to accomodate a customer
Kundenauftragsabwicklungssystem	customer order servicing system

Lagerarbeiter L

Kundenauftragsdisposition	customer order planning and scheduling
Kundendienst	after-sales service; customer service
Kundenforderungen	accounts receivable
Kundennutzen	consumer benefits
kundenorientiert	customer-centred; customer-oriented
Kundenstamm	customer base
▷ Kundenstamm erweitern	to increase the customer base
Kundentreue	consumer loyalty
Kundenzufriedenheit	customer satisfaction
Kundschaft	clientele, customers
▷ anspruchsvolle Kundschaft	sophisticated/demanding clientele
Kurzarbeit	short time; undertime;
▷ kurzarbeiten	to be working short time/undertime
Kurzarbeit fahren	to be working short time
kurzfristig	at short notice

L

Ladung	shipment
Ladungspartie	truckload lot (TL)
Läger	stocks; inventories, inventories held in storage
Lager	storage, store; warehouse, inventories, stocks, inventories held in storage
▷ ab Lager	ex warehouse
▷ auf Lager	in stock
▷ günstig am Markt gelegenes Lager	market positioned warehouse
▷ produktionsnahes Lager	point-of-use storage
▷ Lager abbauen	to cut stocks; to liquidate stocks; to destock
▷ Lager aufnehmen	to take inventory
▷ Lager klein halten	to keep stocks trim; to understock
▷ Lager räumen	to clear stocks
▷ Lager wiederauffüllen	to replenish stocks
Lagerabbau	inventory cutting; stock reduction
Lagerabgangsrate	rate of usage
Lageranteil	ratio of inventory level
Lagerarbeiter	stock clerk, stockkeeper

L Lagerauftrag

Lagerauftrag	stock order
Lagerauslastung	utilization of storage capacity
Lagerautomatisierung	automation of inventory processes
Lagerbehälter	storage bin, storage container
Lagerbehandlung	handling of goods in storage
Lagerbestände	inventories, inventories held in storage
▷ Lagerbestände abbauen	to cut/to run down/to trim inventories
▷ Lagerbestände aufnehmen	to compile inventory
▷ Lagerbestände gehen zu Neige	stocks are running low/short
▷ Lagerbestände niedrig halten	to keep stock levels down; to keep stocks trim
▷ Lagerbestände senken, reduzieren	to reduce/to liquidate inventories; to destock
▷ Lagerbestände sind erschöpft	stocks are depleted
▷ Lagerbestände wiederauffüllen	to replenish/to refill stocks
▷ zu hohe Lagerbestände haben	to overstock
▷ zu kleine Lagerbestände haben	to understock; to have insufficient stocks of items
Lagerbestand	inventory, inventory level; regular stock on hand
▷ eingefrorener Lagerbestand	frozen inventory
▷ Lagerbestand nach Losgröße	lot-size inventory
Lagerbestandsaufstellung	inventory status report
Lagerbestandsbericht	stock status report
Lagerbestandsbewertung	inventory valuation/costing
Lagerbestandsfortschreibung	updating of inventory
Lagerbestandsführung	inventory accounting, inventory control
Lagerbestandsvergleich	comparison of inventory movements
Lagerbewegung	inventory/stock movement
Lagerbuch	stock book; stock ledger
Lagerbuchführung	inventory/stock accounting; inventory record file
Lagerbuchhaltungsabteilung	inventory accounting department
Lagerbudget	inventory budget
Lagerdaten	inventory data; inventory figures
Lagerdauer	period of storage
Lagerdisposition	stock ordering; stockbuilding (activity)
Lagereingänge	inventory additions
Lagereinrichtungen	storage facilities

Lagerkapazität

Lagerentnahme	withdrawal from stock
Lagerfach	storage bin, storage slot
Lagerfachkarte	bin tag
lagerfähig	fit for storage
Lagerfähigkeit	storage life
Lagerfertigung	production to stock; make-to-stock production
Lagerfertigungsprodukt	made-to-stock product
Lagerfinanzierung	inventory financing
Lagerfunktion	inventory function
Lagergebäude	warehouse, storehouse; storage building
Lagergebühren	storage charges
Lagergeld	warehouse charges, storage charges
Lagergeschäft	procurement to stock up inventory; warehousing business
Lagergewinne	inventory profits
Lagergröße	inventory level, stock level
Lagerhalle	storage building
Lagerhaltung	stockpiling, storing; warehousing
▷ Lagerhaltung nach ABC-Klassifikation	ABC inventory control; split inventory method
▷ Lagerhaltung mit konstanten Beständen	cycle system of constant inventory control
Lagerhaltungsabteilung	stores department
Lagerhaltungsanalyse	inventory analysis
Lagerhaltungskosten	inventory carrying costs; warehouse/storage charges
Lagerhaltungsmethode	inventory method
Lagerhaltungsmodell	inventory model
Lagerhaltungsplanung	inventory scheduling
Lagerhaltungsschwankungen	inventory fluctuations
Lagerhaltungssystem	inventory control system
Lagerhaltungszyklus	inventory cycle
Lagerhaus	warehouse, storage building
Lagerhüter	inactive inventory item
Lagerinvestitionen	inventory investment
Lagerist	stockkeeper, storekeeper, stock clerk
Lagerjournal	inventory journal
Lagerkapazität	storage capacity

L Lagerkarte

Lagerkarte	inventory card; stock record card
Lagerkartei	inventory records
Lagerkennzahlen	inventory turnover ratios
Lagerkonto	inventory (assets) account
Lagerkontrolle	inventory audit
lagerlos	stockless
▷ lagerlose Fertigung	stockless production
Lagermaterial	stock on hand
Lagermodell	procurement inventory model
lagern	to stock, to store, to warehouse
Lagerort	stock location
Lagerortkarte	bin tag
Lagerpersonal	inventory clerks
Lagerplanungsmodel	inventory planning model
Lagerraum	storage area/space
▷ Lagerraum bereitstellen	to provide storage space
Lagerreduzierung	destocking
Lagerrisiko	storage risk
Lagerschein	warehouse receipt, warehouse certificate
Lagerspesen	storage charges
Lagerstatistik	inventory statistics
Lagerüberschüsse	excess inventories of items
Lagerüberwachung	monitoring the status of inventory
Lagerumschlag	inventory/stock turnover; inventory-sales ratio; stockturn
Lagerumschlagsrate	rate of inventory turnover
Lagerung	storage, stockkeeping
▷ Lagerung im Kühlhaus	cold storage
▷ Lagerung von Hilfs- und Betriebsstoffen	storage of materials and supplies
Lagerungskosten	storage expenses, storage costs
Lagerverluste	inventory losses
Lagervertrag	warehousing contract
Lagerverwaltung	inventory management
Lagerwirtschaft	inventory control; inventory management
Lagerzeit	(average) inventory period
Lagerzugänge	additions to stock; inventory additions; inventory receipts
Lagerzugangsliste	stock receipts register

Leistungserfüllung L

Landweg, auf dem	by land
▷ auf dem Landweg befördern	to transport by land
Last	load
last-in, first-out (LIFO)	last in, first out (LIFO)
Lastschrift	debit note
Lastschriftanzeige für Versandauftrag	shipping order debit note
Lean Management	lean management
Leck	leak
lecken	to leak
Leerfahrt eines Behälters	dead head
Leerlaufzeit	idle time
▷ Leerlaufzeit (Montageband)	unassigned time
leisten	to perform
Leistung	performance, effort, service
▷ Leistung (Ausführung einer Arbeit)	efficiency
▷ außerordentliche Leistung	outstanding performance
▷ Leistung durch Dritte	performance by a third party
▷ Leistung und Gegenleistung	performance and counter-performance
▷ Leistungen absetzen	to sell goods and services
▷ Leistungen anbieten	to offer services
▷ Leistungen erbringen	to render services, to effect performances
Leistungsabgabe	output
leistungsabhängig	output-related
▷ leistungsabhängige Kosten	output-related costs
Leistungsbeschreibung	performance description
Leistungsbeurteilung	efficiency/service/performance rating; output evaluation
▷ Leistungsbeurteilung des Personals	personnel rating
Leistungsbewertung	efficiency rating; output evaluation
▷ Leistungsbewertung nach Einzelfaktoren	factor rating
Leistungsbewertungsschema	performance measurement system
Leistungsbudget	performance budget
Leistungscenter	performance centre; service centre
Leistungsdaten	performance figures
Leistungsdefizit	performance deficit
Leistungseinheit	output/service unit
Leistungserfüllung	performance, fulfillment of contractual stipulations
▷ Unmöglichkeit der Leistungserfüllung	impossibility of performance, non-fulfillment of contract

L — Leistungserstellung

Leistungserstellung	production/creation/output of goods and services
Leistungsfähigkeit	efficiency, operative capability; productive capacity
Leistungsfaktoren	factors of production; productive resources; inputs
Leistungsgrad	performing level; performance efficiency; performance evaluation; efficiency rate, performance factor
Leistungsgrenze	output maximum; limit of performance
Leistungskontrolle	performance control
Leistungsmaßstab	standard of performance; performance objective
Leistungsmessung	performance measurement
Leistungsnorm	performance standard
Leistungsniveau	performing level
leistungsorientiert	achievement oriented; output oriented
Leistungspotential	capability of a company
Leistungsprofil	capability profile
Leistungsschau	trade fair, trade exhibition
Leistungssoll	production target
Leistungssteigerung	increase in efficiency; improved performances; efficiency gains
Leistungsstörung	default in performance
Leistungsstrom	flow of goods and services
Leistungsumfang	scope of services
Leistungsverkehr	supplies
Leistungsvolumen	volume of output
Leistungsvorgaben	performance targets/standards
Leistungswettbewerb	competition based on efficiency
Leistungszeit	time of performance
Leistungszentren	performance centres
Leistungsziel	performance objective
Leistungszulage	producitvity bonus
Lieferant	supplier, contractor, subsupplier, subcontractor
Lieferantenanalyse	supplier analysis
Lieferantenauftragsdatei	order file of suppliers
Lieferantenauswahlkriterien	supplier selection criteria

Lieferverzug L

Lieferantenbewertung	supplier assessment, supplier evaluation
Lieferantenbeziehungen	supplier relationships
Lieferantenkonto	supplier account
Lieferbedingungen, Preisstellung	delivery terms
Lieferdatum	delivery date; date of delivery
lieferfähig	serviceable
▷ lieferfähig bleiben	to maintain serviceability
Lieferfähigkeit	service ability, customer service
Lieferflexibilität	flexibility in delivery
Lieferkontrolle	supply control
Lieferkosten	delivery costs/expenses; cost of delivery
Liefermenge	order quantity
Liefermengenliste	bill of batches
liefern	to deliver; to supply; to effect/to execute delivery
Lieferort	place of delivery
Lieferplan	delivery schedule, assembly schedule
Lieferquelle	source of supply
Lieferschein	delivery note/order; bill of delivery; packing slip
Lieferservice	delivery service
Liefertermin	delivery date, due date
▷ geänderter Liefertermin	revised due date, changed delivery date
Liefertreue	faithfulness to meet delivery dates, reliability in delivery
Lieferüberwachung	Output Control
Lieferumfang	scope of supplies
Lieferung	delivery; supply
▷ Lieferung beschleunigen	to expedite delivery
▷ zur sofortigen Lieferung bestellen	to order for immediate/prompt delivery
▷ Lieferung durchführen	to effect/to execute delivery
▷ Lieferung einstellen, aussetzen	to suspend delivery
▷ Lieferung zurückstellen	to postpone delivery
▷ Lieferung auf Abruf	delivery on call
▷ Lieferung in Teilmengen	split delivery
▷ Lieferung frei Längsseite Schiff	delivery free alongside ship (FAS)
Liefervertrag	delivery contract
Lieferverzug	delay in delivery, delayed delivery

L Lieferzeit

▷ in Verzug setzen | to set a final deadline for delivery
Lieferzeit | delivery time, delivery period; time of delivery
▷ Lieferzeit einhalten | to deliver goods within the specified time; to observe delivery dates
Lieferzeitplan | delivery schedule
Liegezeit | idle period
Listenpreis | list price
▷ ein Preisnachlaß auf die Listenpreise | a discount off the list prices
Lizenz | licence
▷ eine Lizenz beantragen | to apply for a licence
▷ eine Lizenz erhalten | to acquire a licence
▷ Lizenzen für ein Produkt erwerben | to license products
▷ Lizenzen für ein Produkt vergeben | to license products
Lizenzgebühr | licence fee
Lizenzvergabe | licensing
Logistik | logistics
Logistikkonzepte | logistical concepts
logistisch | logistical
▷ logistisches Denken | logistical thinking
Lohn | wages
Lohnkosten | wage costs
▷ starre Lohnkosten | rigid wage costs
Lohnnebenkosten | non-wage costs
Lohnverhandlungen | wage negotiations
Los | batch, lot
Losbildung | batching, batch sizing, lot sizing
lose | loose; *auch:* in bulk
Losfertigung | batch production
Losgröße | lot size, batch size
▷ Standardlosgröße | standard batch quantity (SBQ)
▷ feste Losgröße | fixed batch size
▷ gleitende wirtschaftliche Losgröße | least unit cost batch size
▷ optimale Losgröße | optimum batchsize, optimal batch size
▷ wirtschaftliche Losgröße | economic batch size
Losgrößenbestimmungstechnik | lot sizing; lot sizing techniques
Losmengenabweichung | batch quantity variation
Luftfracht | air freight
Luftweg, auf dem | by air
▷ auf dem Luftweg befördern | to transport by air
Luxusgüter | luxury goods

M

Machbarkeitsstudie	feasibility study
Mängel (ab Werk)	deficiencies
Mängelrüge	complaint about faulty material and workmanship
Make or Buy**	Make or Buy
Manager	manager, director
Mandant	client
Mangel	shortage
▷ Mangel an qualifizierten Arbeitskräften	shortage of qualified labour
Manteltarifvertrag	industry-wide agreement
Marke	brand
Markenname	brand name
Marketing	marketing
Markt	market, input market
▷ einen Markt bearbeiten	to cover a market
▷ einen Markt beliefern	to supply a market
▷ einen Markt für etwas schaffen	to create an outlet (for)
▷ Konkurrenz vom Markt drängen	to force competitors out of a market
Markt- und Kundenversorgung	market supply
Marktanalyse	market analysis
Marktanteil	market share
▷ Marktanteile gewinnen	to gain market shares
Marktbereich	market segment
Marktdynamik	market dynamics
marktfähig	saleable
Marktforschung	market research
Marktführer	market leader
Marktinformationen	market intelligence
Marktnachfrage	demand
Marktnische	market niche
Marktpreis	current price
Marktsättigung	market saturation
Maschine	machine; engine; Plr: equipment
Maschinenausfall	machine breakdown
Maschinenbau	mechanical engineering
Maschinenbauingenieur	mechanical engineer

M Maschinenbelastung

Maschinenbelastung	machine loading, machine load
▷ mit Kapazitätsgrenze	finite machine loading
▷ ohne Kapazitätsgrenze	infinite machine loading
Maschinengruppe	work centre, work place, work station, machine group
Maschinenkapazität	machine capacity
Maschinenstillstandszeit	machine idle time
Maschinenstörung	machine breakdown
Masse	bulk; volume
Massenausgabe	bulk issue
Massengüter	bulk goods
Massenfertigung	mass production
Massenverarbeitung	mass processing
massig	bulky
Maße	dimensions, measurements
Maßeinheit	unit of measure
▷ Maßeinheit im Einkauf	purchasing unit of measure
maßgeschneidert	tailor-made
Maßstab	scale
Material...	materials
Material	material(s)
▷ auftragsgebundenes Material	allocated/assigned/obligated material
▷ bestelltes Material	material on order
▷ bereitgestelltes Material	staged material
▷ bewährtes Material	reliable material
▷ brennbares Material	combustible material
▷ eingehendes Material	incoming material
▷ fehlerhaftes Material	defective material
▷ rollendes Material	rolling stock
▷ veraltetes Material	obsolete material
▷ verarbeitetes Material	processed material, worked material
▷ verwendetes Material	consumed material
▷ zweckgebundenes Material	earmarked material
▷ im Fertigprodukt enthaltenes Material	direct material**
▷ nicht im Fertigprodukt enthaltenes Material	indirect material**
▷ in Verarbeitung befindliches Material	work in progress (WIP)
▷ Material mit langen Beschaffungszeiten	long lead-time material
▷ Material bereitstellen, beistellen	to provide material, to supply material

Materialbeschreibung M

▷ Material gebrauchen, einsetzen	to use/utilize material
▷ Material gemeinsam einsetzen	to pool material
▷ Material liefern	to supply material
Material- und Herstellungs ...	material and workmanship
Material- und Herstellungsmängel	faulty material and workmanship
▷ frei von Material- und Herstellungsmängeln	free from defects in material and workmanship
Materialabfall	spoilage, scrap
Materialabgang	materials withdrawal
Materialanforderung	(stores) materials requisistion
Materialanforderungsschein	materials requisition slip/form; assembly order
Materialangaben	materials specifications
Materialanlieferung	supply of materials
Materialannahme	materials receiving
Materialannahmeschein	receiving slip
Materialannahmestelle	point of receipt
Materialaufwand	material costs/input
Materialaufzeichnungen	material records
Materialausbeute	material yield; materials accounting
Materialausgabe	materials issue; issuing of materials
Materialausgabeschalter	materials issue counter
Materialausgabeschein	stock issue note, stock issue form
Materialbedarf	material needs/requirements
Materialbedarfsplanung	planning of material requirements
Materialbedarfsrechnung	assessment of material requirements
Materialbedarfsvorhersage	forecasting of material requirements
Materialbegleitkarte	shop traveller
Materialbelege	materials records
Materialbereich	materials management function
Materialbereitstellung	material provision, provision(ing) of material(s); supply of material(s)
Materialbereitstellungsplan	supply-of-materials plan
Materialbeschaffenheit	quality of material(s)
Materialbeschaffung	materials purchasing, procurement of materials
Materialbeschaffungsplan	materials purchase budget
Materialbeschaffungspolitik	materials purchasing policy
Materialbeschreibung	specification

M Materialbestand

Materialbestand, -bestände	materials on hand, materials on stock
Materialbestandskarte	bin card
Materialbestandskosten	material accounts
Materialbestandsrechnung	materials status evaluation
Materialbestimmungskarte	order bill of materials
Materialbewegungen	material movements
Materialbezüge	material purchases
Materialbilanz	materials input-output statement
Materialbuchführung	materials accounting
Materialdisposition	inventory planning, materials planning and scheduling
▷ bedarfsgesteuerte Materialdisposition	material requirements planning
Materialdurchfluß	materials throughput
Materialeingänge	incoming materials
▷ Überprüfung der Materialeingänge	inspection of incoming materials
Materialeingang	incoming materials
Materialeingangskontrolle	material delivery verification
Materialeinheit	unit of material
Materialeinkauf	materials purchasing
Materialeinkäufe	material purchases
Materialeinsatz	input
Materialeinsparungen	materials savings, saving of material
Materialeinzelkosten	cost of direct material
Materialempfangsbescheinigung	receiving slip
Materialentnahme	material(s) withdrawal
Materialentnahmeschein	materials order
Materialermüdung	material fatigue
Materialfehler	defect in material, defective material
▷ Material- oder Herstellungsfehler	defective material and workmanship
Materialfluß	material(s) flow; flow of materials
Materialflußanalyse	analysis of materials flows
Materialflußgestaltung	materials flow layout
Materialflußkontrolle	materials flow control
Materialflußkosten	cost of materials flow
Materialflußoptimierung	materials flow optimization
Materialflußtechnik	materials flow methods
Materialgemeinkosten	materials handling overheads; indirect materials

Materialgemeinkostenzuschlag	materials overhead rate
Materialgesamtkosten	material cost
▷ geringst mögliche Materialgesamtkosten	least total material cost
Material(hilfs)stellen	indirect materials centre
materialintensiv	material/resource intensive
Materialkarte	stock ledger card
Materialknappheit	shortage in materials
Materialkontrolle	materials control
Materialkosten	material(s) costs, cost of materials
▷ unmittelbare Materialkosten	direct material(s) costs
▷ wachsende Materialkosten	increased cost of materials
Materialkostendruck	materials cost pressure
Materialkostenermittlung	material costing
Materialkostenplan	material budget; materials used budget
Materialkostenstelle	materials cost centre
Materialkreislauf	materials cycle
Materiallager	materials stock; stock of materials
Materialliste	materials list
Materialmehraufwand	additional material input
Materialmenge	material shortage
Materialmengenabweichung	materials quantity (of usage) variance
Materialmischung	materials mix
Materialnachweis	material accounting
Materialplanung	materials planning
Materialpreis	materials price
Materialpreisabweichung	materials price variance
Materialprüfung	materials testing; inspection of incoming materials
Materialprüfungskosten	expenses of a materials inspection
Materialqualität	quality of material(s)
Materialrückgabeschein	materials return record
Materialschaden	defective material
Materialschein	bill of materials
Materialschwund	wastage
Materialstapel	stockpile
Materialsteuerung	materials control

M Materialtransport

Materialtransport	material(s) handling
▷ bedarfsorientierter Materialtransport	demand pull
▷ innerbetrieblicher Materialtransport	in-plant materials handling
Materialumarbeitung	reprocessing of materials
Materialverarbeitung	processing of materials
Materialverbesserung	improvement of materials
Materialverbrauch	material(s) usage; utilization of materials
Materialverfügbarkeit	availability of materials
Materialverlust	loss of material
Materialverschleiß	wastage
Materialverschwendung	wasting of materials
Materialverwaltung	materials administration
Materialvorrat	material supplies
▷ Materialvorräte gehen zu Neige	supplies are running low
Materialwiederaufbereitung	reprocessing of materials
Materialwirtschaft**	materials management**
Materialwirtschaftscontrolling	controlling in materials management
Materialzugänge	incoming materials
materiell	materials
Matrix	matrix
Matrixstückliste	matrix bill of material
Mehrarbeit	overtime
Mehrfachverwendung	multiple use
Mehrfachverwendungsteil	multiple usage part; common part
Mehrmaschinenbedienung	multiple machine work
mehrstufig	multi-level, multi-stage
Mehrwert	value added
Mehrwertsteuer	value added tax (VAT)
Menge	quantity
▷ saldierte Menge	balanced quantity
▷ unterlieferte Menge	quantity shortage
Mengenkontrakt	contract (over a stipulated quantity)
Mengenrabatt	bulk discount
Messe	trade fair, trade exhibition, show
Messebauer, Messebaufirma	exhibition contractor
Methode	method
▷ Kritischer-Pfad-Methode	Critical Path Method (CPM)
mieten	to hire, to rent

Mindestbestellmenge	minimum order quantity
Mindestlagerbestand	minimum stock
Mitarbeiter	staff member, member of staff
Mitarbeitermotivation	staff motivation
Mitsprache bei Entscheidungen	participation in decision-making processes
Mitteilung	notice
Mittel	assets, resources; means
▷ liquide Mittel	liquid assets
Mittelpunkt	focus
Mittelsmann	middleman
mittelständisches Unternehmen	medium-sized company
Mittelwert	mean
▷ einfacher Mittelwert	simple mean
Modell	model; series
▷ ein Modell entwickeln	to develop a model
modular	modular
möglich	possible
▷ sobald wie möglich	as soon as possible
▷ sobald es Ihnen möglich ist	at your earliest convenience
Monopol	monopoly
Montage	assembly, fitting, installation
▷ Montage nach Auftrag	finish-to-order; assemble-to-order
Montage (bes. im Anlagenbau)	erection
Montageband	assembly line
▷ Auslastung des Montagebandes	line loading
Montageplan	assembly plan, built schedule
Montagetechniker	installation engineer
Montagewerk	assembly plant
Monteur	fitter
Mühe	effort
multinationaler Konzern	multinational group; multinational
Muster	sample, specimen; pattern
▷ einem Muster entsprechen	to match a sample
Musterkollektion	collection of samples
Muttergesellschaft	parent company, Holding

N

Nacharbeit	rework
Nacharbeitsauftrag	rework order; spoilt work order
Nachberechnung von Lieferungen und Leistungen	invoicing of additional supplies and services
Nachbestellbedarf	re-order requirements
nachbestellen	to reorder
Nachbestellung	repeat order
Nachbestellungskosten	reorder cost
Nachfaßauftrag	follow-up order
Nachfrage	demand
▷ abgeleitete Nachfrage	derived demand
▷ geringe Nachfrage	weak demand
▷ große Nachfrage	strong demand
▷ momentane Nachfrage	current demand
▷ ungedeckte Nachfrage	unsatisfied demand
▷ wachsende Nachfrage	rising demand
▷ Nachfrage und Angebot	supply and demand
▷ Ungleichgewicht zwischen Nachfrage und Angebot	supply and demand imbalance
Nachfragemacht	buyer concentration (of power)
Nachfragemenge	required quantity; quantity demanded
Nachfragerückgang	decline in demand; loss of demand
Nachfrageverschiebungen	changes in demand; shifts in demands; demand trends
Nachkalkulation	ex-post costing
Nachschubvorgänge	supply procedures
nachträglicher Einbau	retrofit
Nachunternehmer	subcontractor
Nachunternehmervertrag	subcontract
Nebenkosten	incidental expenses
Nebenprodukt	by-product
nehmen	to take
Netto	net
Nettobedarfsrechnung, -ermittlung	assessment of net material requirements, net requirements calculation
Nettoeinkommen	net income
Nettogewicht	net weight

Nettogewinn	net profit from business activities
Nettomaterialbedarf	net material requirements
Netz	network
▷ für den lokalen Bereich	local area network (LAN)
▷ für den überregionalen Bereich	wide area network (WAN)
Netzverteilungsstruktur	distribution network structure
Netzwerk	network
neuester Stand der Technik	state-of-the-art
▷ unsere Maschinen sind auf dem neuesten Stand der Technik	our machines are state-of-the-art
Neuplanung	replaning
▷ Neuplanung von unten nach oben	bottom-up replanning
Nichtbeachtung (von)	non-compliance with
Niederlassung	branch
Niedrigstpreis	rock-bottom price
Niveau	level
Norm(en)	standard(s); codes
Normalausführung	standard design, conventional design
Normalkapazität	normal capacity
Normalleistung	standard performance
Normalverteilung	normal distribution
Normierung	standardization
▷ Normierung von Materialien	material standardization
Normteile	standard parts
▷ zugekaufte Normteile	bought-out standard parts
Notierung	quotation
nützen	to benefit
Nullserie	pilot lot
Nutzen	benefit
▷ Nutzen ziehen aus	to benefit from

O

Obergrenze	ceiling
Öffentlichkeitsarbeit	public relations
Operations Research**	operations research**
Optimalität	optimality

O Optimalitätsanalyse

Optimalitätsanalyse	optimality analysis
optionell	optional
Organigramm	organisation chart
Organisation	organisation
▷ Organisation einer Abteilung	departamental organisation
Organisationspyramide	organisational structure/pyramide
▷ flache Organisationspyramide	flat organisational pyramid
▷ hierarchische Organisationspyramide	hierarchical organisational pyramid
Original ...	original
Originalrechnung	original invoice
Output	output
Overengineering**	overengineering**

P

Packliste	list of items
Paket	parcel; package
Parallelbeschaffung	multiple sourcing
Partner	partner
Passiva	liabilities
Pauschalpreis	lump-sum price
Pauschalvertrag	lump-sum contract
periodisch	periodic, cyclic
Personal	personnel, staff
Personalbedarf	manpower requirement
Personalbeschaffung	recruitment
Personaldirektor	Human Resources Manager
Personaleinstellung	recruitment of staff
Personalentwicklung	human resources development
Personalkapazität	manpower
Personalkosten	personnel expenses, staff costs
Personalleiter	personnel manager
Pflege	maintenance, servicing
Pflicht	duty, commitment
▷ Pflichten übertragen	to delegate duties
Pflichtenheft	request for proposal (RFP); request for quote (RFQ)

Preisflexibilität

▷ Pflichtenheft bei Verfahren	System Requirements
Phantom-Stückliste	phantom bill of material
Phase	stage
Plan	plan, program(me)
Planentwürfe	draft plans
Planstelle	vacency
Planung	planning
▷ strategische Planung	strategical planning
▷ taktische Planung	tactical planning
Planungsentwurf	blueprint, draft
Post	post, mail
▷ mit getrennter Post	under separate cover
Posten	item, lot; assortment
Preis	price
▷ angemessener Preis	reasonable price
▷ der äußerst kalkulierte Preis	rock-bottom price
▷ gegenwärtiger Preis	current price, ruling price
▷ geltender Preis	current price
▷ geplanter Preis	planned price
▷ günstiger Preis	favourable price
▷ herabgesetzter/reduzierter Preis	reduced price
▷ konkurrenzfähiger Preis	competitive price
▷ festgesetzter Preis	the stipulated price
▷ zum Preis von DM ... einkaufen	to buy at the price of DM ...
▷ unter Preis einkaufen	to buy below price
▷ über Preis einkaufen	to buy over price
▷ Preise angleichen	to adjust prices
▷ Preise drücken	to force down prices
▷ Preise festsetzen	to set prices
▷ Preise nennen	to quote prices
Preisabsprache	price fixing
Preisanfrage	enquiry (inquiry) for prices
Preisangebot	quotation, bid
▷ angefordertes Angebot	quotation
▷ nicht angefordertes Angebot	bid
Preisanstieg	increase in prices; price increase
Preisaufschlüsselung	breakdown of prices
Preisbildung	price formation, pricing
▷ Preisbildung durch Marktführer	leader pricing
Preisdegression	economies of scale
Preisfestlegung	pricing, stipulation of prices
▷ nach Deckungsbeitrag	contribution margin pricing
▷ zum Lieferzeitpunkt	price prevailing at date of shipment
Preisflexibilität	price elasticity

P Preisgleitklausel

Preisgleitklausel	price escalation clause
Preisgleitung	price escalation
Preisindex	price index
Preis-Leistungs-Verhältnis	value for money ratio, price/performance ratio
Preisliste	price list
▷ aktuelle Preisliste	current price list
Preisnachlaß	discount; *nach Beschwerde:* allowance
Preisniveau	price level
▷ ein Preisniveau erreichen	to match prices
Preisstatistik	price statistics
Preissteigerung	cost increase
Preisstellung	delivery terms
Primärbedarf	primary requirements
Primärbedarfsdisposition	master production scheduling
Primärbedarfsplan	master production schedule (MPS)
Primärbedarfsplanung	master planning
Probe	sample
Probeauftrag	trial order
Probenentnahme	sampling
Probegröße	sample size
Probleme	problems, difficulties
▷ Probleme angehen	to address problems; to tackle difficulties
Produkt	product
▷ erstrangiges Produkt	top of the range product
▷ marktfähiges Produkt	saleable goods
▷ Produkt des täglichen Gebrauchs	product of daily use
▷ ein Produkt auf den Markt bringen	to launch a product
Produktbeschreibung	product specification
Produktdesign, beschaffungsmarktgerechtes	design-to-market
Produktdesign, kostengerechtes	design-to-cost
Produktdesign, prozeßgerechtes	design-to-process
Produktdesign, Veränderungen im	redesign
Produktentwicklung	product development
Produkthaftung	product liabilites
Produktinnovation	product innovation
Produktion	production

Produktionsstufen

▷ Prinzip der kontinuierlichen Verbesserungen in der Produktion | Kaizen, i.e. prinziple of continuous improvements in production
▷ Produktion in Stückzahlen | output
▷ Produktion aufnehmen | to take up production
▷ Produktion beschleunigen | to expedite production
▷ Produktion drosseln | to curb production
▷ Produktion erweitern | to broaden production
▷ Produktion umsiedeln | to relocate production
▷ Produktion zurückfahren | to run down production

Produktionsablauf | production process
▷ Straffung des Produktionsablaufs | to streamline the production process
Produktionsabschnitt | stage (of production)
Produktionsanlagen | manufacturing/production facilities
Produktionsart und -umfang | type and scope of production
Produktionsauftrag | work order
▷ Auftragserfüllung in Teilmengen | flow order
Produktionseinrichtungen | production facilities
Produktionsfaktorenplanung | Manufacturing Resource Planning
Produktionsgüter | producer/production goods
Produktionsgüterindustrie | producer goods industry
Produktionskapazität | manufacturing/productive capability
▷ verfügbare Produktionskapazitäten | available production facilities
Produktionskosten | cost of production; manufacturing expenses

Produktionsleiter | production manager
Produktionslogistik | production logistics
Produktionsmittel | means of production
▷ eingesetzte Produktionsmittel | input
▷ Produktionsplan für Primärbedarf | Master Production Schedule
Produktionsplanung | production planning
Produktionsplanung und -steuerung | production planning and management

Produktionsreihe, -serie | production series, model
Produktionsstätte | factory, plant, production facilities
▷ hochautomatisierte Produktionsstätten | highly automated plants
▷ neue Produktionsstätten bauen | to build new production facilities
▷ Produktionsstätten verlagern | to relocate production facilities
Produktionssteuerung | production/operations management; production control

Produktionsstruktur | pattern of production
Produktionsstufen | stage of production

P Produktionsstückliste

Produktionsstückliste	production bill of material
Produktionssysteme	systems of production
Produktpalette	range of products
Produktvielfalt	product diversification
Produktzentrenfertigung	dedicated production
Produktzentrum (in der Fertigung)	group technology
Produzent	manufacturer, producer
Profit	profit
▷ Profit als Leistungskriterium	profit as criterion of business performance
▷ Profit als Unternehmensziel	profit as business objective
▷ Profite verbuchen, verzeichnen	to be in the red
profitabel	profitable
Profitabilität	profitability
profitorientierte Tätigkeiten	profit-oriented activities
Proforma Rechnung	pro forma invoice
Prognose	forecast
Projekt	project
Projektfinanzierung	project funding
Projektleiter	project manager
Projektteams	project teams
Prokurist	Authorized Signatory (on behalf of a company)
Prospekt	leaflet, brochure
Prospektmaterial	descriptive material, descriptive literature
Protokoll (einer Besprechung)	minutes (of meeting)
Protokoll (einer Verhandlung)	minutes of negotiation
Provision	commission
Prozeß	process
Prozeßkette	process chain
▷ logistische Prozeßketten	logistical process chains
Prozeßkontrolle	process control
▷ statistische Prozeßkontrolle	statistical process control
Prozeßmanagement	process management
Prozeßplanung	process planning
▷ computergestützte Prozeßplanung	computer-aided process planning
Prozeßsteuerung	process orientation, process control
Prozeßverbesserung	process improvements
▷ kontinuierliche Prozeßverbesserung	continuous process improvement (CPI)

Q Qualitätsziele

Prüfauftrag	trial order, test order
Prüfeinrichtung	testing equipment
prüfen	to check, to control, to audit, to examine
Prüffeld	test section
Prüfung	test, audit, control, check; examination
Prüfzeit	test time, inspection time

Q

QS-Anweisungen	quality assurance instructions
QS-Grundsätze	quality policies
QS-Leiter	quality assurance manger
Qualifizierung	qualification
Qualität	quality
▷ erstklassige Qualität	first-class quality
▷ mindere Qualität	inferior/poor quality
▷ mittelwertige Qualität	medium quality
Qualitätsaudit	quality audit
Qualitätsaufzeichnungen	quality records
Qualitätsbewertungsmaßstab	Accepted Quality Level (AQL)
Qualitätskontrolle	quality control
▷ Qualitätskontrolle in der Fertigung	inspection
▷ computergestützte Qualitätskontrolle	computer-aided inspection and testing
▷ mangelhafte Qualitätskontrolle	poor quality control
Qualitätskosten	quality-related costs
Qualitätsmängel	quality deficiencies
Qualitätsmanagement-Handbuch	quality manual
Qualitätsmanagement-System	quality system
Qualitätsnachweis	quality certificate
Qualitätsplan	quality plan
Qualitätssicherung	quality assurance
Qualitätsstandart	quality level
Qualitätssteuerung	quality control
Qualitätstreue	quality standards
Qualitätsware	quality goods
Qualitätsziele	quality targets

Q Quelle

Quelle	source
Querschnittsfunktionen	cross-section functions
Querverweis	cross-reference

R

Rabatt	discount
Rahmen	framework
Rahmenauftrag	blanket order
Rahmenvereinbarung	framework agreement
Rahmenvertrag	basic contract; framework agreement
Rate	rate; instalment
▷ auf Raten zahlen	to pay in instalments
rationalisieren	to streamline
▷ Kosten rationalisieren	to streamline costs
Rationalisierung	rationalization
rationell	efficient
Rechner	computer
▷ Großrechner	high-capacity computer
rechnergestützt	computer-aided
Rechnung	account, bill, invoice
▷ eine Rechnung begleichen	to settle an account; to pay a bill
▷ in Rechnung stellen	to charge, to invoice
▷ Dienstleistungen in Rechnung stellen	to invoice sales and services
Rechnungsabschrift	duplicate invoice, copy of invoice
Rechnungsjahr	financial year, fiscal year, business year
Recht	law, right
Recht . . .	legal
Rechtsansprüche	claims
Rechtsseite	legal part
Recycling	recycling
Recycling- und Entsorgungskosten	recycling and waste disposal costs
Reduktion	reduction
reduzieren	to reduce
Reengineering	reengineering
Regelabweichung	deviation, variance

Rückstand R

Regressforderungen	claims
▷ Regress fördern/anmelden	to claim damages
Reibung	friction
Reichweite von Befugnissen	scope of authorization, level of authorization
Reifegrad	maturity stage, stage of development
Reihenfolge	sequence
Reihenfolgeplanung	sequence planning, sequencing
▷ Reihenfolgeplanung am Montageband	line-set
Reingewinn (nach Versteuerung)	net trading profit
Reingewinn (vor Versteuerung)	net trading surplus
rentabel	economic, profitable
Rentabilität	economic effectiveness, profitability; financial viability
rentieren	to be profitable; to pay for itself
▷ sich innerhalb eines Jahres rentieren	to pay for itself within a year
Reparatur	maintenance; breakdown maintenance
Reparaturauftrag	repair order
Reporting	reporting
Ressourcenliste	list of capacities
Resultat	result, outcome
Revision	audit
▷ innerbetriebliche Revision	internal audit
Richtlinien	guidelines
Richtpreis	benchmark price
Riemen	strap
Risiko	risk
▷ das einer Tätigkeit innewohnende Risiko	inherent risk
Rohstoff	raw material
Rohstofflager	stock of raw materials
Rohstoffmarkt	raw material market
rohstoffreich	rich in raw materials
Rollgeld	cartage
Rollgut	carted goods
Rückkopplung	feedback
Rückstand	backlog (of orders); arrears

R Rückstandsliste

▷ (mit Zahlungen) im Rückstand sein
▷ erwartete Rückstände
Rückstandsliste

to be in arrears
anticipated delays
delay report, back order list, backlog list

rüsten
Rüstkosten
Rüstzeit
▷ interne Rüstzeit
▷ Rüstzeit bei Arbeitsbeginn
▷ Rüstzeit bei Arbeitsschluß

to set up something
set-up cost
set-up time
internal set-up time
start-up time
shut-down time

S

Sättigungspunkt
saisonbedingt
Sammelladung
▷ Sammelladungen zusammenstellen
Sammelladungsverkehr
Sammeltransport

equilibrium point
seasonal
grouped freight
to group freight/cargo
grouped freight
groupage consignment, freight consolidation

Sanierungspläne
Satz
schätzen
Schätzung
Schaden
Schadenersatzforderungen
▷ Schadenersatz fordern
Schadenersatzklage
Schadensbericht
Scheck
▷ einen Scheck einlösen
Schicht
▷ eine zusätzliche Schicht fahren
schicken
Schiedsgerichtsverfahren
Schiff
Schiffsladung
▷ Schiffsladungen löschen
Schiffsverkehr

redevelopment plans
rate
to estimate, to evaluate
estimate, estimation, evaluation
damage
claims, claims for damages
to claim damages
legal action for damages
survey report
cheque
to cash a cheque
shift
to run an additional shift
to send, to dispatch
arbitration
ship, vessel
boatload
to discharge cargoes
shipping traffic

Skala S

Schlechterfüllung einer Leistung	defective performance
Schlichtungsverfahren	arbitration
Schlüssel	key, code
schlüsselfertig	turn key
▷ schlüsselfertiges System	turn-key system
Schlupf	slack
Schlupfzeit	slack time
Schlußdatum für ein Angebot	closing-date, deadline for submitting an offer
Schnittpunkt	intersection
Schnittstelle	interface
schrittweise	step-by-step
Schrott	scrap
Schüttgut	bulk material
Schulden	debts, liabilities
schulden	to owe
Schuldner	debtor
Schutt	debris, scrap
Schwachstelle	weak point; trouble spot; vulnerable areas
▷ Schwachstellen ausfindig machen	to identify vulnerable areas
Schwachstellenanalyse	weak point analysis; analysis of potential trouble spots
Schwarzarbeit	moonlighting
Schwerpunktarbeitsgang	key operation, primary operation
Seeweg, auf dem	by sea, by ship
▷ auf dem Seeweg befördern	to transport by sea/by ship
Selbstkostenpreis	cost price
Sendung	shipment, consignment
senken	to reduce, to cut
Sicherheit	safety, security
Sicherheitsanalyse	safety analysis
Sicherheitsbestand	emergency stock; minimum stock
Sicherheitseinrichtung	safety equipment
Sicherheitsingenieur	safety engineer
Sicherheitstechnik	safety technology, technical safety
Sicherheitsvorschriften	safety regulations
Signatur	signature
Single Sourcing	single sourcing
Skala	scale

S Skonto

Skonto	cash discount
Software	software
Soll	debit
▷ Soll und Haben	debit and credit
Sollauslastung	calculated usage
Soll-Ist-Vergleich	target-performance comparison
Soll-Kapazität	calculated/rated/standing/nominal capacity
Soll-Leistung	rated performance
▷ Soll-Leistung	rated output
Solltermin	target date, due date
Sollwert	target value
Sonderanfertigung	special design
Sonderanfertigungen	goods made to specifications
Sondereinzelkosten	costs, special direct costs
Sonderpreis	special price
Sonderteile	special parts
Sortiment	assortment, range
Spanne	margin
sparsam	economical
Spediteur	forwarder, forwarding agent
Spediteurrechnung	forwarder's note of charges
Spediteurübernahmebescheinigung	forwarder's receipt
Speditionsauftrag	shipping order
Speditionsunternehmen	forwarder, forwarding agent; shipping company
Spesen	expenses
Spitzenmodell	best-selling model, top-of-the-range model
Spitzenprodukt	first-class product, top-of-the-range product
Stahlindustrie	steel industry
Stammbelegschaft	permanent staff
Stammdatei	master file
Stammkunde	regular customer
Stammlieferant	regular supplier
Stand	status
▷ neuester Stand der Technik	state-of-the-art
Standard	standard
Standardabweichung	standard deviation

Stückgüter — S

Standardbehälter	standard container
Standardlosgröße	standard batch quantity (SBQ)
Standardmethoden	standard methods/approaches
▷ statistische Standardmethoden	standard statistical approaches
Standardteile	standard parts
Standardzeitzugabe	standard allowance
Standort	location
Standortvorteile	location advantages
Stapel	batch
Stapelware	staple goods
Starttermin	start date
▷ frühester Starttermin	earliest start date
▷ letzter Starttermin	latest start date
Statistik	statistics
▷ vergleichende Statistiken	comparative statistics
Steuer	tax
steuerfrei	tax free, tax exempt
Steuerjahr	tax year, fiscal year
Stichprobe	random sample
▷ Stichproben nehmen	to take random samples
Stichprobenentnahme	sampling
▷ für Bewertung	acceptance sampling
▷ am Arbeitsplatz	work sampling
Stillstandzeit	idle time
▷ störungsbedingte Stillstandzeit	downtime
▷ Stillstandszeit bei Maschinenschaden	machine down time
Stornierung	cancellation
Stornogebühren	cancellation charges
Stoß	batch
Straßenverkehr	road traffic
Strategie	strategy
▷ Strategien optimieren	to fine-tune strategies
Strategiepläne	action plans
▷ Strategiepläne entwickeln	to develop action plans
Streifencode	bar code
Struktur	structure; fabric
Strukturbruch	structural break
Strukturstückliste	indented explosion, structure bill of material
Stückarbeit	piece work
Stückgüter	general cargo

S Stückkosten

Stückkosten	unit cost
▷ kleinste Stückkosten	least unit cost
Stückkostenrechnung für Massenfertigung	process costing
Stückliste	part/specification list; list of items, bill of materials
▷ Stückliste der Ressourcen	bill of resources
Stücklistenkette	bill-of-material chain
Stücklistenverwaltung	part list management
Stücklohn	piece rate
Stückpreis	price per unit; price each; single price
Stückzeit	piece time, standard time per unit
Stufe	level
stufenweise	step-by-step; level-by-level
Stundenabrechnung	man-hour accounting
Stundenerfassung	man-hour recording
Stundenzettel	time sheet
Supposition	supposition
Synergien nutzen	to use synergies
System	system, scheme; method; framework
▷ schlüsselfertiges System	turn-key system
▷ verteilte Systeme	distributed systems
Systemgestaltung	systems design
Systemorganisation	system-oriented structure
Systemplanung	systems engineering
Systemprogrammierung	systems design
Systemzwänge	structural constraints

T

(t) Tonne	ton, tonne (t)
1 metrische Tonne = 1 mt = 1000 kg	1 metric ton(ne) = 1 mt = 1,000 kilos
1 britische Tonne = 1016 kg	1 long ton(ne) = 1,016 kilos
1 US Tonne = 907,18 kg	1 short ton(ne) = 907.18 kilos
t/Jahr	tpa (tonnes per annum)
t/Tag	tpa (tonnes per day)
Tabelle	chart, table

Terminierung T

▷ Tabelle für wirtschaftliche Losgrößen | EOQ tables (Economic Order Quantity tables)
Tagesordnung | agenda
Tagesordnungspunkt | topic on the agenda (TOP), issue
Tagespreis | current price, ruling price
Taktzeit | cycle time
Taragewicht | tare weight
Team | team
▷ abteilungsübergreifende Teams | cross-functional teams; multi-disciplinary teams
Technik | engineering, technic
▷ Technik zur optischen Zeichenerkennung | optical scanning
▷ neuester Stand der Technik | state-of-the-art
Techniker | engineer
▷ technischer Assistent | technician
▷ Wartungstechniker | service engineer
technisch | technical
▷ technische Änderung | technical alteration, engineering change
▷ technische Daten | specifications, technical data, engineering data
▷ technischer Direktor | head of engineering, chief engineer
▷ technische Zeichnung | technical drawing
Teile | parts
Teilebedarfsmenge | component requirements quantity
Teilekodierung und -klassifizierung | part coding and classification
Teilenachweis | where-used list
Teilesatz | kit
Teilestammdatei | part record
Teilevielfalt | part diversity
Teillast | partial load
Teillieferung | part delivery
Teilzeitarbeit | part-time work
Termin | appointment, meeting
▷ einen Termin vereinbaren | to fix a date for a meeting/delivery etc.
▷ letzter Termin | closing-date, deadline
▷ Liefertermin | delivery date
termingemäß | in time, in due time, according to schedule
Terminierung | scheduling
▷ Terminierung mit Zeitabschnitten | block scheduling

T

Terminkontrolle

▷ Terminierung der Werkstattfertigung	job shop scheduling
Terminkontrolle	expediting
Terminplan	schedule
Terminplanung	scheduling, rescheduling
Termintreue	schedule effectiveness, faithfulness to deadlines
Terminüberwachung	expediting
Textilindustrie	textile industry
Thema	subject, issue, topic
▷ Thema von zentraler Bedeutung	core strategic issue
Tochtergesellschaft	subsidiary
▷ hundertprozentige Tochtergesellschaft	wholly-owned subsidiary
Total Cost of Ownership**	Total Cost of Ownership**
Total Quality Control	Total Quality Control (TQC)
Total Quality Management**	Total Quality Management**
Transport	transport(ation), carriage, conveyance
▷ kombinierter Transport	multimodel transport, intermodal transport
▷ während des Transportes	en route, during transport; in transit
transportieren	to transport, to carry
Transportkosten	carriage charges, cost of transport(ation), transfer costs
▷ interne Transportkosten	internal handling cost
Transportmittel	means of transport
Transportweg, auf dem	in transit
▷ Verlust oder Schaden auf dem Transportweg	damage or loss in transit / during transport
Tratte	draft
treffen	to meet
Trend	trend, tendency
▷ Trends erkennen	to spot trends

U

Überbestand	surplus inventory
überfällig	overdue, past due
Überlieferung	surplus delivery

Überprüfzeit	check time, inspection time
überschneiden	to overlap, to intersect
Überschuß	surplus
Überschußmaterial	excess material
Überschußprodukte	surplus products
Überstunden	overtime
Überstundenzuschlag	overtime bonus
übertragen	to delegate, to transfer
überwachen	to supervise
Überwachung	supervision
Überwachungspersonal	supervisory staff
üblich	usual, customary
Umfang	scope, volume; size; bulk; range
Umfrage	survey
Umgang	handling
▷ Umgang mit Lagerbeständen	handling of goods in storage
umgehen (mit)	to deal with, to handle
Umlaufbestände	work in progress
Umlaufvermögen	current/working assets; floating/working capital
Umsatz	turnover, sale
Umsatzerlöse	sales revenue; sales
Umsatzrate	rate of turnover
Umsatzvolumen	sales volume
Umschlag	transshipment, handling
Umschlaghäufigkeit	turnover ratio; turnover/stockturn rate; rate of inventory turnover
umsiedeln	to relocate, reengineering plans
Umstrukturierungspläne	restructuring plans, reengineering plans
umverteilen	to relocate, to redistribute
Umwelt	environment
umweltpolitisch	environmental
▷ umweltpolitische Belange	environmental concerns
Umweltschutz	environmental protection, environmental pollution control
Umweltschutzvorschriften	pollution control regulations
Umweltverträglichkeitsstudie	eco-compatibility study
Unfallverhütungsvorschriften	rules for the prevention of accidents
unfrei	carriage/freight forward

U ungenau

ungenau	inaccurate
unhandlich	bulky
Universalmaschine	universal tool machine
Unkosten	expenses
Unteilbarkeit	indivisibility
Unterlieferant	subcontractor, subsupplier
Unternehmen	company, business, business enterprise
Unternehmensergebnisse	corporate results
▷ Unternehmensergebnisse verbessern	to improve corporate results
Unternehmensführung	management
Unternehmensgefüge	corporate structure; structure of a company
Unternehmensphilosophie	corporate philosophy
Unternehmensplanung	management planning; business administration
Unternehmensstrategie	corporate strategy
Unternehmensziele	business (*incl.* managerial) objectives/targets; corporate aims
Unternehmer	entrepreneur, businessperson, contractor; employer
Unternehmergeist	entrepreneurial spirit
unternehmerisch	entrepreneurial, managerial, managemental
▷ unternehmerische Entscheidungen	entrepreneurial decisions
Unterschrift	signature
▷ Unterschriftenregelung	sign off rules, sign off levels
▷ unterschreiben	to sign, to sign off
▷ einen Vertrag abzeichnen, paraphieren	to sign off a contract
▷ einen Vertrag unterschreiben	to sign a contract
untersuchen	to enquire, to inquire; to examine, to check, to inspect
Untersuchung	examination; enquiry; study (on), research (on), inspection
unverpackt	loose, not packed; *auch:* in bulk
Ursache	reason; origin, source
Ursprung	source
Ursprungsland	country of origin
Ursprungszeugnis	certificate of origin

V

Value Engineering**	Value engineering**
variabel	variable
▷ variable Kostenkalkulation	direct costing
▷ variable Metallbearbeitungsmaschine	machining centre
▷ variable Preisfestlegung	bid pricing
Variable	variable
Variantenstückliste	modular bill of material
Verarbeitung, Bearbeitung	processing
Verarbeitung, maschinelle	machining
Verabredung	appointment, meeting
veräußern	to sell; to dispose (of)
veranschlagen	to estimate
Veranschlagung	estimate
Verantwortung	responsibility
▷ Verantwortung übernehmen	to accept responsibility
▷ keinerlei Verantwortung übernehmen für	not to accept any responsibility for ...
verarbeiten	to process
▷ verarbeitet	processed
Verarbeitung	processing; finish, fabrik
▷ die Verarbeitung von Waren	the finish/fabrik of goods
Verarbeitungseinheit	processing unit
▷ zentrale Verarbeitungseinheit	central processing unit
Verband	association
verbessern	to improve
Verbindlichkeit	liability
▷ Verbindlichkeiten	liabilities
Verbrauch	consumption, usage; expenditure
verbrauchen	to consume, to use
Verbraucher	consumer
▷ innerbetriebliche Verbraucher	internal customers
Verbraucherbedürfnisse	customer needs
▷ Verbraucherbedürfnisse decken	to meet/to satisfy customer needs
Verbraucherforderungen	customer demands
Verbraucherpreis	consumer price
Verbraucherverhalten	consumer behaviour
Verbraucherwünsche	consumer demands
▷ Verbraucherwünsche umlenken	re-directing consumer demands

V Verbrauchsabweichung

Verbrauchsabweichung	usage variance
Verbrauchsgüter	consumables, consumer goods
▷ dauerhafte Verbrauchsgüter	durable consumer goods
Verbrauchsgüterindustrie	consumer goods industry
Verbrauchsmaterial	supplies
verbrauchsorientiertes System	pull system
verbuchen	to record, to book
verdienen	to earn
Verdienst	earnings
verdrängen	to freeze competitors out of a market
Verdrängungswettbewerb	predatory/destructive competition; predatory price cutting policy
Verein	society; club
▷ eingetragener Verein	incorporated society
vereinbaren	to agree (upon)
Vereinbarung	agreement, settlement
Vereinbarung einer Vertragsstrafe	penalty agreement
vereinheitlichen	to unify, to standardize
vereinigen	to incorporate, to unify
Vereinigung	incorporation
Verfahren	procedure, operations
Verfahrensbeschreibung	operations description
Verfahrenstechniker	process engineer
Verfahrensschritte	process steps
Verfahrenstechnik	process engineering
verfügbar	available
Verfügbarkeit	availability
▷ negative Verfügbarkeit	minus availability
Vergabe	order placement
Vergabeprotokoll	minutes of negotiation on order placement
Vergabeverhandlung	negotiation on order placement
Verhandlungsprotokoll	minutes of negotiation
Vergleichsmessungen mit Bezugspunkten	benchmark measures
Verhältniszahlen	ratios, relatives
Verhandlung	negotiation
Verhandlungsführung	conduct of negotiations
Verhandlungstrick	negotiating ploy
Verkäufer	sales manager; seller, vendor

Verkäuferanalyse	vendor analysis
Verkäuferbewertung	vendor rating
Verkäufermarkt	seller's market
Verkauf	sale
verkaufen	to sell
Verkaufsbedingungen	terms and conditions of sale
Verkaufskosten	cost of sales
Verkaufsleiter	sales manager, head of sales department
Verkaufsniederlassung	sales branch
Verkaufspreis	sales price
Verkaufspunkt	point of sales (POS)
Verkaufsschlager	best-selling model
Verkaufstrend	sales trend
Verkaufsvolumen	sales volume
Verkehr	transport
Verkehrsmittel	means of transport
Verkehrsnetz	transport system
Verknappung	shortcoming, shortage
Verladehafen	port of shipment
verladen	to ship
Verlässlichkeit eines Lieferanten	supplier reliability
Verlagerung	relocation
▷ Produktionsstätten verlagern nach …	to relocate production sites to …
verlangen	to demand, to require
Verlust	loss
▷ Verlust erleiden	to suffer a loss
▷ Verluste verzeichnen	to be in the red
▷ Verlust, möglicher	contingent loss
▷ Verlust, vorhersehbarer	foreseeable loss
▷ Verlust oder Schaden auf dem Transportweg	loss or damage in transit
Verlustunternehmen	loss-making company
vermieten	to hire, to rent
Vermittler	middleman
Vermögensgegenstände, -werte	assets
▷ immaterielle Vermögensgegenstände	fixed intangible assets
▷ festangelegte Vermögenswerte	fixed assets
▷ sonstige Vermögenswerte	other assets
vernachlässigen	to neglect

V Vernachlässigung

Vernachlässigung	negligence
Verordnung	regulation
verpacken	to pack
Verpackung	packing and packaging
▷ Verpackung mit Riemen	strapping
▷ Verpackung und Markierung	packing, packaging and marking
Verpackungsmaterial	packing material, packaging
verpflichtet sein	obliged, to be obliged to
Verpflichtung	liability, obligation
Verrechnungssatzverfahren	standard record method
Verrechnungsschein bei Lieferung	charge ticket
verringern	to reduce, to decrease, to scale down
versäumen	to neglect; to miss
Versäumnis	negligence, omission
Versand	shipment, dispatch
▷ Versand von Waren	shipment of goods
Versandabteilung	shipping department, transport department, dispatch department
Versandangaben	forwarding/shipping instructions
Versandanweisungen	delivery/shipping instructions
Versandanzeige	advice of dispatch; advice note; shipping advice
Versandart	manner of shipment
Versandauftrag	dispatch/shipping order
Versanddatum	date of dispatch
Versanddokumente	shipping documents
Versandgewichte	shipping weights
Versandmenge	shipping quantity
▷ kleinere Versandmenge, als Ladungspartie	less than truckload (LTL)
Versandort	place of dispatch, place of shipment
Versandvorschriften	shipping instructions
Versatz	offset
verschicken	to ship, to dispatch
verschieben	to postpone
Verschiebung	offset
Verschiffung	shipment
Verschiffungsanweisungen	shipment instructions
Verschiffungsanzeige	shipment advice
Verschiffungsdokumente	shipment documents

Vertrag V

Verschiffungsvorschriften	shipment instructions
Verschlüsselung	coding
Verschwendung	wasting of resources
versenden	to dispatch, to ship
Versender	consignor
versichern	to insure, to guarantee
Versicherung	insurance
▷ Versicherung abschließen	to effect insurance
Versicherungspolice	insurance policy
Versicherungsvertreter	insurance agent
Versorgung	supply
▷ Versorgung sicherstellen	to ensure the availability of supplies and services
Versorgungsbetriebe	public utilities
Versorgungseinheit	supply unit
Versorgungskette	supply chain
Versorgungskonzepte	supply concepts
Versorgungsnetz	supply network
Versorgungsschwierigkeiten	supply shortages; supply difficulties/problems
Versorgungswirtschaft	supply mangement
Verspätung	delay
Versuchsauftrag	trial order, test order
vertagen	to adjourn
Verteiler	distributor
Verteilung	allocation; distribution
▷ Verteilung von Zuständigkeitsbereichen	allocation of work responsibilities
Verteilzentrum	distribution centre
verteilte Systeme	distributed systems
Vertrag	contract
▷ ein Vertrag läuft aus	a contract expires
▷ etwas vertraglich festsetzen	to stipulate something in a contract
▷ Vertrag aktualisieren	to update a contract
▷ Vertrag aufheben	to withdraw from a contract
▷ Vertrag auflösen	to terminate a contract
▷ Vertrag sistieren	to suspend a contract
▷ Vertrag stornieren	to cancel a contract
▷ Vertrag unterzeichnen	to sign a contract
▷ Vertrag paraphieren	to sign off a contract
▷ Vertrag verlängern	to prolong a contract
▷ von einem Vertrag zurücktreten	to withdraw from a contract

V Vertragsbestimmung

Vertragsbestimmung	contractual stipulation
Vertragsentwurf	contract draft
Vertragserfüllungsgarantie	guarantee for fulfilment of contract
Vertragsklauseln	contract clauses
Vertragslaufzeit	duration of contract
Vertragspreis	contract price
Vertragssistierung	suspension of contract
Vertragsspediteur	contract carrier
Vertragsstornierung	cancellation of contract
Vertragsstrafe	penalty
▷ eine Vertragsstrafe festsetzen	to stipulate a penalty in a contract
Vertragswesen	contract management
Vertraulichkeitsvereinbarung	confidentiality agreement
Vertreter	representative
Vertrieb	distribution, sales; marketing
Vertriebsbüro	sales office
Vertriebsgemeinkosten	selling expense
Vertriebskosten	cost of distribution
Vertriebsphasen	distribution stages
Vertriebsplanung und -steuerung	distribution planning and management
Vertriebsstelle	outlet
Verursachung	creation, cause
Verwaltung	administration
Verwaltungsgemeinkosten	administrative expense, cost of general administration
Verwendungskette	where-used chain
Verwendungsnachweis	where-used list
▷ einstufiger Verwendungsnachweis	single-level where-used list
▷ mehrstufiger Verwendungsnachweis	multiple-level where-used list
verzeichnen	to record
Verzeichnis	register, schedule
Verzögerung	delay; hold-up
verzollt	duty paid
Verzug	delay
▷ im (Zahlungs-)verzug sein	to be in arreas
▷ im Verzug setzen	to set a final deadline for delivery
Verzugsmeldung	delay notice
Vielfachverwendung	multiple use
Vollkostenrechnung	full absorption costing

Vollmacht	power of attorney
Vollmachten	powers, authority
▷ Vollmachten übertragen	to delegate powers
voraus: im voraus	in advance
Vor(aus)bestellung	advance order
Vorauszahlung	advanced payment, payment in advance
Vorabnahme	preliminary inspection, preliminary acceptance
Vorfertigung	prefabrication, fabrication, parts manufacture
Vorfertigungsauftrag	fabrication order
Vorgabeleistung	performance target
Vorgabe-/Lieferüberwachung	Input-Output Control
Vorgaben	standards, parameter; performance targets
▷ Vorgaben in Kalkulationen	determination of standards
▷ Kostenvorgaben	target standard costs; ideal standard costs
Vorgabetafel	dispatch board
Vorgehen	procedure
Vorgehensweise	tactic, approach
Vorgesetzter	superior
▷ mein Vorgesetzter ist …	I report to …
Vorverhandlung	preliminary negotiation
Vorhersage	forecast
Vorkaufsrecht	option to buy
▷ das Vorkaufsrecht innehaben	to have first option
Vormontage	pre-assembly
vor Ort	en situ, at site
Vorprodukte	primary/preliminary products; prefabricated products, intermediate products (= used for further processing)
Vorrat	stock, store
Vorratssenkung	stock reduction
Vorratsfertigung	stock production
Vorsitzender der Geschäftsführung (UK)	Chairman (of the Board of Directors)
Vorsitzender der Geschäftsführung (USA)	CEO (= Chief Executive Officer)
Vorstand (allg.)	board of directors

V Vorstand

Vorstand (Deutschland)	managing board
Vorstandsvorsitzender	chairman (of the managing board)
Vorteil	benefit
Vorwärtsdurchlaufterminierung	forward flow scheduling
Vorwärtsterminierung	forward scheduling
Vorzugspreis	special price

W

Wachstum	growth
▷ anhaltendes Wachstum	sustainable growth
Währung	currency
▷ ausländische Währung	foreign exchange, foreign currency
Waggon	carriage; *für Güter:* waggon
▷ frei Waggon	free on rail (F.O.R)
Waggonladung	carload lot
wahlweise	optional
Ware	good(s), commodity
▷ ausgewählte Ware	selected goods
▷ beschädigte Ware	damaged goods
▷ gelagerte Ware	goods in stock
▷ leichtverkäufliche Ware	fast-selling goods
▷ schwerverkäufliche Ware	slow-selling goods
▷ zollpflichtige Ware	dutiable goods
▷ Ware mit hoher Umsatzgeschwindigkeit	fast-selling goods
▷ Ware mit geringer Unsatzgeschwindigkeit	slow-selling goods
▷ Ware abholen	to collect goods
▷ Ware termingerecht liefern	to deliver goods within the specified time
▷ Ware zurückweisen	to reject goods, to refuse acceptance of goods
Warenabgang	quantity withdrawn
Warenanalyse	commodity analysis
Warenannahme	acceptance of goods
Warenbedarfsplanung	distribution requirements planning
Warenbeschaffenheit	the nature of goods
Warenbörse	commodity market
Wareneingang	incoming goods (department)
Warenfluß	flow of goods

Werker W

Warenlager	stocks of goods/merchandise; warehouse, storehouse
Warenlagerung	storage/storing/warehousing of goods
Warenlieferung	delivery of goods
▷ Warenlieferung annehmen	to accept delivery of goods
Warenmarkt	commodity market
Warenmuster	sample of merchandise
Warenrechnung	invoice
Warensendung	consignment
Warentransport	conveyance of goods
Waren- und Dienstleistungsfluß	flow of goods and services
Warenverkehr	goods traffic
Warenversand	shipment/dispatch of goods
Warenverteilung	distribution
Warenwirtschaft	commodities management
Warenzeichen	trade mark
▷ eingetragenes Warenzeichen	registered trade mark
Warenzeichenpolitik	branding
Warenzugang	quantity received
Wartung	maintenance
▷ Wartung, Reparatur und Betriebsstoffe	maintenance, repair and operating supplies (MRO)
Wartungsgarantie	maintenance guarantee
Wartungshandbuch	maintenance manual
Wechsel	bill of exchange; draft
Werbeagentur	advertising agency
Werbebrief	sales letter
Werbebudget	advertising budget
werben	to advertise
Werbung	advertising
▷ vergleichende Werbung	competitive advertising
Werbungskosten	marketing costs
Werk	factory
▷ ab Werk	ex factory; ex mill; ex works
▷ Werk zur Fertigung neuer Produkte	pilot plant
Werker	direct labo(u)r
▷ Werker orientierte Instandhaltung plus fortlaufende Verbesserung an Maschinen und Anlagen für einen reibungslosen Materialfluß	total productive maintenance

W Werksleiter

Werksleiter	plant manager; production manager
Werksnormen	works standards
Werkstatt	shop
▷ Werkstatt mit Fließfertigung	flow shop
Werkstattbestand	in-process inventory
▷ auftragsbezogener Werkstattbestand	work in progress, inventory in process, work in process
▷ Werkstattbestand an Verbrauchsgütern	floor stocks
Werkstattfertigung	job shop production/manufacturing
▷ Terminierung der Werkstattfertigung	job shop scheduling
Werkstattsteuerung	shop floor control
Werkzeuglager	tool room
Werkzeugmaschine	machine tool
Werkzeugsatz	set of tools
Werkzeugwechselzeit	tool allowance
Wert	value
▷ Wert der Roh- und Betriebsstoffe	value of raw materials and supplies
Wertanalyse	value analysis**
Wertfestlegung	valuation
Wertkontrakt	framework agreement for part families, stipulating budgets rather than quantities or types
Wertminderung	deterioration, devaluation
Wertpapiere	securities
Wertschöpfung	value added, added value; real net output
Wertschöpfungskette	value added chain
Wertschöpfungspartnerschaft	value added partnership
Wertschöpfungsvolumen	total value added, total added value
▷ angestrebtes Wertschöpfungsvolumen	targeted added value
Wertzeitregel	value time rule
Wettbewerb	competition
▷ leistungsgerechter Wettbewerb	competition based on efficiency
▷ rücksichtsloser Wettbewerb	relentless competition
▷ unlauterer Wettbewerb	unfair competition
▷ starker Wettbewerb	fierce competition, keen competition
Wettbewerbsdruck	competitive pressures
wettbewerbsfähig	competitive

Wochenarbeitszeit

Wettbewerbsvorteil	competitive advantage
▷ beträchtliche Wettbewerbsvorteile	substantial competitive advantages
▷ einen Wettbewerbsvorteil erzielen	to achieve a competitive edge
Wiederaufbereitung	recycling
wiederauffüllen	to refill, to replenish
Wiederauffüllung	refilling, replenishing
wiederausschreiben	to rebid
Wiederausschreibung	rebid
Wiederbeschaffung	reorder
Wiederbeschaffungsauftragsmenge	reorder quantity; replacement order quantity
Wiederbeschaffungsdurchlaufzeit	procurement lead time; replacement lead time
Wiederbeschaffungsfrist	replacement deadline
Wiederbeschaffungszeit	replacement period, procurement lead time, replacement time
Wiederholfertigung	repetitive manufacturing, repetitive production
Wiederverkäufer	resaler
Wiederverwertung	recycling, reuse
▷ Wiederverwertung von Materialien durch teilweise Wiederverwertung	blend off, reuse
Wirkungsgrad	efficiency
Wirtschaft	economy
▷ angebotsorientierte Wirtschaft	supply-sight economy
Wirtschaft	economic
wirtschaften	to manage
▷ schlecht wirtschaften	to mismanage
▷ sparsam wirtschaften	to economize
wirtschaftlich	economical, cost-effective, low-cost
▷ wirtschaftliche Effizienz	economic efficiency
Wirtschaftlichkeit	cost effectiveness, profitability
Wirtschaftlichkeitsanalyse	economic feasibility analysis
Wirtschaftlichkeitsbeurteilung	economic feasibility evaluation
Wirtschaftlichkeitsstudie	feasibility study
Wirtschaftsanalyse	economic analysis
Wirtschaftskreislauf	economic cycle; business process
Wirtschaftssystem	economy
Wochenarbeitszeit	hours worked per week

Z zahlen

zahlen	to pay
Zahlung	payment
▷ Zahlung innerhalb von 60 Tagen	payment within 60 days
▷ Zahlung innerhalb von 14 Tage 2 % Skonto 30 Tage netto	payment within 14 days 2 % cash discount 30 days net
▷ Zahlung in Raten (1. Rate, 2. Rate usw.)	payment in instalments (1st instalmend, 2nd instalmend, etc.)
Zahlung erfolgt	payment to be effected
▷ nach Endabnahme	after final inspections and acceptance
▷ nach Lieferung	after receipt of goods
▷ nach Vorabnahme	after preliminary acceptance
Zahlung gegen Bankgarantie	payment against presentation of bonds (bank guaranties)
Zahlungsaufforderung	reminder
Zahlungsbedingungen	terms of payment
Zahlungseingänge	payments received
Zahlungsverfahren	payment procedure
Zahlungsziel, offenes	open account terms
zeichnen	to draw
Zeichnung	drawing
Zeit	time
▷ die zur Einführung eines neuen Produktes benötigte Zeit	time-to-market
Zeitbegrenzung	deadline, time limit
▷ Zeitbegrenzung für Preisangebot	quotation expiration date, deadline for submitting an offer
Zeitfenster	time fence
Zeitlohn	time work
Zeitlohnsatz	time work rate
Zeitplan	schedule
▷ dem Zeitplan voraus	ahead of schedule
▷ dem Zeitplan hinterher	behind schedule
Zeitraum	time span, period of time
▷ vorgegebener Zeitraum	time fence
Zellenfertigung	cellular manufacturing
Zentrale	headquarters, main office
▷ zentrale Verarbeitungseinheit	central processung unit (CPU)
▷ zentralisierte Güterabfertigung	centralized dispatching
zerbrechlich	fragile

Zulieferstamm

zerbrochen	broken
zerlegen	to dismantle, to knock down
Zertifikat	certificate
Zertifikat gemäß ISO ...	certification according to ISO ...
▷ zertifiziert sein gemäß	to be certified according to
Ziel	target, objective, aim
Zielgruppe	target group, target market
Zielkosten	target cost
Zielkostenbetrachtung	target costing
Ziellagerbestand	target inventory level
Zinsen	interests
Zinssatz	interest rate
Zoll (Behörde)	customs
Zoll (Maßangabe)	inch (")
Zollabfertigung	customs clearance
Zollabfertigungskosten	clearance costs
Zollgebühr	customs duty
Zollager	bonded warehouse
zollfreie Zone	duty-free zone
zollpflichtige Waren	dutiable goods
Zollverschluß	bond
Zubehörteile	accessories
Zufriedenheit des Kunden	customer satisfaction
Zukaufteil	bought-out part
Zulassung	approval
▷ zugelassen sein durch	to be approved by
Zulieferer	supplier(s), subcontractor(s), direct suppliers
▷ erstklassige Zulieferer	first-rate suppliers
▷ preisgünstiger Zulieferer	low-cost supplier
▷ teurer Zulieferer	high-cost supplier
▷ Zulieferer für ein Werk	supplier to a plant
▷ Zulieferer verpflichten	to subcontract
Zulieferindustrie	ancilliary industry, supply industry
▷ Schwächen der Zulieferindustrie	weaknesses of the supply industry
Zulieferprozeß	supply process
Zulieferschwierigkeiten	supply problems
Zulieferstamm	supplier base
▷ Umfang des Zulieferstammes verringern	to reduce the supplier base

Z Zulieferteile

Zulieferteile	supplied/purchased parts, bought-out parts
Zulieferung	supply
zuordnen	to allocate (to)
Zusammenarbeit	cooperation
▷ abteilungsübergreifende Zusammenarbeit	interfunctional cooperation, cross-functional cooperation
Zusammenfassen	to incorporate, to integrate, to unite, to unify, to group
▷ Zusammenfassen von Lieferanten	supplier clustering
▷ zusammengefaßte Prozesse	blocked operations, grouped operations
zusammenschließen	to incorporate; to unify
Zusammenschluß	incorporation, merger
zuständig sein für	to be in charge (of), to be responsible (for)
Zustand	status, condition
zustellen	to deliver
Zustimmung	approval
zuteilen	to assign, to allocate
Zuteilung	allocation
▷ Zuteilung von Waren	allocation of goods
Zuteilungskalkulation (Vollkostenrechnung)	absorption costing, total costing, total cost analysis
zuweisen	to assign, to allocate
Zwang	constraint
Zweigstelle	branch
Zwischenhändler	resaler; middleman
Zwischenlager	intermediate store
Zwischenlagerung	temporary storage, interim stock
Zyklus	cycle
▷ zyklische Fertigungssteuerung	cyclical production control
▷ zyklischer Vorrat	cycle stock

Vocabulary
Wörterverzeichnis

B.
English – German
Englisch – Deutsch

A

abatement	Verminderung
ABC classification	ABC-Klassifikation
ABC evaluation analysis	ABC-Analyse
ABC (system of) inventory control	Lagerhaltung nach ABC-Klassifikation
absorption costing	Zuteilungskalkulation (Vollkostenrechnung)
acceptance	Annahme; Akzept
▷ acceptance of goods	Warenannahme
acceptance criteria	Abnahmekriterien
acceptance instruction	Abnahmevorschrift
acceptance sampling	Stichprobenentnahme für Bewertung
acceptance specification	Abnahmevorschrift
accessories	Zubehörteile
accompanying	beigefügt, beigelegt
according to schedule	termingemäß
account	Konto; Einkaufsrechnung
▷ accounts receivable	Kundenforderungen
▷ to settle accounts	eine Rechnung begleichen
account purchases (A/P)	Abrechnung des Einkaufskommissionärs
account sales	Kontoverkäufe
account terms	Zahlungsziel
▷ open account terms	offenes Zahlungsziel
accounted stock	buchmäßiger Lagerbestand
accounting	Buchhaltungs- und Finanzwesen, Rechnungswesen
▷ completed accounting quantity	gebuchte Fertigungsmenge
accounting code	Buchungsschlüssel
accounting ratios	finanzwirtschaftliche Kennzahlen
accounting year	Geschäftsjahr
to accumulate	akkumulieren
to achieve	erreichen, erzielen
▷ to achieve a competitive edge	einen Wettbewerbsvorteil erzielen
▷ to achieve effective control of supply sources	eine effektive Kontrolle von Lieferquellen erzielen
▷ to achieve optimum control of materials	eine optimale Materialkontrolle erzielen
achievement oriented	leistungsorientiert

acknowledgement	Bestätigung, Anerkennung
▷ acknowledgement of order	Auftragsbestätigung
acquisition	Einkauf, Besorgung, Beschaffung; Akquisition
acquisition value	Beschaffungswert
Act of God	höhere Gewalt
action	Handlung; Wirkung; Klage
▷ action for damages	Schadenersatzklage
▷ to take legal action	den Rechtsweg beschreiten
action plans	Strategiepläne
actual cost(s)	Ist-Kosten
actual cost system	Ist-Kosten-Rechnung
added value	Mehrwert; Wertschöpfung; Wertsteigerung
▷ targeted added value	angestrebte Wertschöpfung
▷ total added value, total value added	Wertschöpfungsvolumen
added value activity	Wertschöpfung, Wertschöpfungsprozeß
added value chain	Wertschöpfungskette
added value partnership	Wertschöpfungspartnerschaft
additional charges	Aufschläge
additional demand	Mehrbedarf, Zusatzbedarf, Querbedarf
additional effort	Mehraufwand
additional material input	zusätzlicher Materialaufwand
additional requirements	Mehrbedarf, Zusatzbedarf, Querbedarf
additions to stock	Lagerzugänge
to adjourn	vertagen
adjustment	Angleichung, Einstellung; Regelung
▷ adjustment of complaints	Beschwerdebeilegung
administration	Verwaltung
administrative expenses	Verwaltungsgemeinkosten
to adopt	annehmen, sich zu eigen machen
▷ to adopt more customer-oriented approaches	eine mehr kundenorientierte Haltung einnehmen
advance	Vorsprung, Verbesserung
▷ in advance	im voraus
▷ advanced payment	Vorauszahlung
advance order	Vorbestellung, Vorausbestellung
advance payment	Vorauszahlung
advantage	Vorteil

A to advertise

▷ competitive advantage	Wettbewerbsvorteil
to advertise	werben für; inserieren, annoncieren
advertising	Werbung
advertising agency	Werbeagentur
advertising budget	Werbebudget
advice of dispatch	Versandanzeige
advice note	Versandanzeige
after-sales service	Kundendienst
after-tax charges	Kosten nach Abzug der Steuern
agenda	Tagesordnung
▷ topic on the agenda (TOP)	Tagesordnungspunkt (TOP)
air freight	Luftfracht
alignment	Abstimmung, Korrekur
to allocate (to)	zuordnen
allocation	Zuteilung, Zuordnung
▷ allocation of goods	Zuteilung von Waren
▷ allocation of work responsibilities	Aufgabenverteilung; Verteilung von Zuständigkeitsbereichen
allowance	Gutschrift; Preisnachlaß (nach Beschwerden); Zeitzugabe
▷ standard allowance	Standard-Zeitzugabe
alteration planning	Bedarfsänderung
alternate loading time	Ersatzbelegungszeit
alternate machine	Ausweichmaschine
alternate material	Ausweichmaterial
alternative materials	Ersatzmaterialien, Ausweichmaterialien
to amalgamate	fusionieren
amalgamation	Fusion
American Standard Code for Information Interchange (ASCII)	Amerikanischer Standardcode für den Informationsaustausch (ASCII)
amount	Betrag
▷ the amount owing	der geschuldete Betrag
analysis of materials flow	Materialflußanalyse
analysis of potential trouble spots	Schwachstellenanalyse
Andler's batchsize formula	Andlersche Losgrößenformel
annual account	Jahresbericht
annual requirements	Jahresbedarf
annual review	Jahresprüfung
application for payment	Zahlungsaufforderung
appointment	Termin, Verabredung

approval	Zustimmung, Zulassung
▷ to be approved by	zugelassen sein durch
arbitration	Schiedgerichtsverfahren
area	Bereich, Gebiet
arrears	Rückstände
▷ to be in arrears	(mit Zahlungen) im Verzug sein
arrival date	Ankunftstag, Fälligkeitsdatum
assembly	Montage
▷ final assembly	Endmontage
▷ ready for assembly	einbaufertig
▷ assemble-to-order	auftragsbezogene Montage
assembly line	Fließband
assembly line production	Fließfertigung
assembly line worker	Fließbandarbeiter
assembly list	Bauliste
assembly order	Materialanforderungsschein; Montageauftrag
assembly plan	Montageplan
assembly plant	Montagewerk
assembly schedule	Lieferplan
assessment	Einschätzung, Beurteilung
▷ assessment of material requirements	Materialbedarfsrechnung
▷ assessment of (net) material requirements	Nettobedarfsrechnung, -ermittlung
assessment of sub-contractors	Beurteilung von Unterlieferanten
asset management	Anlagenwirtschaft
assets	(Kapital-)Werte, (finanzielle und andere) Mittel
▷ current assets	Umlaufvermögen
▷ financial assets	Finanzanlagen
▷ fixed assets	Anlagevermögen
▷ fixed intangible assets	immaterielle Vermögensgegenstände
▷ fixed tangible assets	Sachanlagen
▷ other assets	sonstige Vermögenswerte
▷ physical assets	materielle Güter
▷ assets and liabilities	Aktiva und Passiva
to assign	zuteilen, zuweisen; einteilen; bestimmen
assignment	Abordnung
assortment	Auswahl, Sortiment
attachment	Anlage, Beiwerk
audit	Kontrolle; Prüfung
to audit	Bücher prüfen

A to authorize

to authorize	genehmigen, freigeben
authorization	Genehmigung, Freigabe, Entscheidungskompetenz
▷ to obtain authorization (for)	Genehmigung einholen (für)
level of authorization	Reichweite von Entscheidungsbefugnissen
authorized	befugt, freigegeben
▷ to be authorized to sign	zeichnungsberechtigt, unterschriftsbevollmächtigt
▷ authorized dealer	autorisierter Händler
▷ Authorized Signatory	Prokurist
automation	Automatisierung
▷ automation of inventory processes	Lagerautomatisierung
to automatize	automatisieren
auxiliary material	Hilfs- und Betriebsstoffe
availability	Verfügbarkeit
▷ availability of materials	Materialverfügbarkeit
▷ to ensure the availability of supplies and services	die Versorgung sicherstellen
availability calculation	Verfügbarkeitsrechnung
availability code	Verfügbarkeitscode
availability control	Verfügbarkeitskontrolle
availability date	Verfügbarkeitstermin
available	verfügbar
▷ available capacity	verfügbare Kapazität
▷ available production facilities	verfügbare Produktionskapazitäten
▷ available stock	verfügbarer Bestand, verfügbarer Lagerbestand
average	Durchschnitt
▷ average costs	Durchschnittskosten
▷ floating average cost	gleitender Durchschnittspreis
▷ average cost curves	durchschnittliche Kostenkurven
▷ average demand	durchschnittlicher Bedarf
▷ average outgoing quality level (AOQL)	durchschnittliche Fehlermenge
▷ average price	Durchschnittspreis

B

B-parts	B-Teile
B-part ordering key	B-Teile Bestellschlüssel
backlog	Rückstand

backlog of orders, back orders	Auftragsüberhang; Auftragsrückstand, unerfüllter Auftragsrückstand
backlog of work	Arbeitsrückstand
backorder	Auftrag mit Terminverzug
balance sheet	Kontoauszug
bale	Ballen
to bale	in Ballen packen
bar code	Streifencode, Strichcode
bar coding	Balkencodeerkennung, Barcode-Dekoder
base index	Basisindex
base inventory level	Basisbestand
basic commodities	Bedarfsgüter
basic data	Grunddaten
basic goods, basic materials	Grundstoffe
basic goods industry	Grundstoffindustrie
basic industry	Grundstoffindustrie
basic part	Grundteil, Standardteil
basic producer	Hersteller der Grundstoffindustrie
batch	Stapel, Stoß; zusammengefaßte Bestellmenge
batch production	Losfertigung
batch quantity	Losmenge, Losgröße
▷ standard batch quantity (SBQ)	Standardlosgröße
▷ batch quantity variation	Losmengenabweichung
batching	Losbildung, Losgrößenbildung
batch size	Losgröße
▷ economic batch size	wirtschaftliche Losgröße
▷ fixed batch size	feste Losgröße
batchsizing	Losbildung, Losgrößenbildung
Bayesian analysis	Bayes'sche Analyse
to be	sein
▷ to be in the black	Profite verzeichnen
▷ to be in the red	Verluste verzeichnen
benchmark measures	Vergleichsmessung mit Bezugspunkten
benchmark price	Richtpreis, Fixpreis
benchmarking**	Benchmarking**, Kennzahlenvergleich
benchmarking figures, benchmarks	Eckwerte, Kennzahlen
benefit	Vorteil, Nutzen, Gewinn

B — to benefit

▷ the benefit-cost ratio | Kosten-Nutzen-Verhältnis
to benefit | nützen, fördern; Nutzen ziehen aus
best-selling model | Spitzenmodell, Verkaufsschlager
bid | Angebot (bei Ausschreibungen); Gebot

bid pricing | variable Preisfestlegung
bill of delivery | Lieferschein
bill of exchange | Wechsel
bill of lading | Konnossement
▷ clean-on-bord bill of lading | reines Bordkonnossement
bill of material | Materialschein; Stückliste
▷ construction bill of material | Konstruktionsstückliste
▷ manufacturing bill of material | Fertigungsstückliste
▷ master bill of material | Ausgangsstückliste
▷ production bill of material | Fertigungsstückliste
▷ structure bill of material | Strukturstückliste
▷ variant bill of material | Variantenstückliste
bill of quantities | Materialauszug
bill of resources | (Ressourcen-)Stückliste
bin | Behälter
bin card | Materialbestandskarte
bin tag | Lagerortkarte, Lagerfachkarte; Behälterkennzeichnung

blank purchase | Blankobezug
blanket order | Rahmenauftrag
blend-off | Recycling von Material durch teilweise Wiederverwertung

block | Block
blocked operations | zusammengefaßte Prozesse
block control | Fertigungsphasenüberwachung
block scheduling | Terminierung mit Zeitabschnitten
blocked operations | Werkstattfertigung; funktionsorientierte Fertigung

blocked operations facility | Fertigungseinrichtung zur Herstellung verschiedener Produkte

blue print | Blaupause, Planungsentwurf
board of directors | *allg.:* Vorstand; *in GB + USA:* Verwaltungsrat

boatload | Schiffsladung
bonds | Bankgarantien
bonded warehouse | Zollager

bulk production **B**

to book	buchen, verbuchen
▷ to book orders	Aufträge einholen
book value of a company's brand	Buchwert einer Firma
bottleneck	Engpaß
▷ infrastructural bottleneck	infrastruktureller Engpaß
bottom-up replanning	Neuplanung von unten nach oben
bought-out	zugekauft
▷ bought-out components	zugekaufte Fertigteile
▷ bought-out standard parts	zugekaufte Normteile
branch	Zweigstelle, Niederlassung, Filiale
brand	Marke
brand name	Markenname
branding	Warenzeichenpolitik
break in production	Betriebsstörung, Störung in der Fertigung
breakdown	Zusammenbruch; Panne
▷ breakdown of machinery	Betriebsstörung, Maschinenstillstand
breakdown of prices	Preisaufschlüsselung
▷ to break down a price	einen Preis in seine Komponenten aufschlüsseln
▷ to break down costs	Kosten einzeln auflisten
breakdown maintenance	Reparaturservice
break-even point	Kostenrechnungspunkt, Gewinnschwelle
break point	Meßpunkt
to broaden production	die Produktion erweitern
broken, broken down	zerbrochen, kaputt
bucket	Zeitabschnitt, Planungsperiode
bucket system	Dispositionssystem mit Zeitabschnitten
budget	Budget, Haushalt
budget lines	Budgetgrenzen, Budgetrahmen
to build	bauen, errichten, herstellen; aufbauen
building trade	Bauwirtschaft
bulk	Umfang, Größe, Masse
▷ in bulk	lose, unverpackt; en gros
bulk discount	Mengenrabatt
bulk goods	Massengüter
bulk issue	Massenausgabe
bulk material	Schüttgut
bulk production	Großfertigung

B — bulk purchaser

bulk purchaser	Großhändler, Großabnehmer
bulk storage	Großlager
bulk order	Großbestellung
bulky	massig, sperrig, unhandlich
▷ bulky goods	sperrige Güter
buoyant markets	boomende Märkte
business	Geschäft, Unternehmen
▷ to conduct/manage/operate a business	ein Geschäft führen, leiten, betreiben
business administration	Unternehmensplanung
business behavio(u)r	Geschäftsgebahren
business case studies	Fallstudien
business conduct	Geschäftsgebahren
business context	Geschäftsumfeld
business enterprise	Unternehmen
business environment	Geschäftsumfeld, Geschäftslage
businessman/businesswoman	Geschäftsmann/Geschäftsfrau
business logistics**	Business Logistics**
business (incl. managerial) objectives	Unternehmensziele
business performance	Betriebsleistung
business plan	Wirtschaftsplan
business planning	Wirtschaftsplanung, Zielplanung
business practice	Geschäftspraxis
business reengineering**	Business Reengineering
business report	Geschäftsbericht
business reputation	Geschäftsruf
business structure	Betriebsaufbau
business transactions	Geschäftsabschlüsse
business trip	Geschäftsreise
business unit	Geschäftseinheit
▷ strategic business unit	strategische Geschäftseinheit
business year	Geschäftsjahr
to buy	kaufen, einkaufen, beschaffen
▷ to buy at the price of DM . . .	zum Preis von DM . . . einkaufen
buyer	Einkäufer, Beschaffer
▷ industrial buyer	Einkäufer für die Industrie
▷ non-resident buyer	im Ausland ansässiger Einkäufer
▷ resident buyer	ortsansässiger Einkäufer
▷ at buyer's risk and expense	auf Rechnung und Gefahr des Käufers
buyer code	Einkäuferschlüssel

buyer concentration (of power) | Nachfragemacht
buyer credit | Beschaffungskredit
buyer's market | Käufermarkt
buying | Einkauf
▷ centralized buying | zentralisierter Einkauf
▷ decentralized buying | dezentralisierter Einkauf
▷ rigidly centralised buying | streng zentralisierter Einkauf
▷ wholesale buying | Engroseinkauf
buying agent | Einkäufer, Einkaufsvertreter
buying and sales department | Einkaufs- und Verkaufsabteilung
buying and selling | Ein- und Verkauf
buying capacity | Kaufkraft
buying cartel | Beschaffungskartell
buying centre (USA: center) | Beschaffungsgruppe; Einkaufsgremium eines Unternehmens
buying commission | Einkaufsprovision
buying department | Einkaufsabteilung
buying letter of credit | Einkaufsakkreditiv
buying programme | Beschaffungsplan, Beschaffungsprogramm
buying quota | Einkaufskontingent
buying resource | Bezugsquelle, Beschaffungsquelle
buying task | Beschaffungsaufgabe
by-product | Nebenprodukt

C

C-part ordering key | C-Teile Bestellschlüssel
cachet | Gütesiegel, Qualitätsnachweis
calculation | Berechnung, Kalkulation
▷ calculation of costs | Kostenkalkulation
▷ calculation for depreciation | Abschreibungsrechnung
▷ calculation of requirements | Bedarfsrechnung
▷ calculation of stock | Bestandsrechnung
calibration | Eichung
call for tenders | Ausschreibung
to call off a delivery | eine Lieferung abrufen
to call off a meeting | einen Termin absagen
call off times | Abrufzeiten

C — to cancel

to cancel	stornieren
▷ to cancel a contract	von einem Vertrag zurücktreten
cancellation	Absage, Stornierung
▷ cancellation of orders	Auftragsstornierung
cancellation charges	Stornogebühren
cancellation contract	Aufhebungsvertrag
cancellation of contract	Vertragsstornierung
cancellation of order (in case of non-delivery) and subsequent acquisition of goods from another source, with supplier having to pay for additional costs and expenses	Deckungskauf
capability	Fähigkeit, Befähigung
▷ capability of a company	Leistungspotential
capability profile	Leistungprofile
capacity	Kapazität
▷ actual capacity	Ist-Kapazität
▷ capacity required	Kapazitätsbedarf
▷ customer order capacity load overview	auftragsbezogene Kapazitätsbelastungsübersicht
▷ rated capacity	Soll-Kapazität
capacity alignment	Kapazitätsabgleich
capacity calculation	Kapazitätsrechnung
capacity level(l)ing	Kapazitätsabgleich
capacity load calculation	Kapazitätsbelastungsrechnung
capacity load overview	Kapazitätsbelastungsübersicht
Capacity Requirements Planning (CRP)	Kapazitätsbedarfsplanung
capacity scheduling	Kapazitätsterminierung
capacity where-used list	Kapazitätsverwendungsnachweis
capital	Kapital
▷ to procure capital	Kapital beschaffen
▷ to tie up capital	Kapital binden
capital assets	Kapitalwerte
capital budgeting	Kapitalbedarfsrechnung
capital cost	Investitionskosten
capital goods	Investitionsgüter
capital goods industry	Investitionsgüterindustrie
capital investment	Geldinvestitionen
capital lockup	Kapitalbindung
capital procurement	Kapitalbeschaffung
capital procurement costs	Kapitalbeschaffungskosten
capital reserves	Kapitalrücklagen

capital resources	Kapitalausstattung
capital stock	Grundkapital
capital turnover	Kapitalumschlag
to capitalize	kapitalisieren; Kapital schlagen aus
▷ capitalized value	Ertragswert
careless storage	unsachgemäße Lagerung
carload lot	Waggonladung
carriage	Beförderung, Transport
▷ carriage forward	unfrei, Fracht bezahlt der Empfänger
▷ carriage paid	frachtfrei, Fracht bezahlt
carriage charges	Transportkosten, Frachtgebühren
carrier	Frachtführer
▷ contract carrier	Vertragsspediteur
carrier's liability	Haftung des Frachtführers
to carry	befördern, transportieren
cartage	Rollgeld
carted goods	Rollgut
cash	Bargeld
▷ to pay in cash	in bar zahlen
cash account	Kassakonto
cash discount	Skonto
cash flow	Kapitalfluß
▷ low cash flow	geringe Kostenelastizität
cash payment	Barzahlung
cash purchases	Bareinkäufe
cash requirements	Bedarf an liquiden Mitteln
to cash a cheque	einen Scheck einlösen
catalogue	Katalog, Broschüre
CEO (= Chief Executive Officer)	Vorsitzender der Geschäftsführung (USA)
certificate	Zertifikat, Zertifizierung
▷ certificate according to ISO 9001	Zertifizierung gemäß ISO 9001
▷ to be certified accoring to ISO 9001	zertifiziert sein gemäß ISO 9001
certificate of compliance	Bestätigung der Vertragserfüllung
certificate of origin	Ursprungszeugnis
certificate of inspection	Beschaffenheitszeugnis; Abnahmeprotokoll
Chairman (of the Board of Directors)	Vorsitzender der Geschäftsführung (UK)
chairman (of the managing board)	Vorstandsvorsitzender
changes	Veränderungen
▷ changes in demand	Nachfrageverschiebungen

C — to charge

to charge	berechnen, in Rechnung stellen
to be in charge (of)	zuständig sein (für)
charges	Kosten
cheap imports	Billigimporte
chemical industry	Chemieindustrie
chief buyer	Chefeinkäufer
circular flow	Kreislauf
▷ circular-flow economy	Kreislaufwirtschaft
circulating capital	Betriebsmittel
circulation of goods	Güterumlauf
civil engineering	Baukonstruktion
civil works	Bauarbeiten
claim	Forderung
▷ claim for damages	Schadensersatzforderung; Regreßforderung
to claim	fordern
▷ to claim damages	Regreß anmelden
claim management	Durchsetzung von vertraglichen Ansprüchen bei Nichterfüllung
claims	Rechtsansprüche
classification	Eingruppierung
classification numbers	Gliederungszahlen
to classify	klassifizieren
to cleanse	säubern; entsorgen
clearance	Lagerräumung; Zollabfertigung
clearance costs	Zollabfertigungskosten
client	Kunde; Mandant
clientele	Kundschaft
▷ sophisticated clientele	anspruchsvolle Kundschaft
closing-date	Schlußdatum/letzter Termin für ein Angebot
code	Norm; Kennzeichen
coding	Verschlüsselung
cold storage	Lagerung im Kühlhaus
cold store	Kühlhaus
to collect goods	Waren abholen
collection of samples	Musterkollektion
commerce	Handel
commercial agent	Handelsvertreter, Händler
commission	Provision

completition card C

▷ commission on purchase | Einkaufsprovision
commission buyer | Einkaufskomissionär
commissioning | Handhabung; Inbetriebnahme
commissioning team | Anfahrmannschaft
commodities management | Warenwirtschaft
commodity | handelsübliche Ware, Gut, Handelsartikel
commodity analysis | Warenanalyse
commodity market | Warenmarkt, Warenbörse
common part | Wiederholteil; Mehrfachverwendungsteil

company | Firma, Gesellschaft, Unternehmen
▷ a reputed/renowned company | eine renommierte Firma
company agreement | Betriebsvereinbarung
comparative statistics | vergleichende Statistiken
to compare | vergleichen, gegenüberstellen
comparison | Vergleich, Gegenüberstellung
▷ comparison of inventory movements | Lagerbestandsvergleich

to compete | konkurrieren, wetteifern um
competence | Fachkompetenz
competence centre | Kompetenzstelle, Kompetenzträger
competition | Wettbewerb, Konkurrenz; Konkurrenzkampf
▷ destructive competition | Verdrängungswettbewerb
▷ unfair competition | unlauterer Wettbewerb
▷ keen/stiff competition | starke Konkurrenz
▷ competition in efficiency | Leistungswettbewerb
▷ to face keen/stiff competition | starker Konkurrenz ausgesetzt sein
competitive | konkurrierend; wettbewerbsfähig
▷ competitive advertising | vergleichende Werbung
▷ competitive advantage | Wettbewerbsvorteil
▷ substantial competitive advantages | beträchtliche Wettbewerbsvorteile
▷ competitive pressures | Wettbewerbsdruck
▷ competitive price | konkurrenzfähiger Preis
competitor | Konkurrent
competitor analysis | Konkurrenzanalyse
to compile inventory | Lagerbestände aufnehmen
complaint about faulty material and workmanship | Mängelrüge

complete | völlig, komplett
▷ completely knocked down (CKD) | komplett zerlegt
completion card | Fertigungskarte, Rückmeldekarte

C component

component	Bestandteil; Baugruppe, Bauteil, Bauelement
component requirements quantity	Teilebedarfsmenge
computer	Computer, Rechner
▷ computer-aided design (CAD)	rechnergestützte Konstruktion
▷ computer-aided manufacturing (CAM)	computergestützte Fertigung
▷ computer-aided process planning (CAPP)	computergestützte Prozeßplanung
▷ computer-aided inspection and testing	computergestützte Qualitätskontrolle
▷ computer-aided engineering	computergestützte technische Entwicklung
▷ computerized production control	maschinelle Fertigungssteuerung
▷ high-capacity computer	Großrechner
concentration of purchasing power	Einkaufskonzentration
concept of modular assembly	Baukastenprinzip
condition	Zustand
▷ in fully operative condition	voll betriebsfähig
conditions	Bedingungen
▷ to adhere to conditions	sich an Bedingungen halten
▷ to agree to conditions	Bedingungen zustimmen
▷ to alter conditions	Bedingungen ändern
conduct	Führung, Leitung; Verhalten
confidentiality agreement/clause	Vertraulichkeitsvereinbarung
confirmation	Bestätigung
▷ written confirmation	schriftliche Bestätigung
▷ confirmation of order	Auftragsbestätigung
consigned component production	Fremdfertigung mit Beistellung (von Teilen oder Baugruppen)
consignee	Empfänger
consignment	(Waren-)Sendung
consignment note	Frachtbrief
consignment stock	Konsignationslager
consignor	Versender, Absender
constraints	Zwänge
▷ structural constraints	Systemzwänge
construction	Konstruktion; Baugewerbe
construction and erection	Bau und Montage
construction bill of material	Konstruktionsstückliste
consumables	Verbrauchsgüter
to consume	verbrauchen, konsumieren

consumer	Verbraucher, Konsument; Bedarfsträger
consumer behavio(u)r	Konsumentenverhalten, Verbraucherverhalten
consumer benefits	Kundennutzen
consumer goods	Konsumgüter, Verbrauchsgüter; Bedarfsgüter
consumer goods industry	Verbrauchsgüterindustrie
consumer loyalty	Kundentreue
consumer price	Verbraucherpreis
consumer-supplier relationship	Abnehmer-Lieferanten-Beziehungen
consumption	Verbrauch, Konsum
consumption forecast	Verbrauchsprognose
container	Container
▷ container on railroad flatcars (COFC)	Flachwagencontainer (Bahn/Lkw)
containership	Containerschiff
contingent loss	möglicher Verlust
continuous process production	Fließ- und Prozeßfertigung
contract	Vertrag
▷ contract (over a stipulated quantity)	Mengenkontrakt
▷ contract of carriage	Frachtvertrag
▷ contract of sale	Kaufvertrag
▷ to cancel a contract	Vertrag stornieren
▷ to prolong a contract	Vertrag verlängern
▷ to sign a contract	Vertrag unterzeichnen
▷ to sign off a contract	Vertrag paraphieren
▷ to stipulate something in a contract	etwas vertraglich festsetzen
▷ to suspend a contract	Vertrag sistieren
▷ to terminate a contract	Vertrag auflösen
▷ to update a contract	Vertrag aktualisieren
▷ to withdraw from a contract	Vertrag aufheben
▷ a contract expires	ein Vertrag läuft ab
▷ duration of contract	Vertragslaufzeit
contract clauses	Vertragsklauseln
contract draft	Vertragsentwurf
contract management	Vertragswesen
contract period	Auftragsabwicklungszeit
contract price	Vertragspreis
contract-specific QA manual	auftragsbezogenes QS-Handbuch
contractual stipulation	Vertragsbestimmung
fulfillment of contractual stipulations	Leistungserfüllung
non-fulfillment of contractual stipulations	Nichterfüllung vertraglicher Verpflichtungen

contractor	Unternehmer; (Groß-)Lieferant
contribution	Beitrag
▷ to make contributions	Beiträge leisten
controlling**	Controlling**
▷ controlling in materials management	Materialwirtschaftscontrolling
convenience	Bequemlichkeit
▷ at your earliest convenience	sobald es Ihnen möglich ist
conventional design	Normalausführung
to convert	umrüsten
to convey	befördern, transportieren
conveyance	Beförderung, Transport
▷ conveyance of goods	(Waren-)Transport
core competence	Kernkompetenz
▷ to concentrate on one's core competence	sich auf seine Kompetenz konzentrieren
core strategic issues	Thema von zentraler strategischer Bedeutung
core time	Kernarbeitszeit
corporate	betriebs-, betrieblich
corporate aims	Unternehmensziele
corporate function	betriebliche Teilaufgabe
corporate philosophy	Unternehmensphilosophie
corporate strategy	Unternehmensstrategie
corporate structure	Betriebsstruktur
▷ distribution-oriented corporate structure	vertriebsorientierte Betriebsstruktur
▷ manufacturing-oriented corporate structure	produktionsorientierte Betriebsstruktur
▷ supply-oriented corporate structure	beschaffungsorientierte Betriebsstruktur
cost(s)	Kosten, Aufwand
▷ fixed costs	Fixkosten
▷ projected costs	veranschlagte Kosten
▷ running costs	laufende Kosten
▷ substantial costs	beträchtliche Kosten
▷ reimbursable costs	zu erstattende Kosten
▷ special direct costs	Sondereinzelkosten
▷ still expected costs	noch zu erwartende Kosten
▷ unforeseen costs	unvorhergesehene Kosten
▷ variable costs	variable Kosten
▷ cost of acquisition	Beschaffungskosten, Einkaufspreis
▷ cost of capital	Kapitalkosten
▷ cost of delivery	Lieferkosten
▷ cost of direct material	Materialeinzelkosten

cost price

▷ cost of distribution	Vertriebskosten
▷ cost of general administration	allgemeine Verwaltungskosten
▷ cost of launching a new venture	Anlaufkosten eines Unternehmens
▷ cost of materials	Materialkosten
▷ cost of materials flow	Materialflußkosten
▷ cost of production	Produktionskosten
▷ cost of supplies	Beschaffungskosten
▷ cost of transactions	Abwicklungskosten
▷ cost of transport(ation)	Transportkosten, Frachtkosten
▷ to cut back costs	Kosten reduzieren
▷ to cut costs to the bone	Kosten so niedrig wie möglich kalkulieren
▷ to meet costs	für Kosten aufkommen
▷ to reduce costs	Kosten reduzieren
▷ to write off costs	Kosten abschreiben
to cost	kosten
cost abatement	Kostendämpfung
cost adjustment	Kostenangleichung
cost accounting	Kostenrechnung
cost calculation	Kostenkalkulation
▷ actual cost calculation	Ist-Kosten-Kalkulation
cost centre, cost center	Kostenstelle
cost centre number	Kostenstellennummer
cost-conscious	kostenbewußt, preisbewußt
cost-covering	kostendeckend
cost curves	Kostenkurven
▷ average cost curves	durchschnittliche Kostenkurven
▷ long-run cost curves	langfristige Kostenkurven
▷ short-run cost curves	kurzfristige Kostenkurven
cost effective	kostenwirksam
cost-effectiveness, profitability	Wirtschaftlichkeit
cost engineering	Kostenengineering; Kostenplanung
cost improvement techniques	Kostenoptimierungsmethoden
cost increase	Preissteigerung
cost management	Kostenmanagement
costs	Kosten
▷ to allocate costs	Kosten zuordnen
costs for subcontracted supplies and services	Fremdleistungskosten
costs incur	Kosten fallen an
cost structure	Kostengefüge
costly	kostspielig, teuer
cost price	Beschaffungspreis; Selbstkostenpreis

C   cost-ratio plan

cost-ratio plan	Kostendeckungsplan
cost variance analysis	Abweichungsanalyse
costing method using burden rates	Zuschlagskalkulation
counterfoil (of delivery costs)	Empfangsschein
counter-offer	Gegenangebot
countermeasure	Gegenmaßnahmen
country of destination	Bestimmungsland
country of origin	Ursprungsland
cover	Deckung, Sicherheit
▷ under separate cover	mit getrennter Post
to cover	decken, abdecken; versichern
▷ to cover a market	einen Markt bearbeiten
▷ to cover requirements	Bedarf decken
cover note	Deckungsbestätigung, vorläufige Deckungszusage
to create	schaffen
▷ to create an outlet (for)	einen Markt für etwas schaffen
creation	Verursachung, Hervorrufung
credit	Guthaben, Kredit-(seite), Haben
▷ unlimited credit	der unbeschränkte Kredit
▷ long-term credit	langfristiger Kredit
▷ medium-term credit	mittelfristiger Kredit
▷ short-term credit	kurzfristiger Kredit
▷ letter of credit (L/C)	Akkreditiv
▷ line of credit	Kreditlinie
credit note	Gutschrift
creditor	Gläubiger
creditors	Gläubiger; Verbindlichkeiten
Critical-Path Method (CPM)	Kritischer-Pfad-Methode
cross-functional cooperation	funktionsübergreifende Zusammenarbeit
cross-section functions	Querschnittsfunktionen
to curb	reduzieren, drosseln
▷ to curb production	Produktion drosseln
current	gegenwärtig, aktuell; gültig
▷ current account	Girokonto
▷ current assets	Umlaufvermögen
▷ current demand	momentane Nachfrage
▷ current order	laufender Auftrag
▷ current overhead	Ist-Gemeinkosten
▷ current price	Tagespreis, geltender Preis
▷ current price list	aktuelle/gültige Preisliste
▷ current quantity released	aktuelle Abrufmenge
▷ current unit cost	momentane Kosten pro Einheit

customary	üblich
customer	Kunde, Abnehmer; Bedarfsträger
▷ demanding customers	anspruchsvolle Kunden
▷ prospective customer	potentieller Kunde
▷ regular customer	Stammkunde
▷ to accomodate a customer	einem Kunden entgegenkommen
▷ to attract customers	Kunden anziehen
customer base	Kundenstamm
▷ to increase the customer base	den Kundenstamm erweitern
customer-centred approaches	kundenorientierte Haltung/ Strategien
▷ to adopt a more customer-centred approach	eine mehr kundenorientierte Haltung einnehmen
customer demands	Verbraucherforderungen
customer needs	Verbraucherbedürfnisse
▷ to meet/to satisfy customer needs	Verbraucherbedürfnisse decken
customer order servicing system	Kundenauftragsabwicklungssystem
customer planning and scheduling	Kundenauftragsdisposition
customer satisfaction	Zufriedenheit der Kunden
custom made	kundenspezifische Anfertigung
customs	Zoll
customs clearance	Zollabfertigung
customs duties	Zollgebühren
cut	Abbau, Kürzung
to cut	schneiden; kürzen; senken; reduzieren
▷ to cut back costs	Kosten reduzieren
▷ to cut prices to the bone	Kosten so niedrig wie möglich kalkulieren
cycle	Kreislauf; Laufzeit; Bearbeitungszeit für ein Stück pro Arbeitsgang
cycle time	Taktzeit; Zeit je Arbeitsvorgang
cyclical production control	zyklische Fertigungssteuerung

D

damage	Schaden
▷ damaged goods	beschädigte Waren
▷ to claim damages	Schadensersatzforderungen anmelden
data	Daten
▷ to input data into a system	Daten in ein System eingeben

D — data base

data base	Datenbank
data communications	Datenaustausch
data processing	Datenverarbeitung
data security	Datenschutz
date	Datum
▷ to fix a date	einen Termin vereinbaren
▷ date of delivery	Lieferdatum
▷ date of dispatch/shipment	Versanddatum
day-to-day needs	alltäglicher Bedarf
dead head	Lehrfahrt eines Behälters
deadline for delivery	letzter Liefertermin
deadline for submitting an offer	Angebotsfrist
deadline for tenders	Ausschreibungsfrist
deal	Geschäft
▷ one-off deal	Einmalgeschäft; Einzelgeschäft
dealer	Händler
debit	Soll, Belastung
debit and credit	Soll und Haben
debit note	Lastschrift
debris	Schutt
debtor	Schuldner
debts	Schulden, Verbindlichkeiten, Forderungen
decision-making process	Entscheidungsfindungsprozeß
decline	Abnahme, Rückgang
▷ decline in demand	Nachfragerückgang
dedicated production line	Fertigungsstraße (zur Herstellung eines Endprodukts)
default	Versäumnis, Nichterfüllung, Verzug
▷ default in performance	Leistungsstörung
defect	Mangel, Fehler
▷ defect in material	Materialfehler
defective	fehlerhaft
▷ defective material and workmanship	Material- oder Herstellungsfehler
▷ defective performance	Schlechterfüllung einer Leistung
deficiencies	Mängel (ab Produktion), Qualitätsmängel
del credere	Delkredere
delay	Verzögerung, Verspätung, Verzug
▷ delay in delivery, delayed delivery	Lieferverzug
▷ delayed acceptance	Annahmeverzug

demand D

to delegate | delegieren, übertragen
▷ to delegate duties | Pflichten übertragen, Aufgaben verteilen
▷ to delegate powers | Vollmachten übertragen
delegation of work responsibilites | Aufgabenverteilung
to deliver | liefern, zustellen
▷ to deliver goods within the specified time | Waren termingerecht liefern, die Lieferzeit einhalten
delivery | Lieferung, Anlieferung
▷ delivery on call | Abruflieferung
▷ part delivery | Teillieferung
▷ partial delivery | Teillieferung
▷ split delivery | Lieferung in Teilmengen
▷ surplus delivery | Überlieferung
▷ to effect/to execute delivery | Lieferung durchführen, liefern
▷ to set final deadline for delivery | in Verzug setzen
delivery contract | Liefervertrag
delivery costs/expenses | Lieferkosten
delivery date | Lieferdatum
delivery deadline | Lieferfrist
delivery dependability | Liefertreue
delivery due date | Liefertermin
delivery note | Lieferschein
delivery notice | Liefermeldung
delivery on call | Abruflieferung
delivery period | Lieferzeit
delivery schedule | Lieferplan
delivery services | Lieferservice
delivery specifications | Liefervorschrift
delivery terms | Lieferbedingungen, Preisstellung
delivery time | Lieferzeit
demand (for) | Bedarf, Nachfrage (nach)
▷ additional demand | zusätzlicher Bedarf, Mehrbedarf, Querbedarf
▷ anticipated demand | voraussichtlicher Bedarf
▷ average demand | durchschnittlicher Bedarf
▷ current/imminent demand | aktueller Bedarf
▷ deferred demand | zurückgestellter Bedarf
▷ dependent demand | mittelbar entstandener Bedarf
▷ effective demand | echter Bedarf
▷ excessive demand | übermäßiger Bedarf
▷ increased demand | gesteigerter Bedarf, Bedarfszunahme
▷ interplant demand | Bedarf der eigenen Werke
▷ joint demand | gemeinschaftlicher Bedarf

D to demand

▷ low demand | geringer Bedarf
▷ original demand | ursprünglicher Bedarf
▷ potential demand | möglicher Bedarf
▷ rising demand | wachsende Nachfrage
▷ secondary demand | Nebenbedarf
▷ strong demand | große Nachfrage
▷ supplementary demand | Mehrbedarf, Zusatzbedarf, Querbedarf
▷ tertiary demand | Tertiärbedarf
▷ unsatisfied demand | ungedeckte Nachfrage
▷ urgent demand | dringender Bedarf
▷ weak demand | geringe Nachfrage
▷ assessment of a demand | Bedarfsermittlung, Bedarfsrechnung
▷ changes/shifts in demands | Nachfrageverschiebungen
▷ (cost-optimal) coverage of demands | (kostenoptimale) Bedarfsdeckung
▷ creation of a demand | Bedarfsauslösung
▷ emergence of a demand | Bedarfsentstehung
▷ meeting of a demand | Bedarfsdeckung
▷ satisfaction of a demand | Bedarfsbefriedigung
▷ to coordinate/synchronize demands | Bedarfsbündelung

to demand | fordern, erfordern, verlangen
demand analysis | Bedarfsanalyse
demand-controlled materials planning | bedarfsgesteuerte Disposition
demand-covering objective | Bedarfsziel
demand determination | Bedarfsbestimmung
demand forecasting | Bedarfsprognose
demand gap | Bedarfslücke
demand oriented | bedarfsorientiert
▷ demand-oriented production | bedarfsorientierte Fertigung
demand planning | Bedarfsmengenplanung
▷ consumption-fxed demand planning | bedarfsgebundene Bedarfsmengenplanung
▷ short-term demand planning | kurzfristige Bedarfsmengenplanung
▷ long-term demand planning | langfristige Bedarfsmengenplanung
▷ qualitative demand planning | qualitative Bedarfsmengenplanung
▷ quantitative demand planning | quantitative Bedarfsmengenplanung
demand rate | Bedarfsrate
demand research | Bedarfsforschung
demand trends | Nachfrageverschiebungen
departamental | Abteilungs . . .
departmental expenses | Abteilungskosten
departamental organisation | Organisation einer Abteilung
department | Abteilung; Fach, Bereich
depreciation | Abwertung, Wertminderung; Abschreibung

▷ replacement method of depreciation | Abschreibung auf Wiederbeschaffung
depth of production | Fertigungstiefe
derivation of cost functions/cost curves | Ableitung von Kostenfunktionen/Kostenkurven
descriptive literature | Prospektmaterial
design | Konstruktion
to design | entwerfen, konstruieren
design and construction office | Konstruktionsbüro
design and construction overheads | Konstruktionsgemeinkosten
design input | Designvorgaben
design-to-cost | Produktdesign, kostengerechtes
▷ Design-to-Cost** | Design-to-Cost**
design-to-market | Produktdesign, beschaffungsmarktgerechtes
design-to-process | Produktdesign, prozeßgerechtes
to destock | Läger abbauen/reduzieren
destocking | Lagerreduzierung, Lagerabbau
destructive competition | Verdrängungswettbewerb
deterioration | Wertminderung
determinants | Bestimmungsfaktoren
devaluation, depreciation | Abwertung
to develop | entwickeln; erschließen
▷ to develop a model | ein Modell entwickeln
deviation | Abweichung
▷ mean absolute deviation (MAD) | mittlere absolute Abweichung
device | Vorrichtung; Gerät
dimensions | Maße, Abmessungen
direct labo(u)r (cost) | direkte Lohnkosten
to discharge cargoes | Schiffsladungen löschen
discount | Preisnachlaß, Rabatt; Diskont
▷ bulk discount, quantity discount | Mengenrabatt
▷ cash discount | Skonto
▷ discount off the net price list | Preisnachlässe auf die Nettopreisliste
to discount | abziehen, abrechnen; diskontieren
dismantling | Abbauen, Abrüsten
dismantling time | Abrüstzeit
dispatch | Absendung, Versand
▷ dispatch by rail | Bahnversand
to dispatch | versenden, absenden, verschicken
dispatch department | Versandabteilung

dispatch order	Versandauftrag, Speditionsauftrag
to dispose (of)	erledigen, beseitigen; veräußern
▷ to dispose of waste	Abfall entsorgen
distribution	Vertrieb
distribution costs	Vertriebskosten
distribution planning and management	Vertriebsplanung und -steuerung
distribution stages	Vertriebsphasen
distributor	Verteiler; Großhändler; Generalvertreter
division	(Ver-)Teilung; Abteilung; Geschäftsbereich, Sparte
▷ division of labo(u)r	Arbeitsteilung
dock receipt	Kaiübernahmebescheinigung
document of title	Eigentumsnachweis
documentary collection	Dokumenteninkasso
documentary credits	Dokumentenakkreditv
domestic trade	Binnenhandel
to dominate	herrschen, beherrschen
▷ to dominate a sector	eine Branche beherrschen
down payment	Anzahlung
downtime	störungsbedingte Stillstandzeit
draft	Entwurf
▷ draft of a drawing	Zeichnungsentwurf
▷ contract draft	Vertragsentwurf
to draft	entwerfen
draft plans	Planentwürfe
to draw	zeichnen
drawing	Zeichnen; Zeichnung
drop shipment	Direktlieferung eines Unterlieferanten an den Kunden
dual sourcing	Dual Sourcing: Bezug bei mehr als einem Zulieferer
due	fällig
due date	Liefertermin, Fälligkeitstermin
dumping price	Dumpingpreis
duplicate invoice	Rechnungsabschrift
durable	haltbar, dauerhaft
▷ durable consumer goods	dauerhafte Verbrauchsgüter, Gebrauchsgüter
dutiable goods	zollpflichtige Waren

E

early	früh
▷ earliest finish date	frühester Endtermin
▷ earliest start date	frühester Starttermin
early order	frühzeitige Bestellung
early order discount	Frühdispositionskredit
to earn	verdienen; einbringen
earning capacity	Ertragskraft
earnings	Verdienst; Einkommen, Einkünfte
▷ to lift earnings	das Betriebsergebnis steigern
eco-compatibility study	Umweltverträglichkeitsstudie
economic	(staats-, volks-)wirtschaftlich, wirtschafts...
economical	sparsam, wirtschaftlich
economic analysis	Wirtschaftsanalyse
economic cycle	Wirtschaftskreislauf
economic effectiveness	Rentabilität, wirtschaftliche Effizienz
economic feasibility evaluation	Wirtschaftlichkeitsbeurteilung
Economic Order Quantity (EOQ)	wirtschaftliche Bestellmenge
economies of scale	Preisdegression
▷ Economy of Scale	volumenabhängige Wirtschaftlichkeit
to economize	sparsam wirtschaften
economy	Wirtschaft, Wirtschaftssystem
to effect delivery	Lieferung ausführen, liefern
effective date (of a contract)	Inkrafttreten (eines Vertrages)
efficiency	Wirkungsgrad
efficiency bonus	Leistungszulage
efficiency gains	Effizienz-/Leistungssteigerung
efficiency rating	Leistungsbeurteilung, Leistungsbewertung
efficient	effizient; leistungsfähig; rationell, wirtschaftlich
effort	Anstrengung, Mühe, Bemühung
▷ to make an effort	sich anstrengen, sich bemühen
electrical engineering industry	elektrotechnische Industrie
electricity industry	Elektrizitätswirtschaft
electronic data interchange (EDI)	papierlose Datenübertragung
electronic data processing (EDP)	elektronische Datenverarbeitung (EDV)

E — electronic engineering

electronic engineering	Elektrotechnik
to employ	beschäftigen, einstellen; anwenden
employee	Arbeitnehmer(in), Angestellte(r), Arbeiter(in)
employer	Arbeitgeber(in), Unternehmer(in)
empowerment	verstärkte Übertragung von Entscheidungskompetenz an Mitarbeiter
to empower a person	eine Person bevollmächtigen, ermächtigen
en route	während des Transportes
en situ, at site	vor Ort
to enclose	beilegen
to endorse	indossieren
endorsement	Indossament
engineer	Techniker; Ingenieur
▷ service engineer	Wartungstechniker
▷ chief engineer	technischer Leiter
engineering	Maschinenbau; technische Leistung; technische Entwicklung
engineering change	technische Änderung
engineering change application	Änderungsantrag
engineering change history	Änderungsgeschichte
engineering change notice	Änderungsmitteilung
engineering data	technische Daten
engineering order	Entwicklungsauftrag
to enquire (auch: inquire)	anfragen; untersuchen, prüfen
enquiring procedure	Anfrageverfahren
enquiry (auch: inquiry)	Anfrage, Nachfrage; Prüfung, Untersuchung
entitlement	Berechtigung
▷ to be entitled to	berechtigt sein
entrepreneur	Unternehmer
entrepreneurial	unternehmerisch
▷ entrepreneurial decisions	unternehmerische Entscheidungen
▷ entrepreneurial spirit	Unternehmergeist
environment	Umwelt
environmental	Umwelt
▷ environmental concerns	umweltpolitische Belange
▷ environmental protection	Umweltschutz
environmental protection, environmental pollution control	Umweltschutz

EOQ tables	Tabelle für wirtschaftliche Losgrößen
equilibrium point	Sättigungspunkt
equipment	Ausrüstung, Einrichtung, Maschinen
equipment (goods)	Ausrüstungsgüter
equity capital	Eigenkapital
erection	Montage (bes. im Anlagenbau)
error	Fehler
error message	Fehlermeldung
error note	Fehlermeldung
escalation clause	Preisgleitklausel
estimate	Schätzung, Veranschlagung, Kostenvoranschlag
to estimate	abschätzen, einschätzen; veranschlagen; beurteilen
estimation	Meinung, Achtung, Wertschätzung, Bedarfsabschätzung
▷ management estimation	Bedarfsabschätzung durch die Geschäftsleitung
to evaluate	schätzen, festsetzen, bewerten
evaluation	Schätzung, Bewertung
ex	aus
▷ ex factory/ex mill/ex works	ab Werk
▷ ex warehouse	ab Lager
excess	Überschuß
▷ excess inventories of items	Lagerüberschüsse
▷ excess materials	Überschußmaterial
to execute	ausführen
▷ to execute delivery	Lieferung ausführen, liefern
▷ to execute orders	Aufträge ausführen
execution of an order	Auftragserfüllung
executive	leitender Angestellter
exempt from purchase tax	einkaufssteuerfrei
exhibition	Ausstellung, Messe
exhibition centre	Ausstellungszentrum, Messegelände
exhibition contractor	Messebaufirma
expediting	Terminkontrolle
to expedite	beschleunigen; überwachen
▷ to expedite delivery	Lieferung beschleunigen
▷ to expedite delivery dates	Liefertermine überwachen
▷ to expedite production	Produktion überwachen
expenditure	(Kosten-)Aufwand, Ausgaben, Verbrauch

F — expense accounts

expense accounts	Aufwandskonten
expenses	Kosten, Aufwendungen; Unkosten, Spesen
▷ extraordinary expenses	außerordentliche Aufwendungen
▷ expenses for maintaining inventory levels	Lagerhaltungskosten
▷ expense of materials inspection	Kosten einer Materialüberprüfung
expertise	Erfahrung, Fachwissen
explosion	Auslösung (von Bedarf)
explosion level code	Dispositionsstufencode
export	Ausfuhr, Export
export restrictions	Ausfuhrauflagen
to export	ausführen, exportieren
ex-post costing	Nachkalkulation
extended capacity tie-up	hohe Kapitalbindung
external trade	Außenhandel

F

to fabricate	fertigen
fabricated component	Eigenfertigungsteil
fabrication	Fertigung, Fabrikation
fabrication order	Vorfertigungsauftrag
facility	Betriebsanlage, Einrichtung
facilities management	Anlagenwirtschaft
factor rating	Leistungsbewertung nach Einzelfaktoren
factors of production	Leistungsfaktoren
factory	Fabrik, Produktionsstätte
factory cost	Herstellungskosten
factory structure data	Betriebsstrukturdaten
failure	Ausfall, Versagen
▷ failure analysis	Ausfallanalyse
faithfulness to deadlines	Termintreue
familiarization time	Einarbeitungszeit
fast-selling goods	leichtverkäufliche Ware; Ware mit hoher Umsatzgeschwindigkeit
faulty	fehlerhaft
favourable	vorteilhaft, günstig

fiscal year F

▷ favourable price | günstiger Preis
feasibility | Durchführbarkeit
▷ feasibility of criteria | Durchführbarkeit von Kriterien
▷ feasibility of solutions | Durchführbarkeit von Lösungsansätzen
feasibility study | Wirtschaftlichkeitsstudie
fee | Gebühr
feedback | Rückkopplung
to fill | anfüllen, ausfüllen; erfüllen; ausführen
▷ to fill a need | einen Bedarf befriedigen
▷ to fill orders | Aufträge ausführen
fill-in reorder | Bestellung zur Ergänzung des Lagers
final assembly | Endmontage
final assembly schedule | Endmontageplan
final construction | Endmontage
final consumer | Endverbraucher
final inspection and acceptance | Endabnahme
finance | Finanzwesen, Finanzen
to finance | finanzieren
financial | finanziell; Finanz . . .; Geld . . .
financial planning | Budgetierung
financial viability | Rentabilität
financial year | Geschäftsjahr, Rechnungsjahr
to find a market | Absatz finden
to fine-tune strategies | Strategien optimieren
to finish | beenden
finish | Ende, Vollendung
▷ the finish of goods | Verarbeitung von Waren
▷ finish-to-order | Montieren nach Auftrag
finished goods | Fertigwaren, Endprodukte
finished product inventories | Endproduktbestände
finishing lead time | Endbearbeitungszeit
finite production planning | Fertigungsfeinplanung
finite scheduling | Feinterminierung
firm offer | verbindliches Angebot, Festangebot
first-class quality | erstklassige/erstrangige Qualität
first cost | Einkaufspreis
first order | Erstbestellung
first-rate supplier | erstklassiger Zulieferer
fiscal year | Geschäftsjahr

F — fit for storage

fit for storage	lagerfähig
fitter	Monteur
fitting	Installation; Einbau, Montage
▷ ready for fitting	einbaufertig
fittings	Ausstattung
fixed assets	Anlagevermögen, festangelegte Vermögenswerte
fixed charges/costs	fixe Kosten
fixed order point	fester Bestellpunkt
fixed period ordering	Bestellung in festen Zeitintervallen
flexibility in delivery	Lieferflexibilität
float	Werkstattbestand; Losfüller (bei festen Losgrößen)
floating average cost	gleitender Durchschnittspreis
floating capital	Umlaufvermögen
floor	Untergrenze; Werkstatt
▷ on the floor	in der Werkstatt
floor stock	freier Werkstattbestand (billige Teile und Massenteile)
flow	Fluß
▷ flow of goods	Warenfluß
▷ flow of goods and services	Leistungsstrom; Waren- und Dienstleistungsfluß
▷ flow of materials	Materialfluß
▷ flow of new orders	Auftragswelle
flow chart	Fließ-Schaubild
flow-line/flow-shop production	Fließfertigung, Fließproduktion
flow process	Fließverfahren
flow rate	Flußrate
flow shop	Werkstatt mit Fließfertigung
focus	Brennpunkt, Mittelpunkt
to focus efforts (on)	Bemühungen auf etwas konzentrieren
follow-up contract/order	Folgeauftrag
foot (')	Fuß (Maßeinheit)
to force down prices	Preise drücken
force majeure**	höhere Gewalt
forecast	Vorhersage, Prognose
▷ forecast-based material planning	prognosegesteuerte Disposition
foreign currency, foreign exchange	Devisen
foreign trade	Außenhandel
foreseeable loss	Verlust, vorhersehbarer

global sourcing

formality	Formalität
form-fits-function	Form-folgt-Funktion
to forward	transportieren, befördern, weitersenden
forwarder	Spediteur, Speditionsunternehmen
forwarder's note of charges	Spediteurrechnung
forwarder's receipt	Spediteurübernahmebescheinigung
forwarding agent	Spediteur, Speditionsunternehmen
forwarding instructions	Versandangaben
fragile	zerbrechlich
▷ fragile goods	zerbrechliches Gut
framework	Rahmen, System
framework agreement	Rahmenvereinbarung
free	frei
▷ free carrier (FCR)	frei Frachtführer
▷ free on board (FOB)	frei Schiff
freight	Fracht
▷ unitized freight	vereinheitlichte Fracht
freight consolidation	Sammeltransport
freight costs	Frachtkosten, Transportkosten
friction	Reibung
frozen	gefroren
▷ frozen inventory	eingefrorener Lagerbestand
▷ frozen order	gefrorener Auftrag
full absorption costing	Vollkostenrechnung
function	Funktion; Abteilung
▷ function-oriented structure	Funktionsorganisation
▷ function-related service	funktionsspezifische Leistung
functional budget	Funktionsbudget
functional departamentation	Funktionsgliederung

G

general cargo	Stückgüter
general costs	Gemeinkosten
general terms and conditions	AGBs, Allgemeine Geschäftsbedingungen
global sourcing	internationale Beschaffung, Global Sourcing

G goods

goods	Güter, Waren
▷ damaged goods	beschädigte Waren
▷ faulty goods	fehlerhafte Waren
▷ fragile goods	zerbrechliche Ware
▷ luxury goods	Luxusgüter
▷ selected goods	ausgewählte Waren
▷ stapel goods	Stapelware
▷ goods in process	Halbfertigwaren, Halbfabrikate
▷ goods in stock	Läger, gelagerte Waren
▷ goods in transit	auf dem Transportweg befindliche Güter
▷ goods made to specifications	Sonderanfertigungen
▷ goods ready for dispatch	versandbereite Güter
goods received notice	Wareneingangsmeldung
goods tariff	Gütertarif
goods traffic	Warenverkehr
go-slow	Bummelstreik
graduate engineer	Diplomingenieur
to grant	gewähren, einräumen
gross	brutto
▷ gross cost price	Bruttoeinkaufspreis
▷ gross domestic product (GDP)	Bruttosozialprodukt
▷ gross national product (GNP)	Bruttonationalprodukt
▷ gross purchase price	Bruttoeinkaufspreis
▷ gross requirements	Bruttobedarf
▷ gross requirements calculation	Bruttobedarfsermittlung
▷ gross weight	Bruttogewicht
group	Gruppe; Konzern
to group something	etwas zusammenfassen, zusammenstellen
▷ to group freight/cargo	Sammelladungen zusammenstellen
▷ grouped traffic	Sammelladungsverkehr
group classification	Gruppenklassifizierung
group classification code	Gruppenklassifizierungscode
group production	Gruppenfertigung
group technology	Fertigung von Teilefamilien; produktorientierte Fertigungsgruppe; Produktzentrum (in der Fertigung); Inselfertigung; Nestfertigung
group work centre	Gruppenarbeitsplatz
groupage consignment	Sammeltransport
growth	Wachstum
▷ sustainable growth	anhaltendes Wachstum

guarantee	Garantie
▷ guarantee for availability of spare parts	Ersatzteilversorgungsgarantie
▷ guarantee for fulfillment of contract	Vertragserfüllungsgarantie
▷ bank guarantee	Bankerfüllungsgarantie
to guarantee	garantieren, versichern, Garantie leisten für
guidelines	Richtlinien

H

hand-to-mouth buying	Beschaffung für die lagerlose Fertigung bei Sofortbedarf
handling	Abwicklung
to handle	umgehen mit; bedienen; abwickeln; durchführen
▷ to handle a complaint	eine Beschwerde abwickeln
handling (of)	Abwicklung, Umschlag; Umgang
▷ handling of goods in storage	Lagerbehandlung; Umgang mit Lagerbeständen
▷ hazardous materials handling	Umgang mit Gefahrgütern
head company	Führungsgesellschaft
head office	Hauptverwaltung, Zentrale
headquarters	Hauptsitz, Zentrale
head of the purchasing department, head of purchasing	Chefeinkäufer, Einkaufsleiter
hedge inventories	spekulativer Bestand
hedging	spekutive Bestandsbildung
highly automated	hochautomatisiert
▷ highly automated plants	hochautomatisierte Produktionsstätten
to hire	mieten, vermieten
hire purchase	Einkauf auf Raten/Einkauf auf Anzahlung
hold order	angehaltener Auftrag
hold-up	Verzögerung
(at) home and abroad	im In- und Ausland
hours worked per week	Wochenarbeitszeit
human resources development	Personalentwicklung
Human Resources Manager	Personaldirektor

to identify	ausfindig machen, identifizieren
▷ to identify vulnerable areas	Schwachstellen ausfindig machen
idle period	Liegezeit
idle time	Ausfallzeit, Stillstandzeit, Brachzeit, Leerzeit
illustrations	Abbildungen
immediate delivery	sofortige Lieferung
to implement	ausführen, durchführen
implementation	Ausführung, Durchführung
▷ implementation of purchasing objectives	Durchführung von Einkaufszielen
implicit interest charges for average inventory periods	Lagerzins bei durchschnittlichen Lagerzeiten
import	Import, Einfuhr
to import	importieren, einführen
import quotas	Importquoten
import restrictions	Einfuhrauflagen
importer	Importeur
to impose	verhängen
▷ to impose new regulations	neue Bestimmungen verhängen
impossibility of performance	Unmöglichkeit der Erfüllung einer Leistung
to improve	verbessern, erhöhen, steigern
▷ improved performance	Leistungssteigerung
▷ to improve corporate results	Unternehmensergebnisse verbessern
improvement	Verbesserung
▷ improvement of materials	Materialverbesserung
inaccurate data	ungenaue Daten/Angaben
inactive inventory item	Lagerhüter
inch (″)	Zoll (Maßeinheit)
incidental expenses	Nebenkosten
incidental procurement expenses/costs	Beschaffungsnebenkosten
income	Einkommen; Einkünfte
▷ targeted (net) income	geplantes Betriebsergebnis
income distribution	Einkommensverteilung
income tax	Einkommensteuer
incoming materials	Materialzugänge
incoming orders	Auftragseingänge
in-company	innerbetrieblich

to incorporate	vereinigen, zusammenschließen
incorporated company	(USA) Aktiengesellschaft
incorporated society	eingetragener Verein
incorporation	Vereinigung, Zusammenschluß; Eintragung
increase	Anstieg, Zuwachs
▷ increase in earnings	Einkommenszuwachs
▷ increase in efficiency	Leistungssteigerung
▷ increase in productivity	Produktivitätssteigerung
▷ increased cost of materials	wachsende Materialkosten
indent	Einkaufsauftrag
indemnification	Ersatzvornahme
▷ to claim indemnification	Schadenersatz fordern
index numbers	Indexzahlen
indirect costs	Gemeinkosten
indirect material**	Materialgemeinkosten; Hilfsstoffe
indirect materials center	Material(hilfs)stellen
indivisibility	Unteilbarkeit
industrial	industriell, Industrie ...
▷ industrial enterprise	Industrieunternehmen
▷ industrial equipment	Betriebsausrüstung, Betriebsausstattung
▷ industrial management	Betriebsführung
▷ industrial products	Industrieerzeugnisse
▷ industrial properties	Industriegelände
▷ industrial unit	industrielle Betriebseinheit
▷ industrial zone	Industriegebiet
industry	Industrie, Industriezweig
industry-wide agreement	Manteltarifvertrag
inferior quality	minderwertige Qualität
information flow	Informationsfluß
information channels	Informationswege
inherent risk	das einer Tätigkeit innewohnendes Risiko
in-house	firmenintern
▷ in-house parties	firmeninterne Parteien
▷ in-house user groups	firmeninterne Bedarfsträger/ Konsumenten
initial order	Erstbestellung
in-plant	innerbetrieblich
▷ in-plant demand	Bedarf der eigenen Werke
▷ in-plant materials handling	innerbetrieblicher Materialtransport
input	eingesetzte Produktionsmittel, Materialeinsatz; Dateneingabe

input market

input market	Beschaffungsmarkt
Input-Output Control (I/OC)	Eingang-Ausgang-Kontrolle; Vorgabe-Liefer-Überwachung
input price	Einstandspreis, Einkaufspreis
inquiry	Anfrage
▷ inquiry for prices	Preisanfrage
inspection	Abnahme
▷ final inspection	Endabnahme
▷ inspection in manufacturing	Qualitätskontrolle (in der Fertigung); Revision
▷ inspection of incoming materials	Überprüfung der Materialeingänge
to install	installieren, einbauen
installation	Installation, Einbau; Anschluß; Anlage, Einrichtung
▷ ready for installation	einbaufertig
installation engineer	Montagetechniker
instal(l)ment	Rate
▷ first instalment	Anzahlung
▷ to pay in instalments	auf Raten zahlen
instructions	Arbeitsanweisung
instruction sheet	Arbeitsanweisung
insufficient	ungenügend, unzureichend
▷ insufficient stocks of items	zu kleine Lagerbestände
insurance	Versicherung
▷ to effect insurance	Versicherung abschließen
insurance agent	Versicherungsvertreter
insurance policy	Versicherungspolice
to insure	versichern; sicherstellen
to integrate	integrieren, eingliedern
▷ integrated materials management	integrierte Materialwirtschaft
▷ integrated production control system	integriertes Fertigungssteuerungssystem
integration	Integration
intercompany material purchases	Materialbezüge innerhalb eines Unternehmens
interests	Zinsen
interest rate	Zinssatz
interface	Schnittstelle
interfunctional co-operation	abteilungsübergreifende Zusammenarbeit
intermediate product	Vorprodukt; Zwischenprodukt
intermittent production	(losweise) Werkstattfertigung

inventory fluctuations

internal	innerbetrieblich
▷ internal audit	interne Revision
▷ internal customers	innerbetriebliche Verbraucher/ Konsumenten
▷ internal relationships	innerbetriebliche Beziehungen
international	international
▷ international markets	internationale Märkte
▷ international procurement	internationale Beschaffung
to intersect	überschneiden
introductory discount	Einführungsrabatt
inventories	Läger, Lagerbestände, Vorräte
▷ reduction of inventories	Lagerabbau
▷ to cut/to run down/to trim inventories	Lagerbestände abbauen
▷ to destock (inventories)	Lagerbestände senken
▷ to reduce/to liquidate inventories	Lagerbestände senken/reduzieren
inventory	Lagerbestand; Bestandsliste
▷ inventory held in storage	Lager, Lagerbestände
inventory accounting	Lagerbestandsführung; Lagerbuchführung
inventory accounting department	Lagerbuchhaltungsabteilung
inventory additions	Lagerzugänge, Lagereingänge
inventory analysis	Lagerhaltungsanalyse
inventory (assets) account	Lagerkonto
inventory audit	Lagerkontrolle
inventory budget	Lagerbudget, Lagerplan
inventory card	Lagerkarte
inventory carrying/holding costs	Lagerhaltungskosten
inventory changes	Bestandsveränderungen
inventory clerks	Lagerpersonal
inventory control	Lagerbestandsführung, Lagerwirtschaft
▷ cycle system of constant inventory control	Lagerhaltung mit konstanten Beständen
inventory control system	Lagerhaltungssystem
inventory cost	Lagerkosten
inventory costing	Lagerbestandsbewertung
inventory cutting	Lagerabbau
inventory cycle	Lagerhaltungszyklus
inventory data/figures	Lagerdaten
inventory financing	Lagerfinanzierung
inventory fluctuations	Lagerhaltungsschwankungen

inventory function

inventory function	Lagerfunktion
inventory investment	Lagerinvestitionen
inventory journal	Lagerjournal
inventory level	Lagergröße, Lagerbestand
inventory losses	Lagerverluste
inventory management	Lagerverwaltung, Lagerwirtschaft
inventory method	Lagerhaltungsmethode
▷ split inventory method	Lagerhaltung nach ABC-Klassifikation
inventory model	Lagerhaltungsmodell
inventory movements	Lagerbewegungen
inventory planning	Materialdisposition
inventory planning model	Lagerplanungsmodell
inventory profits	Lagergewinne
inventory receipts	Lagerzugänge
inventory record file	Lagerbuchführung
inventory records	Lagerkartei
inventory-sales ratio	Lagerumschag
inventory scheduling	Lagerhaltungsplanung
inventory statistics	Lagerstatistik
inventory status report	Lagerbestandsaufstellung
inventory turnover	Lagerumschlag
▷ rate of inventory turnover	Lagerumschlagsrate
inventory turnover ratios	Lagerkennzahlen
inventory valuation	Lagerbestandsbewertung
inventory write-off	Bestandsabwertung, Bestandsabschreibung
inventory write-up	Bestandsaufwertung
to invest	investieren, (Geld/Mittel) anlegen
investment	Investition; (Kapital-)Anlage; Anlagekapital
investor	Investor, Kapitalanleger
invoice	(Waren-)Rechnung
▷ amended invoice	berichtigte Rechnung
invoice price	(Einkaufs-)Rechnungspreis
invoicing of additional supplies and services	Nachberechnung von Lieferungen und Leistungen
to invoice	fakturieren, in Rechnung stellen
▷ to invoice sales and/or services	(Dienst-)Leistungen in Rechnung stellen
▷ invoiced purchase price	(Einkaufs-)Rechnungspreis

iron and steel industry	eisenschaffende Industrie
ironworking industry	die eisenverarbeitende Industrie
issue/issuing of materials	Materialausgabe

J

job costing	Auftragskostenermittlung
job order	Fertigungsauftrag
job order costing	Auftragskostenermittlung
job shop	Werkstattfertigungs-Werkstatt
job shop production	Werkstattfertigung
job shop scheduling	Terminierung der Werkstattfertigung
job-lot production	losweise Werkstattfertigung
joint demand	gemeinschaftliche Nachfrage, komplementäre Nachfrage
job description	Arbeitsplatzbeschreibung
joint order	Verbundbestellung, Auftragsverbund
job production	Einzelfertigung
job site	Baustelle
joint-stock company	GB: Kapital- oder Aktiengesellschaft *USA:* Offene Handelsgesellschaft auf Aktien
joint venture	Gemeinschaftsunternehmen; Joint Venture
just-in-time (JIT)**	Just-in-Time
just-in-time principle	Just-in-Time-Prinzip
just-in-time purchasing	Beschaffung für die lagerlose Fertigung; Just-in-Time-Beschaffung

K

Kaizen	Prinzip der kontinuierlichen Verbesserungen in der Produktion
to keep	halten, behalten
▷ to keep down stock levels	Lagerbestände niedrig halten
▷ to keep stocks trim	Lagerbestände niedrig halten

L — key

key (adj.)	wichtig, zentral
▷ key criteria	wichtige Kriterien
▷ key criterion	wichtiges Kriterium
▷ key data	Eckwerte
▷ key data in materials management	Kennzahlen der Materialwirtschaft
▷ key date	erster Tag eines Planungszeitraums
▷ key operation	Schwerpunktsarbeitsgang
▷ key supplier	Stammlieferant; A-Lieferant
to knock down	zerlegen
▷ completely knocked down (CKD)	komplett zerlegt

L

labo(u)r	Arbeit, Arbeitskräfte; Lohnkosten
labo(u)r intensive	arbeitsintensiv
▷ labour-intensive industries	arbeitsintensive Industriezweige
▷ labour-intensive tasks	arbeitsintensive Aufgaben
▷ to carry out labour-intensive tasks	arbeitsintensive Aufgaben ausführen
labo(u)r rate per hour	Lohnsatz pro Stunde
labo(u)r shortages	Arbeitskräftemangel
labo(u)r ticket	Ist-Zeit-Meldung (bei Fertigungsauftrag)
large enterprise	Großunternehmen
large-scale production	Großserienproduktion
large-scale user	Großabnehmer
last-in, first-out (LIFO)	last-in, first-out (LIFO)
to launch a product	ein Produkt auf den Markt bringen
layout	Anordnung
▷ functional layout	funktionelle Anordnung
law	Gesetz
lawer	Rechtsbeistand, Rechtsanwalt
legal	rechtlich, Gesetzes-, Rechts-
legal department	Rechtsabteilung
legal regulations	rechtliche Verordnungen
lead time	Beschaffungszeit; Bearbeitungszeit
lead time management	Beschaffungszeitmanagement
leaflet	Faltblatt, Broschüre
leak	Leck
▷ to leak, to be leaky	lecken
lean management	Lean Management

loading   **L**

least processing time rule	kürzeste Operationszeitregel
least total material cost	geringstmögliche Materialgesamtkosten
least unit cost batchsize	wirtschaftliche Losgröße
Letter of Credit (L/C)	Akkreditiv
letter of intent (LOI)	Absichtserklärung; gegebenenfalls gesetzlich bindende Verpflichtung eine bestimmte Ware zu einem bestimmten Zeitpunkt abzunehmen
level	Niveau, Ebene; Stufe der Produktion
▷ level by level	stufenweise
▷ level of explosion	Dispositionsstufe
▷ level of service	Lieferbereitschaft
liability	Haftung, Gesamthaftung
▷ liabilities	Verbindlichkeiten
licence	Lizenz
▷ to acquire a licence	eine Lizenz erhalten
▷ to apply for a licence	eine Lizenz beantragen
▷ to licence products	Lizenzen für ein Produkt erwerben/vergeben
licence fee	Lizenzgebühr
licensing	Lizenzvergabe
to lift	aufheben
▷ to lift restrictions	Einschränkungen aufheben
limit	Grenze
▷ limit of performance	Leistungsgrenze
line balancing	Belastungsausgleich
line loading	Auslastung des Montagebandes
line-set	Reihenfolgeplanung am Montageband
liquid assets	liquide Mittel
listing	Auflisten
list price	Listenpreis
load	Last, Belastung
load centre	Belastungsgruppe
load chart	Belastungsübersicht
load level(l)ing	Belastungsausgleich, Belastungsglättung
load projection	Belastungshochrechnung
loading	Auslastung, Belastung (von Maschinen), Belegung
▷ balanced loading	geglättete Maschinenauslastung, abgeglichene Belastung

L

loading factor

▷ finite loading | Maschinenbelastung mit Kapazitätsgrenze
▷ infinite loading | Maschinenbelastung ohne Kapazitätsgrenze
loading factor | Auslastungsfaktor
loading period | Belegungszeit
loading plan | Belastungsplan, Belegungsplan (von Kapazitäten)
loading rate | Auslastungsgrad
loading time | Belegungszeit
loan | Darlehen, Kredit
▷ loan to finance purchase | Einkaufsdarlehen
location advantages | Standardvorteile
logistical | logistisch
▷ logistical concepts | Logistikkonzepte
▷ logistical thinking | logistisches Denken
loss | Verlust
▷ loss for year | Jahresfehlbetrag
▷ loss of demand | Nachfragerückgang
▷ loss of materials | Materialverlust
▷ loss or damage in transit | Verlust oder Schaden auf dem Transportweg
▷ loss-making companies | Verlustunternehmen
▷ to suffer a loss/losses | Verlust/Verluste erleiden
lot | Posten, Los
▷ truckload lot | Ladungspartie
lot size | Losgröße
▷ lot-size inventory | Lagerbestand nach Losgrößen
lot sizing | Losgrößenbestimmung
lot sizing technique | Losgrößenbestimmungstechnik
lot splitting | Losteilung
lump-sum contract | Pauschalvertrag
lump-sum price | Pauschalpreis

M

machine | Maschine
▷ alternate machine | Ausweichmaschine
machine capacity | Maschinenkapazität
machine centre | Belastungsgruppe
machine down time | störungsbedingte Stillstandzeit

to manufacture — M

machine idle time	Maschinenstillstandszeit
machine key	Maschinenschlüssel
machine load, machine loading	Maschinenbelastung, Maschinenbelegung
machine run time	Maschinenlaufzeit
machine tool	Werkzeugmaschine
machining	Verarbeitung, maschinelle
machining cell	Fertigungsnest
main contractor	Hauptvertragsnehmer
maintenance	Wartung, Instandhaltung, Pflege
▷ maintenance, repair and operating supplies (MRO)	Wartung, Reparatur und Betriebsstoffe
maintenance guarantee	Wartungsgrantie, Leistungsgarantie
maintenance manual	Wartungshandbuch
maintenence	Wartung
Make or Buy**	Make or Buy**
make-to-stock production	Lagerfertigung
management	Geschäftsleitung, Unternehmensführung
▷ management by objectives	Führung nach Zielvorhaben
management planning	Unternehmensplanung
management policies	Arbeitgeberpolitik
manager	Führungskraft, Manager, Geschäftsführer
managerial	Führungs-, Management-
▷ on managerial level	auf Führungsebene
▷ managerial staff	Führungskräfte
managing board	Vorstand *(BRD)*
managing director	Generaldirektor, geschäftsführender Direktor; Betriebsleiter
man-hour	Arbeitsstunde (eines Arbeitnehmers)
man-hour accounting	Stundenabrechnung
man-hour recording	Stundenerfassung
manner of shipment	Versandart
manpower	Arbeitskräfte, Personalkapazität
manpower provision, hiring of personnel	Arbeitnehmerüberlassung
manpower requirement	Personalbedarf
manufacture	Fertigung, Herstellung, Erzeugung
▷ repetitive manufacture	Wiederholfertigung
to manufacture	herstellen, verarbeiten

M manufactured goods

manufactured goods	Fertigwaren
manufacturer	Hersteller, Produzent
manufacturing	Herstellung, Produktion, Fertigung; verarbeitende Industrie
manufacturing capability	Produktionskapazität
manufacturing control	Fertigungssteuerung
manufacturing costs/expenses	Produktionskosten, Herstellungskosten
manufacturing facilities	Produktionsanlagen, Fertigungsanlagen
manufacturing industry	die verarbeitende Industrie
manufacturing instruction	Fertigungsanleitung
manufacturing inventory	Fabrikbestand
manufacturing lead time	Fertigungsdurchlaufzeit, Kettenlaufzeit
▷ composite manufacturing lead time	kumulative Fertigungszeit
manufacturing lead time scheduling	Durchlaufterminierung
manufacturing resource planning	Produktionsfaktorenplanung
Manufacturing Resource Planning (MRPII)	Gesamtproduktionsplanung
margin	Spanne
▷ contribution margin	Deckungsbeitrag
▷ profit margin	Deckungsbeitrag
market	Markt, Absatzmarkt
▷ a buoyant market	ein boomender Markt
▷ a flat market	ein flauer Markt
market analysis	Marktanalyse
market dynamics	Marktdynamik
market intelligence	Marktinformation
market leader	Marktführer
market niche	Marktnische
market research	Marktforschung
market saturation	Marktsättigung
market segment	Marktbereich
market share	Marktanteil
▷ to gain market shares	Marktanteile gewinnen
market supply	Markt- und Kundenversorgung
marketing	Vertrieb, Marketing
marketing costs	Werbungskosten
marketing tools	Werbemittel
mass processing	Massenverarbeitung

material costs

mass producer	Massenfertigung
mass production	Massenfertigung
Master Production Schedule	Primärprogramm, Produktionsprogramm für Primärbedarf
master production scheduling	Primärbedarfsdisposition
to match	entsprechen, zusammenpassen; übereinstimmen
▷ to match prices	ein Preisniveau erreichen
▷ to match a sample	einem Muster entsprechen
material	Material, Stoff
▷ allocated/assigned/obligated material	auftragsgebundenes Material
▷ alternative material	Ausweichmaterial, Ersatzmaterial
▷ combustible material	brennbares Material
▷ consumed material	verwendetes Material
▷ defective material	fehlerhaftes Material, Materialschaden
▷ direct material	im Fertigprodukt vorkommendes Material
▷ indirect material	nicht unmittelbar im Fertigprodukt vorkommendes Material
▷ earmarked material	zweckgebundenes Material
▷ incoming material	eingehendes Material
▷ long lead-time material	Material mit langen Beschaffungszeiten
▷ obsolete material	veraltetes Material
▷ on order material	bestelltes Material
▷ processed material	verarbeitetes Material
▷ reliable material	bewährtes Material
▷ semiprocessed material	Halbzeug
▷ staged material	bereitgestelltes Material
▷ material on hand	Materialbestand
▷ to pool material	Material gemeinsam einsetzen
▷ to provide material	Material bereitstellen
▷ to supply material	Material bereitstellen, zuliefern
▷ to utilize material	Material gebrauchen, benutzen, einsetzen
material accounts	Materialbestandskonten
material and workmanship	Material- und Herstellungs ...
▷ faulty material and workmanship	Material- und Herstellungsmängel
▷ free from defects in material and workmanship	frei von Material-und Herstellungsmängeln
material budget	Materialkostenplan
material costing	Materialkostenermittlung
material costs	Materialkosten, Materialaufwand
▷ direct material(s) costs	unmittelbare Materialkosten

material defect

material defect	Materialfehler
material delivery verification	Materialeingangskontrolle
material demand	Materialbedarf
material description	Materialbeschreibung
material fatigue	Materialermüdung
material handling	Materialtransport
material input	Materialaufwand
▷ additional material input	Materialmehraufwand
material intensive	materialintensiv
▷ material-intensive industries	materialintensive Industriezweige
material movement	Materialbewegungen
material needs	Materialbedarf
material overheads	Bereitstellungskosten
material planning	Disposition
▷ material planning by order point	verbrauchsgesteuerte Disposition
▷ material planning for dependent requirements	bedarfsgesteuerte Disposition
material provision	Materialbereitstellung
material records	Materialaufzeichnungen
material requirements	Materialbedarf
material requirements planning (MRP)	Materialbedarfsplanung; bedarfsgesteuerte Disposition
material shortage	Materialknappheit
material standardization	Normierung von Materialien
material supplies	Materialvorrat
material usage	Materialverbrauch
material usage variance	veranschlagte Materialmenge
material withdrawal	Materialentnahme
material yield	Materialausbeute
materials	Material . . .; materiell
▷ materials and supplies	Hilfs- und Betriebsstoffe
materials accounting	Materialnachweis; Materialausbeute, Materialbuchführung
materials administration	Materialverwaltung
materials budgeting	Bedarfsmengenplanung
materials control	Materialkontrolle, Materialsteuerung
materials cost	Materialkosten
materials cost center	Materialkostenstelle
materials costing	Materialkostenermittlung
materials cost pressure	Materialkostendruck

materials cycle	Materialkreislauf
materials flow	Materialfluß
▷ costs of materials flows	Materialflußkosten
materials flow control	Materialflußkontrolle
materials flow layout	Materialflußgestaltung
materials flow methods	Materialflußtechnik
materials flow optimization	Materialflußoptimierung
materials flow system	Materialflußsystem
materials handling	Materialtransport
materials handling overheads	Materialgemeinkosten
materials input-output statement	Materialbilanz
materials issue	Materialausgabe
materials issue counter	Materialausgabe(schalter)
materials list	Materialliste
materials management**	Materialwirtschaft
materials management function	Materialbereich
materials mix	Materialmischung
materials order	Materialentnahmeschein
materials overhead rate	Materialgemeinkostenzuschlag
materials planning	Materialplanung
materials price	Materialpreis
materials price variance	Materialpreisabweichung
materials purchase budget	Materialbeschaffungsplan
materials purchased to fill a particular order	Bedarfsmaterial
materials purchasing	Materialbeschaffung, Materialeinkäufe
materials purchasing policy	Materialbeschaffungspolitik
materials quantity (of usage) variance	Materialmengenabweichung
materials receiving	Materialannahme
materials records	Materialbelege
materials requirements	Materialbedarf
▷ assessment of materials requirements	Materialbedarfsrechnung
▷ forecasting of materials requirements	Materialbedarfsvorhersage
▷ planning of materials requirements	Materialbedarfsplanung; bedarfsgesteuerte Disposition
materials requisition	Materialanforderung
materials requisition slip/form	Materialanforderungsschein
materials return record	Materialrückgabeschein

M materials savings

materials savings	Materialeinsparungen
materials specifications	Materialangaben
materials status evaluation	Materialbestandsrechnung
materials stocks	Materiallager, Materialbestände
materials testing	Materialprüfung
materials throughput	Materialdurchfluß
materials usage	Materialverbrauch
materials used budget	Materialkostenplan
materials withdrawal	Materialabgang; Materialentnahme
to maximise	maximieren
▷ to maximise business benefits	Geschäftsgewinne maximieren
means of production	Arbeitsmittel, Fertigungsmittel
means of transport	Verkehrsmittel, Transportmittel
measurements	Maße, Abmessungen
mechanical engineer	Maschinenbauingenieur
mechanical	mechanisch, maschinell
▷ mechanical engineering	Maschinenbau
▷ mechanical manufacture	mechanische Fertigung
medium	Mittel...
▷ medium-priced	mittlere Preislage
▷ medium-sized	mittelgroß, mittelständisch
▷ medium quality	mittelwertige Qualität
to meet	treffen; bestreiten; entsprechen
▷ to meet demands/needs/requirements	Bedarf decken
▷ to meet orders	Aufträge ausführen
medium-sized company/enterprise	mittelständisches Unternehmen
merchandise	Güter, Handelsware, Handelsgut
merchant	(Groß-)Händler; Handel...
to merge	fusionieren
merger	Firmenzusammenschluß, Fusion
middleman	Mittelsmann, Vermittler
minimum	Minimum, Mindest...
▷ minimum of average total costs	Betriebsoptimum, Gewinnschwelle
▷ minimum order quantity	Mindestbestellmenge
▷ minimum stock	Mindestlagerbestand
minutes of meeting	Protokoll einer Besprechung
minutes of negotiation	Verhandlungsprotokoll
mode of operation	Betriebsart
mode of procurement	Beschaffungsart
model	Baureihe, Modell

modular	modular
▷ modular assembly	Baukastenprinzip
▷ modular bill of material	modulare Stückliste
▷ modular building block system	modulares Bausteinsystem
module	Baustein
to monitor	beobachten, überwachen
▷ to monitor possible threats	mögliche Gefahren beobachten
▷ to monitor the status of inventory	Lagerüberwachung
monopoly	Monopol
moonlighting	Schwarzarbeit
multi-disciplinary teams	interdisziplinäre Teams
multi-functional teams	abteilungsübergreifende Teams
multimodal transport	kombinierter Transport
multinational	multinationaler Konzern; Multi
multiple machine operating factor	Mehrmaschinen-Bedienungsfaktor
multiple source buying	Beschaffung bei mehreren Quellen: Multiple Source Buying
multiple machine work	Mehrmaschinenbedienung
multiple usage part	Mehrfachverwendungsteil
multiple use	Mehrfachverwendung
multiple-level where-used list	mehrstufiger Verwendungsnachweis
"must order by" date	spätester Bestellzeitpunkt

N

necessaries	Bedarfsgüter
need	Bedarf, Bedürfnis
need date	Bedarfszeitpunkt
need identification	Bedarfsanalyse
need satisfaction	Bedarfsdeckung
to neglect	versäumen, vernachlässigen
negligence	Versäumnis, Vernachlässigung
to negotiate	verhandeln, aushandeln; besprechen
negotiating ploy	Verhandlungstrick
negotiation	Verhandlung
net	netto
▷ net income	Nettoeinkommen
▷ net income from operations	Unternehmensgewinn
▷ net material requirements	Nettomaterialbedarf

N network

▷ net profit from business activities | Nettogewinn
▷ net trading profit | der Reingewinn nach Versteuerung
▷ net trading surplus | der Reingewinn vor Versteuerung
▷ net weight | Nettogewicht
network | Netz, Netzwerk
▷ Distribution Network Structure | Netzverteilungsstruktur
▷ Local Area Network (LAN) | Netzwerk für den lokalen Bereich
▷ Wide Area Network (WAN) | Netzwerk für überregionalen Bereich
noise | Verzerrung zwischen ermittelten Daten und dem echten Vorgang

non-compliance (with) | Nichtbeachtung (von)
non-repetitive production | Einmalfertigung
non-tariff | außertariflich
non-wage costs | Lohnnebenkosten
normal capacity | Kannkapazität
not-for-profit organisation | gemeinnützige Organisation
notice | Notiz, Mitteilung
▷ at short notice | kurzfristig
notification | Benachrichtigung

O

obliged | verpflichtet
▷ to be obliged to | verpflichtet sein
to observe | beobachten, beachten
▷ to observe delivery dates | Lieferzeiten einhalten
obsolete | veraltet
off-loading | abladen
offer | Angebot
▷ firm offer | Festgebot; verbindliches Angebot
▷ offer subject to confirmation | freibleibendes Angebot
▷ to study an offer | ein Angebot eingehend prüfen
▷ to submit an offer | ein Angebot unterbreiten
to offer | anbieten
offeree | Angebotsempfänger
offeror | Anbieter
offset | Versatz, Verschiebung
offsetting | Rückwärtsterminierung
old-type industries | überholte Industriezweige
one-off deal | Einmalgeschäft; Einzelgeschäft

optimality analysis O

operating capital	Betriebskapital
operating costs/expenditures	Betriebskosten, Betriebsaufwand
operating cycle	Betriebskreislauf
operating data	Betriebsdaten
operating data collection	Betriebsdatenerfassung
operating expense	Betriebskosten
operating funds/resources	Betriebsmittel
operating manual	Betriebshandbuch
operating requirements	Betriebsanforderungen
operating result	Betriebsgewinn, Betriebsergebnis
operating staff	Betriebspersonal
operation	Arbeitsgang, Arbeitsvorgang, Betrieb
▷ alternate operation	alternativer Arbeitsgang, Ausweicharbeitsgang, Index-Position
▷ large-scale operation	Großbetrieb
▷ small-scale operation	Kleinbetrieb
▷ to be in operation	in Betrieb sein
operation attachment parts	zugesteuerte Teile
operation chart	Fertigungsablaufplan
operation costing	Betriebskostenrechnung
operation description	Arbeitsgangbeschreibung
operation manual	Bedienungsanleitung
operation number	Arbeitsgangnummer
operation scheduling	Arbeitsgangterminierung, Ablaufplanung
operation time	Bearbeitungszeit
operational	betriebs-, betrieblich, operativ
▷ at operational level	auf betrieblicher Ebene
▷ operational activities	Betriebsaktivitäten
▷ operational analysis	Betriebsanalyse
▷ operational planning	Budgetierung
▷ operational procedure	Betriebsablauf
▷ operational results	Betriebsergebnis
operations management	Produktionssteuerung
operations path	Fertigungsablauf
operations planning	Arbeitsplanung
operations planning and scheduling	Arbeitsvorbereitung
operations research**	Operations Research**
operative capability	Leistungsfähigkeit
operator	Bediener einer Maschine
optimality analysis	Optimalitätsanalyse

O — optimum cost/output

optimum cost/optimum output	Betriebsoptimum, Gewinnschwelle
optimum order quantity	wirtschaftliche Auftragsmenge
option (to buy)	Vorkaufsrecht
▷ to have first option	das Vorkaufrecht innehaben
optional	optionell, wahlweise, zusätzlich
order	Auftrag, Bestellung
▷ oral order	mündlich erteilter Auftrag
▷ flow order	Produktionsauftragserfüllung in Teilmengen
▷ follow-up order	Nachfaßauftrag
▷ rush order	Eilauftrag
▷ work order	Produktionsauftrag
▷ written order	schriftlich erteilter Auftrag
▷ orders in hand, order backlog	Auftragsbestand
▷ orders received	Auftragseingang
▷ orders shipped	ausgelieferte Aufträge
▷ to secure orders	Aufträge einholen
▷ orders fall back	Aufträge gehen zurück
to order	bestellen, ordern
▷ to order for immediate delivery	zur sofortigen Lieferung bestellen
order bill of materials	Materialbestimmungskarte
order book	Auftragsbuch
order centres	Auftragszentren
Order Control	Auftragssteuerung, Auftragsverfolgung
order file of suppliers	Lieferanten-/Auftragsdatei
order finish card	Auftragsabschlußkarte
ordering	Auftragsvergabe
ordering costs	Bestellkosten
ordering deadline	Beschaffungsfrist
ordering key	Beschaffungsschlüssel
order intake	Auftragseingang
order letter	Bestellschreiben
order number	Auftragsnummer
order planning	Auftragsplanung
order placement	Auftragsvergabe
▷ negotiation on order placement	Vergabeverhandlung
▷ minutes on negotiation on order placement	Vergabeprotokoll
order point	Beschaffungszeitpunkt, Bestellzeitpunkt; Bestellbestand
▷ double order point system	Doppelbestellpunktsystem
order processing	Auftragsabwicklung

order processing times	Auftragsdurchlaufzeiten
order quantity	Auftragsmenge, Bestellmenge
order register	Auftragsbuch, Bestellbuch
orders in hand, order backlog	Auftragsbestand
order scheduling	Auftragseinplanung
order sequence	Auftragsfolge
order sheet	Bestellformular
order system	Bestellsystem
▷ periodic order system	periodisches Auftragssystem
organisation	Organisation
organisation chart	Organigramm
organisational structure/pyramid	Organisationsstruktur, Organisationspyramide
▷ flat organisational structure	flache Organisationspyramide
▷ hierarchical organisational structure	hierarchische Organisationspyramide
original	Original; Ur...
▷ original invoice	Originalrechnung
▷ original price	Einkaufspreis
outcome	Ergebnis, Resultat
outlet	Absatzmarkt; Vertriebsstelle
out-of pocket cost	Barzahlungen eines Unternehmens vor Eingang von Kundenzahlungen
output	Leistungsabgabe; Ertrag; Produktion; Output, Ausstoß
output control	Lieferüberwachung
output evaluation	Leistungsbeurteilung
output maximum	Leistungsgrenze
output oriented	leistungsorientiert
output-related costs	leistungsabhängige Kosten
output unit	Leistungseinheit
outside production	Fremdfertigung
outside shop	Fremdfertigung mit enger Bindung an die Eigenfertigung
outside supply	Fremdbezug
outsourcing	Auslagerung von bislang internen Prozessen und Produkten zu Fremdfertigern
to outsource	Prozesse und Produkte auslagern bzw. fremdfertigen lassen
outstanding accounts	Außenstände
outstanding amount	offenstehender Betrag

O outstanding performance

outstanding performance	außerordentliche Leistung
over-delivery	Überlieferung
overdue	überfällig
overengineering**	Overengineering**
overhead costs/ expenses	Gemeinkosten
overhead pool	Gemeinkosten pro Produktgruppe
overheads	Gemeinkosten
▷ costly overheads	hohe Gemeinkosten
to overlap	überschneiden
overtime	Mehrarbeit, Überstunden
overtime bonus	Überstundenzuschlag
to overstock	zu hohe Lagerbestände haben
ownership	Besitz, Eigentum
▷ transfer of ownership	Eigentumsübergang

P

package	Paket, Packung
to pack, packing	verpacken
packaging	Verpackung
packing, packaging and marking	Verpackung und Material
packing slip	Lieferschein
parallel conversion	Einführung eines neuen Systems parallel zum bestehenden System
parallel schedule	gleichzeitige Fertigung eines Arbeitsganges an mehreren Maschinen
parameter card	Parameterkarte
parent item	Artikel der höheren Dispositionsstufe
parent company	Muttergesellschaft, Holding
part coding and classification	Teilekodierung und Klassifizierung
part delivery	Teilelieferung
part diversity	Teilevielfalt
part(s) family	Teilefamilie
partial load	Teillast
part list	Stückliste
part lists management	Stücklistenverwaltung
part period balancing	Teilperiodenabstimmung

performance P

part record	Teilestammdatei
part shipment	Teillieferung
part-time work	Teilzeitarbeit
part type	Artikeltyp
participation in decision making	Mitsprache bei Entscheidungen
partner	Partner, Geschäftspartner
partnership	Partnerschaft
parts	Teile
parts code	Teile-Code
parts family	Teilefamilie
parts list	Bauliste, Teileliste
parts manufacture	Vorfertigung
parts master	Teilestamm
parts master file	Teilestammdatei
parts movement list	Teilebewegungsliste
past due	überfällig
pattern	Muster
▷ pattern of production	Produktionsstruktur
to pay	zahlen
▷ to pay for itself within a year	sich innerhalb eines Jahres amortisieren
payment	Zahlung
▷ payment within 60 days	Zahlung innerhalb von 60 Tagen
▷ payment after final inspection and acceptance	Zahlung nach Endabnahme
▷ payment against presentation of bonds	Zahlung gegen Bankgarantie
▷ payment in instalments	Ratenzahlung
▷ payment procedure	Zahlungsverfahren
▷ payments received	Zahlungseingänge
▷ payment to be effected ...	Zahlung erfolgt ...
▷ after receipt of goods	nach Wareneingang
▷ after preliminary acceptance	nach Vorabnahme
▷ in advance	im voraus
▷ payment within	Zahlungsbedingungen
▷ 14 days 2 % cash discount, 30 days net	14 Tage 2 %, 30 Tage netto
penalty	Vertragsstrafe
▷ to stipulate a penalty in a contract	vertraglich eine Vertragsstrafe festsetzen
penalty agreement	Vereinbarung einer Vertragsstrafe
to perform	leisten; erfüllen; durchführen
performance	Leistung
▷ actual performance	Ist-Leistung

P — performance budget

▷ rated performance	Soll-Leistung
▷ performance by a third party	Leistung durch Dritte
▷ performance and counter performance	Leistung und Gegenleistung
performance budget	Leistungsbudget
performance centre	Leistungszenter
performance deficit	Leistungsdefizit
performance description	Leistungsbeschreibung
performance efficiency	Leistungsgrad
performance evaluation	Leistungsbewertung
performance factor	Leistungsfaktor
performance figures	Leistungsdaten
performance measurement	Kontrolle von Abläufen
performance measurement system	Leistungsbewertungsschema
performance objective	Leistungsziel
performance planning	Erfolgsplanung
performance target	Vorgabeleistung, Leistungsvorgabe
performing level	Leistungsgrad, Leistungsniveau
period of storage	Lagerdauer
periodic ordering	Auftragserteilung in konstanten Intervallen
periodic order quantity	Auftragsplanung nach festen Zeitintervallen
perishable goods	verderbliche Güter
permanent staff	Stammbelegschaft
personnel	Personal, Angestellte, Belegschaft
▷ to hire temporary personnel	Zeitarbeiter einstellen (auch für: Arbeitnehmerüberlassung)
personnel expenses	Personalkosten
personnel manager	Personalleiter
personnel rating	Leistungsbeurteilung des Personals
phantom list of material	Phantom-Stückliste
phase-out part	Auslaufteil
physical assets	materielle Güter
picking date	Entnahmedatum
picking list	Entnahmeliste, Bereitstelliste
piece list	Stückverzeichnis
piece part	Einzelteil
piece rate	Akkordsatz
piece time	Stückzeit

power of attorney

piece value	Stückwert
piece work	Stückarbeit, Akkordarbeit
pilot	Pilot...
pilot lot	Anlaufserie, Nullserie
pilot plant	Werk zur Fertigung neuer Produkte oder Entwicklung neuer Verfahren
pilot production	Anlaufserie, Nullserie
pipeline inventory	im Verteilsystem befindlicher Bestand
place of delivery	Lieferort
place of dispatch/shipment	Versandort
place/point of destination	Bestimmungsort
placing of orders	Auftragsvergabe
planning	Planung
▷ strategical planning	strategische Planung
▷ tactical planning	taktische Planung
plant	Fabrik, Betriebsanlage, Produktionsstätte
plant assets	Betriebsanlagenwerte
plant construction	Anlagenbau
plant manager	Werksleiter
plant manufacture	Anlagenbau
plant supplies	Betriebsmaterial
point of receipt	Materialannahmestelle
point of sales (POS)	Verkaufspunkt
point-of use storage	produktionsnahes Lager
pollution control regulations	Umweltschutzvorschriften
pool of costs	Kostenblock
poor quality	minderwertige Qualität
port of destination	Bestimmungshafen
port of shipment	Verladehafen
to postpone	aufschieben, verschieben; zurückstellen
▷ to postpone delivery	Lieferung zurückstellen
potential customer	möglicher Kunde
power, effect	Kraft
▷ to take effect, to come into effect	in Kraft treten
power engineering	Energietechnik
power industry	Energiewirtschaft
power of attorney	Vollmacht

pre-assembly	Vormontage
predatory competition	Verdrängungswettbewerb
▷ predatory price cutting policy	Verdrängungswettbewerb
pre-expediting	fertigungsbegleitende Mengen-/ Terminüberwachung
prefabrication	Vorfertigung
preference system	Bedarfsstruktur
preliminary products	Vorprodukte
preliminary acceptance/inspection	Vorabnahme
preliminary negotiation	Vorverhandlung
pre-material	Halbzeug
prepaid	(gegen) Vorauszahlung
pre-tax profits	Gewinn vor Steuer
to press competitors out of the market	Konkurrenten vom Markt drängen
price	Preis; (Börsen-)Kurs
▷ actual price	tatsächlicher Einkaufspreis
▷ agreed price	vereinbarter Preis
▷ current price	aktueller/gültiger Preis
▷ fixed price	Festpreis
▷ lump-sum price	Pauschpreis
▷ planned price	geplanter Preis
▷ projected price	geplanter Preis
▷ price each; price per unit	Stückpreis
▷ price prevailing at date of shipment	Preisfestlegung zum Lieferzeitpunkt
▷ stipulated price	festgesetzter Preis
▷ to adjust prices	Preise angleichen
▷ to set a price	einen Preis festsetzen
▷ to price consumers out of a market	Konkurrenten durch Preispolitik aus dem Markt drängen
price elasticity	Preisflexibilität
price escalation	Preisgleitung
price escalation clause	Preisgleitklausel
price fixing	Preisabsprache
price formation	Preisbildung
price increase	Preissteigerung
price index	Preisindex
price level	Preisniveau
price list	Preisliste
price point	Einstiegspreis
price statistics	Preisstatistik
pricing	Preisfestlegung
▷ leader pricing	Preisbildung durch führende Unternehmen einer Branche

procurement channel   P

pricing margin	Kalkulationsspielraum
primary products	Grundstoffe, Vorprodukte
private limited company	*entspricht in BRD etwa:* GmbH
procedure	Verfahren, Vorgehen, Ablauf
procedure manual	Handbuch für innerbetriebliche Abläufe
proceeds	Ertrag
to process	bearbeiten, verarbeiten, behandeln
▷ processed	verarbeitet
process average	durchschnittliche Fertigungsqualität
process chains	Prozeßkette
▷ logistical process chains	logistische Prozeßketten
process chart	Ablaufdiagramm
process control	Arbeitsablaufsteuerung, Prozeßsteuerung
▷ continuous process control	kontinuierliche Prozeßkontrolle
process costing	Stückkostenrechnung für Massenfertigung
process engineer	Verfahrenstechniker
process engineering	Verfahrenstechnik
process improvement	Prozeßverbesserung
▷ continuous process improvement	kontinuierliche Prozeßverbesserung
processing	Bearbeitung, Verarbeitung
▷ processing of materials	Materialverarbeitung
processing times	Durchlaufzeit, Bearbeitungszeiten
processing unit	Verarbeitungseinheit
▷ central processing unit (CPU)	zentrale Verarbeitungseinheit
process management	Prozeßmanagement
process orientation	Prozeßsteuerung
process sheet	Arbeitsplan
process stocks	Bestand an unfertigen Erzeugnissen im Verlauf der Produktion
process time	Bearbeitungszeit
to procure	beschaffen, besorgen
procurement**	Beschaffung, Einkauf
▷ procurement of materials	Materialbeschaffung
▷ procurement to stock up inventory	Lagergeschäft
procurement authorisation	Beschaffungsermächtigung
procurement budget	Beschaffungsplan, Beschaffungsbudget
procurement channel	Beschaffungsweg

P procurement contract

procurement contract	Beschaffungsvertrag
procurement costs	Beschaffungskosten
▷ incidential procurement costs	Beschaffungsnebenkosten
procurement facilities	Beschaffungseinrichtungen
procurement function	Beschaffungsfunktion
procurement inventory model	Lagermodell
procurement marketing	Beschaffungsmarketing
procurement planning	Beschaffungsplanung
▷ detailed procurement planning	Beschaffungsvollzugsplanung
procurement policy	Beschaffungspolitik
procurement problem	Beschaffungsproblem
procurement research	Beschaffungsforschung
procurement statistics	Beschaffungsstatistik
to produce	produzieren, herstellen
producer	Hersteller, Produzent
producer goods	Produktionsgüter
producer goods industry	Produktionsgüterindustrie
producer's price	Erzeugerpreis
product	Produkt, Erzeugnis, Ware
▷ finished products	Fertigprodukte
▷ made-to-stock product	Lagerfertigungsprodukt
▷ product of daily use	Produkt des täglichen Gebrauchs
▷ semi-finished products	Halbfertigerzeugnisse
product development	Produktentwicklung
product diversification	Produktvielfalt
product innovation	Produktinnovation
production	Produktion
productivity bonus	Leistungszulage
product lifecycle	Produktlebenszyklus
product liability	Produkthaftung
product line	Produktserie
product number	Artikelnummer
product positioning	Produktplazierung
product specification	Produktbeschreibung
product quality	Produktqualität
product unit	Kostenträger Produkt
production	Produktion, Herstellung, Fertigung
▷ production of goods and services	Fertigung von Waren und Dienstleistungen
▷ production to stock	Lagerfertigung
▷ production to order	auftragsbezogene Fertigung

production schedule

▷ to broaden production	Produktion aufnehmen
▷ to curb production	Produktion drosseln
▷ to expedite production	Produktion überwachen
▷ to relocate production	Produktion umsiedeln
▷ to run down production	Produktion zurückfahren
▷ to take up production	Produktion aufnehmen
production break note	Störungsmeldung
production control	Produktionssteuerung
▷ computerized production control	maschinelle Produktionssteuerung
production cost	Herstellungskosten
production data	Betriebsdaten, Fertigungsdaten
production documents	Fertigungsunterlagen, Fertigungsbelege
production equipment and facilities	Betriebsmittel, Fertigungsmittel
production facility	Produktionsstätte, Produktionseinrichtung; Fertigungsanlage
▷ to relocate production facilities	Produktionsstätten verlagern
production goods	Produktionsgüter
production lead time	Kettenlaufzeit; Fertigungsdurchlaufzeit
production level	Baustufe, Fertigungsstufe, Produktionsgrad
production logistics	Produktionslogistik
production manager	Produktionsleiter, Betriebsleiter
production method	Fertigungsverfahren
production method of depreciation	leistungsbezogene Abschreibung
production order	Fertigungsauftrag, Betriebsauftrag, Werkstattauftrag
production planning	Produktionsplanung
production planning and control	PPS
production planning and management	Produktionsplanung und -steuerung
production process	Produktionsablauf
production range	Fertigungsspektrum, Produktionsspektrum
production report	Fertigungsbericht
production release	Fertigungsfreigabe
production resource	Produktionsfaktor
production run schedule	Durchlaufterminierung
production schedule	Fertigungsprogramm, Produktionsprogramm
▷ master production schedule (MPS)	Hauptproduktionsplan, Primärbedarfsplan

P production target

production target	Leistungssoll
productive capacity	Leistungsfähigkeit, Produktionskapazität
productive factors/resources	Leistungsfaktoren
productivity	Produktivität, Ergiebigkeit, Rentabilität
professional skills	Fachkenntnisse
profit	Profit, Gewinn
▷ profit for year	Jahresüberschuß
▷ profit before tax	Bruttogewinn
▷ profit/loss account	Gewinn-Verlust-Rechnung
▷ profit as business objective	Profit als Unternehmensziel
▷ profit as criterion of business performance	Profit als Leistungskriterium
profit and loss account	Gewinn- und Verlustrechnung
profitability	Profitabilität, Rentabilität
profitable	profitabel, gewinnbringend
profit margin	Gewinnspanne
profit orientation	Erfolgsorientierung
profit-oriented activities	profitorientierte Tätigkeiten
profit planning	Erfolgsplanung
profit ratio	Betriebsquote
pro forma invoice	Proforma-Rechnung
progress control	Arbeitsfortschrittsüberwachung
progress payment	Abschlagszahlung
progress report	Fortschrittsbericht
project coordinator	Auftragskoordinator
projected usage per year	voraussichtlicher Jahresbedarf
project execution, project handling	Auftragsabwicklung
project funding	Projektfinanzierung
project manager	Projektleiter
projection	Hochrechnung
project organization chart	Auftragsorganisationsplan
project planning	Projektplanung; Projektierung
project team	Auftragsteam
proliferation	Nachbau
to promote	fördern, unterstützen
▷ to promote the sale of a product	den Absatz eines Produktes fördern
prompt delivery	sofortige Lieferung
proposal	Vorschlag
prospective customer	möglicher/potentieller Kunde

purchase traveller **P**

prospects for the sale of a product	Absatzaussichten
to prove	beweisen, sich erweisen
▷ to prove defective	sich als fehlerhaft erweisen
to provide	bereitstellen, beliefern, auch: beistellen
▷ to provide storage/warehouse space	Lagerraum bereitstellen
▷ to provide materials and/or equipment	Material und/oder Ausrüstung beistellen
provisional production	provisorische Fertigung
provision(ing)	Bereitstellung, auch: Beistellung
▷ provision(ing) of material(s)	Materialbereitstellung, Beistellung von Material
pseudobill of material	Phantom-Stückliste
public limited company (plc)	*entspricht in BRD etwa:* Aktiengesellschaft (AG)
public relations	Öffentlichkeitsarbeit
public utilities	Versorgungswirtschaft, Versorgungsbetriebe
pull principle	Holprinzip
pull system	verbrauchsorientiertes System
purchase	Kauf, Einkauf
▷ purchase and sale	Ein- und Verkauf
to purchase	einkaufen, beschaffen, besorgen
▷ purchased parts	Fertigteile, Zulieferteile, Kaufteile
purchase book	Einkaufsbuch
purchase discount	Einkaufsrabatt
purchase journal	Einkaufsbuch
purchase order (form)	Einkaufsauftrag, Bestellschein
purchase planning	Einkaufsplanung
purchase price	Einkaufs-/Beschaffungspreis
▷ purchase price paid (PPP)	gezahlter Einkaufspreis
▷ to buy at purchase price	zum Einkaufspreis beschaffen
▷ to buy below purchase price	unter Einkaufspreis beschaffen
purchase price variance	variabler Einkaufspreis
purchase quota	Einkaufskontingent
purchase requisition	Bedarfsmeldung, Bestellschein
purchase requisition form	Einkaufsanforderung(schein)
purchase tax	Einkaufssteuer
purchase tax-free	einkaufssteuerfrei
purchase tender	Einkaufsangebot
purchase terms and conditions	Einkaufsbedingungen
purchase traveller	Beschaffungsbegleitkarte

purchase variance

purchase variance	Einkaufsabweichung
purchaser	Einkäufer
purchasing**	Einkauf, Beschaffung
▷ direct purchasing	Bezug beim Hersteller
▷ entrepreneurial purchasing	unternehmerische Beschaffung
▷ indirect purchasing	Einkauf beim Handel
▷ international purchasing	internationale Beschaffung
▷ strategic purchasing	strategische Beschaffung
▷ traditional purchasing	klassischer Einkauf
purchasing account	Einkaufskonto
purchasing agency	Einkaufsgesellschaft
purchasing agent	Einkaufsvertreter
purchasing association/cooperation	Einkaufsverband, Einkaufsgenossenschaft
purchasing assistant, junior purchaser	Mitarbeiter/Sachbearbeiter im Einkauf mit begrenzter Entscheidungskompetenz
purchasing authorization	Einkaufsgenehmigung
purchasing branch office	Einkaufsniederlassung
purchasing control	Einkaufskontrolle
purchasing department	Einkaufsabteilung
purchasing lead time	Bestelldurchlaufzeit
purchasing manager, senior purchaser	Einkaufsleiter, Einkäufer mit weitreichender Entscheidungskompetenz
purchasing manual	Einkaufshandbuch
purchasing organisation	Beschaffungseinrichtung
purchasing permit	Einkaufsermächtigung
purchasing policy	Beschaffungspolitik
purchasing power	Kaufkraft
purchasing staff	Einkaufspersonal, Einkäufer
purchasing techniques	Einkaufstechniken, Beschaffungsmethoden
purchasing terms and conditions	Einkaufsbedingungen
purchasing time	Beschaffungszeit
purchasing tools	Einkaufswerkzeug
purchasing unit of measure	Maßeinheit im Einkauf
purchasing volume	Einkaufsvolumen
push principle	Bringprinzip
to put	legen, stellen; tun
▷ to put into operation	in Betrieb setzten

Q

qualification	Qualifizierung, Befähigung, Eignung
quality	Qualität, Güteklasse
▷ first-class quality	erstklassige Qualität
▷ inferior quality	mindere Qualität
▷ medium quality	mittelwertige Qualität
▷ poor quality	schlechte Qualität
▷ quality of material(s)	Materialbeschaffenheit, Materialqualität
quality assurance	Qualitätssicherung
quality assurance instructions	QS-Anweisungen
quality assurance manager	QS-Leiter
quality certificate	Qualitätsnachweis
quality control	Qualitätssteuerung
▷ poor quality control	mangelhafte Qualitätskontrolle
quality deficiencies	Qualitätsmängel
quality description	Beschaffenheitsangabe
quality engineering	Qualitätssteuerung
quality goods	Qualitätsware
quality level	Qualitätsstandard
quality manual	Qualitätsmanagement-Handbuch
quality policies	QS-Grundsätze
quality protection	Beschaffenheitssicherung, Qualitätssicherung
quality records	Qualitätsaufzeichnungen
quality system	Qualitätsmanagement-System
quality targets	Qualitätsziele
quality-related costs	Qualitätskosten
quantity	Menge
▷ quantity received	Warenzugang
▷ quantity withdrawn	Warenabgang
quay	Kai
▷ ex quay	ab Kai
quota	Kontingent
quotation	Preisangebot, verlangtes Angebot; Notierung
quotation evaluation	Angebotsauswertung
to quote	ein Angebot machen
▷ to quote prices	Preise nennen, angeben

R

railway traffic	Eisenbahnverkehr
random sample	Stichprobe
range	Umfang, Bandbreite; Auswahl
▷ range of production	Produktpalette, Produktionsserie
▷ range of products	Produktionsreihe
rate	Satz, Rate
▷ rate of depreciation	Abschreibungsrate
▷ rate of inventory turnover	Umschlaghäufigkeit
▷ rate of turnover	Umsatzrate
▷ rate of usage	Lagerabgangsrate
rated	Soll
▷ rated capacity	Soll-Kapazität
▷ rated output	Soll-Leistung (Ausstoß)
▷ rated performance	Soll-Leistung
▷ rated value	Soll-Wert
rationalization	Rationalisierung
ratios	Verhältniszahlen, Kennzahlen
▷ management ratios	betriebswirtschaftliche Kennzahlen
▷ ratio of inventory level	Lageranteil; Anteil der Lagerbestände
raw material	Rohstoff
▷ rich in raw materials	rohstoffreich
raw material market	Rohstoffmarkt
real net output	Wertschöpfung
reasonable	vernünftig; angemessen
▷ reasonable price	angemessener Preis
to rebid	wiederausschreiben
▷ to rebid a requirement	einen Bedarf neu ausschreiben
receipt	Eingang; Eingangsbestätigung
receiving materials	Materialeingang
receiving report	Eingangsbericht
receiving slip	Materialempfangsbescheinigung, Materialannahmeschein
reciprocity	Gegenseitigkeit
to record	verzeichnen, aufzeichnen, verbuchen
▷ to record profits	Gewinne verzeichnen
recruitment	Personalbeschaffung
recruitment of staff	Personaleinstellung
recycling	Recycling, Wiederaufbereitung
▷ recycling of materials	Materialwiederaufbereitung

to reorder **R**

recycling and waste disposal costs	Recycling- und Entsorgungskosten
red tape	Papierkrieg
▷ the process is causing a lot of red tape	dieser Vorgang verursacht ein Unmaß an Verwaltungsarbeiten
redesign	Produktdesign, Veränderungen im
redevelopment plans	Sanierungspläne
to reduce	reduzieren, kürzen
▷ to reduce production	Produktion zurückfahren
reduction	Reduktion, Abbau
reengineering	Reengineering, Umstrukturierung
reference	Bezug; Referenz
▷ with reference to	in Bezug auf
reference figures	Eckwerte
to refill	wiederauffüllen
▷ to refill stocks	Lagerbestände wiederauffüllen
refilling	Wiederauffüllung
to refuse	ablehnen, verweigern
▷ to refuse acceptance	Annahme verweigern
▷ to refuse to take delivery of goods	die Annahme von Waren verweigern
to register	verzeichnen, eintragen
▷ registered company	ins Handelsverzeichnis eingetragene Firma
▷ registered trade mark	eingetragenes Warenzeichen
regular	regelmäßig, üblich
▷ regular customer	Stammkunde
▷ regular stock on hand	Lagerbestände
▷ regular supplier	Stammlieferant
regulation	Verordnung, Bestimmung
legal regulation	Rechtsverordnungen, Rechtsbestimmungen
reject	ablehnen, zurückweisen
▷ to reject goods	Waren zurückweisen
relatives	Verhältniszahlen
relentless competition	rücksichtsloser Wettbewerb
to relocate	umsiedeln, umverteilen
▷ to relocate production sites to …	Produktionsstätten verlagern nach …
▷ to relocate production	Produktion verlagern
relocation	Verlagerung
removal	Abzug, Entzug; Abschaffung
to remove	aufheben
to render services	Dienste leisten
to reorder	nachbestellen

173

reorder cost	Nachbestellungskosten
reorder requirements	Nachbestellbedarf
repeat order	Nachbestellung
replacement	Ersatz, Ersatzteil; Austauschmaterial
▷ replacement method of depreciation	Abschreibung auf Wiederbeschaffung
replacement order	Ersatzauftrag
replacement period	Wiederbeschaffungszeit
replacement staff	Aushilfspersonal
replacement time	Wiederbeschaffungszeit
to replenish	wiederauffüllen
▷ to replenish stocks	Lagerbestände wiederauffüllen
report	Bericht
▷ delay report	Bericht über Verzögerung
▷ over, short, and damaged report (OS & D)	Bericht über Über-, Unter- oder beschädigte Lieferung
reporting	Berichtswesen, Reporting
representative	Vertreter
reprocessing	Umarbeitung, Aufarbeitung
▷ reprocessing of materials	Materialumarbeitung, Materialwiederaufbereitung
reprimand	Abmahnung
request	Bitte, Anfrage
▷ request for proposal (RFP)	Angebotsausschreibung
▷ request for quote (RFQ)	Angebotsausschreibung
to request	anfragen, erbitten; anfordern
to require	erfordern, anfordern
▷ required	erforderlich, erfordert
requirement(s)	Bedarf
requirements alteration	Bedarfsänderung
requirements alteration method	Bedarfsänderungsmethode
requirements control	Bedarfsmengenkontrolle
requirements definition	Bedarfsbeschreibung
requirements description	Anforderungsbeschreibung
requirements notice	Bedarfsmeldung
requirements planning	Bedarfsrechnung, Bedarfsplanung, Bedarfsermittlung
resaler	Wiederverkäufer, Zwischenhändler
research	Forschung
▷ research and development department (R + D)	Forschungs- und Entwicklungsabteilung (F + E)

resource; resources	(Geld-)Mittel, (Boden- und Natur-)Schätze; Beschaffungsquellen
resource intensive	materialintensiv
resource requirements	Betriebsmittelbedarf
resource requirements planning	Betriebsplanung
resourcing	Beschaffung
response	Antwort
responsibility	Verantwortung
▷ to accept responsibility (for)	Verantwortung übernehmen (für)
to restrict	begrenzen, einschränken
restructuring plans	Umstrukturierungspläne
results	Resultate; Bilanz, Profite
retailer	Einzelhändler
retail trade	Einzelhandel
retrofit	nachträglicher Einbau
returns	Ertrag, Gewinn
▷ return on investment (ROI)	Anlageertrag; Betriebsrendite
revenue	Ertrag, Gewinn
▷ extraordinary revenue	außerordentliche Erträge
revenue reserves	Gewinnrücklagen
rework	Nacharbeit
rework order	Nacharbeitungsauftrag
rigid	starr, unbewegt
▷ rigid wage costs	starre Lohnkosten
risk	Risiko
transfer of risk	Gefahrenübergang
RO-RO (roll on-roll off)	Ro-Ro
road traffic	Straßenverkehr
rock-bottom price	Niedrigstpreis; der äußerst kalkulierte Preis
rolling stock	rollendes Material
to rule	herrschen, beherrschen
▷ ruling price	Tagespreis; gegenwärtiger Preis
rules for the prevention of accidents	Unfallverhütungsvorschriften
to run	*Grundbedeutung:* rennen, laufen
▷ running costs	laufende Kosten
▷ to run out of an article	ein Artikel geht aus
▷ to run down production	Produktion zurückfahren
rush	Ansturm
▷ rush of orders	Auftragswelle

S

safety	Sicherheit
safety analysis	Sicherheitsanalyse
safety engineer	Sicherheitsingenieur
safety equipment	Sicherheitseinrichtung
safety technology, technical safety	Sicherheitstechnik
safety regulations	Sicherheitsvorschriften
safety, security	Sicherheit
salary	Gehalt
sale	Verkauf; Absatz, Umsatz; Ausverkauf
▷ sales and production plan	Absatz- und Produktionsplan
▷ sale of materials	Materialverkauf
▷ to achieve satisfactory sales	befriedigenden Absatz erzielen
sales assistant	Verkäufer
sales forecasts	Absatzprognosen
sales letter	Werbebrief
sales manager	Verkaufsleiter
sales office	Vertriebsbüro
sales organisation	Absatzorganisation
sales planning	Absatzplanung
sales price	Verkaufspreis
sales revenue	Umsatzerlös
sales trends	Verkaufstrends
sales volume	Umsatzvolumen, Verkaufsvolumen
sample	Muster
▷ sample of merchandise	Warenmuster
▷ random sample	Stichprobe
▷ to take random samples	Stichproben entnehmen
sample size	Probengröße
sampling	Probenentnahme
satisfaction of demands/requirements	Bedarfsbefriedigung
to satisfy	befriedigen, decken, abdecken
▷ to satisfy demands/needs/requirements	Bedarf/Bedürfnisse decken
savings	Einsparungen, Ersparnisse
▷ saving of material	Materialeinsparung
scale	Skala, Maßstab; Ausmaß, Umfang
▷ to scale down	verringern
▷ to scale up	erhöhen

series

schedule	Zeitplan, Terminplan; Aufstellung; Verzeichnis
▷ ahead of schedule	dem Zeitplan voraus
▷ behind schedule	dem Zeitplan hinterher
▷ scheduled time of arrival	planmäßige Ankunftszeit
▷ scheduled load	geplante Maschinenbelastung
schedule effectiveness	Termintreue
scheduling	Terminierung
▷ forward flow scheduling	Vorwärtsdurchlaufterminierung
▷ forward scheduling	Vorwärtsterminierung
scheme	System; Plan; Schema
scope	Umfang, Ausmaß
▷ scope of authority	Reichweite von Befugnissen
scope of services	Leistungsumfang
scope of supplies	Lieferumfang
scrap	Materialabfall, Schrott
seasonal	jahreszeitlich-, saisonbedingt
seawater seepage	Einsickern von Seewasser
secrecy agreement	Geheimhaltungsvereinbarung
section	Geschäftseinheit
▷ section specific	geschäftseinheitsspezifisch
security	Sicherheit
sector/segment of industry	Branche
▷ narrow segment of industry	kleiner Industriesektor
▷ usual in a sector	branchenüblich
selection	Auswahl
▷ selection of a suitable source of supply	Auswahl einer geeigneten Bezugsquelle
to sell	verkaufen, absetzen, führen, vertreiben
▷ to sell goods and services	Leistungen absetzen
▷ to sell well	guten Absatz finden
seller	Verkäufer(in)
seller's market	Verkäufermarkt
selling expense	Vertriebsgemeinkosten
semi-fabricated products, semi-finished products	Halbfertigwaren, Halbfabrikate
semi-processed items	Halbfabrikate
semi-processed material	Halbzeug
to send	schicken, verschicken
▷ to send off	abschicken, wegschicken
sequencing	Ablaufplanung
series	Baureihe, Modell

S service

service	Dienstleistung, Service
▷ to purchase services	Dienstleistungen beschaffen
▷ to render services	Dienstleistungen anbieten
▷ to render smooth services	reibungslose Dienste leisten
▷ to render services to foreign customers	Dienste für ausländische Auftraggeber leisten
▷ to render services tailored to customers' needs	auf die Bedürfnisse der Kunden zugeschnittene Dienste leisten
service centre	Leistungscenter
service-output method of depreciation	leistungsbezogene Abschreibung
service rating	(Dienst-)Leistungsbeurteilung
service unit	Leistungseinheit
serviceability	Lieferfähigkeit
▷ to maintain serviceability	lieferfähig bleiben
to settle	klären, begleichen, bezahlen, ausgleichen
▷ to settle an account/invoice	eine Rechnung begleichen
▷ to settle a complaint	eine Beschwerde beilegen
settlement	Vereinbarung, Klärung, Beilegung
▷ settlement of complaint	Beschwerdebeilegung
to set-up	rüsten, aufrüsten
set-up time	Rüstzeit
▷ internal set-up time	interne Rüstzeit
share	Anteil, Aktie
▷ share company	Aktiengesellschaft
shareholder	Aktieninhaber, Aktionär
shift	Schicht
▷ to run (additional) shifts	(zusätzliche) Schichten fahren
to ship	verschicken, versenden; verschiffen
shipment	Versand, Ladung, Sendung
▷ shipment of goods	Warenversand
shipping	Auslieferung
shipping advice	Versandanzeige, Verschiffungsanzeige
shipping company	Speditionsunternehmen
shipping documents	Versanddokumente, Verschiffungsdokumente
shipping instructions	Versandanweisungen, Verschiffungsvorschriften
shipping list	Frachtliste
shipping order	Versandauftrag, Speditionsauftrag
shipping order debit	Lastschriftenanzeige für Versandauftrag

sourcing

shipping point	ausliefernde Stelle
shipping route optimization	Tourenoptimierung
shipping traffic	Schiffsverkehr
shipping weights	Versandgewichte
shop	Werkstatt
shop floor control	Werkstattsteuerung
shop planning	Auftragseinplanung je Maschine
shop traveller	Materialbegleitkarte
shortage	Mangel, Knappheit
▷ shortage in materials	Materialknappheit
▷ shortage in weight	Fehlgewicht
▷ shortage of qualified labour	Mangel an qualifizierten Arbeitskräften
shortcoming (in)	Verknappung
signature	Unterschrift, Signatur
▷ sign off rules	Unterschriftenregelung
▷ sign off levels	Unterschriftenregelung
▷ to sign a contract	einen Vertrag unterzeichnen
▷ to sign off a contract	einen Vertrag paraphieren
single line system	Fertigungssystem mit zentralem Montageband
single-level explosion	Baukastenstückliste
single price	Stückpreis
single sourcing	Single Sourcing: Beschaffung bei einer Quelle
size	Größe, Umfang
▷ size of the supplier base	Umfang des Zuliefererstammes
skilled worker	gelernter Arbeiter
slack-time	Schlupfzeit
slow-selling goods	schwerverkäufliche Ware; Ware mit geringer Umsatzgeschwindigkeit
small company/enterprise	kleiner Betrieb, Kleinfirma, Zwergbetrieb
software	Software
sole agent	Alleinvertreter
sole distributor	Alleinimporteur
source	Quelle, Ursache, Ursprung
▷ source of supply	Lieferquelle
▷ sole source of supply	einzige Bezugsquelle
▷ sole source supplier	einziger Anbieter, Monopolist
sourcing**	Bezugsquellenforschung, Beschaffungsmarktforschung, Beschaffung
▷ multiple sourcing	Parallelbeschaffung

S — spare part, spares

▷ strategic sourcing | strategische Beschaffungsquellen-forschung
spare part, spares | Ersatzteil
special parts | Sonderteile
special price | Sonderpreis, Vorzugspreis
specification list | Stückliste
specifications | technische Daten, Materialbeschreibung

specimen | Muster, Probe
spoilage | Materialabfall
staff | Personal, Belegschaft, Angestellte
staff costs | Personalkosten
staff development | Personalentwicklung
staff member | Mitarbeiter
staff motivation | Mitarbeitermotivation
stage (of production) | Phase, Produktionsabschnitt
stake | Anteil, Beteiligung
▷ to have a 10% stake in a company | eine zehnprozentige Beteiligung an einer Firma haben

standard | Norm, Standard
▷ standard of performance | Leistungsnorm, Leistungsvorgabe
standard industrial classification (SIC) | Industrienorm
standard parts | Normteile, Standardteile
standard statistical approaches | statistische Standardmethoden
standardization | Normierung
standing order | Dauerauftrag
staple goods | Stapelware
start-up | Anfahren, Beginn; Inbetriebnahme
start-up phase of a project | Anlaufphase eines Projekts
state-of-the-art | neuester Stand der Technik
▷ our machines are state-of-the-art | unsere Maschinen sind auf dem neuesten Stand der Technik

statistical process control | statistische Prozeßkontrolle
status | Zustand
statutory regulations | gesetzliche Vorschriften
steel industry | Stahlindustrie
stipulations | Vorschriften
to stipulate something in a contract | etwas in einem Vertrag festlegen/vorschreiben

contractual stipulations | Vertragsvorschriften

stockpiling

stipulated	festgesetzt, vorgeschrieben
step-by-step	schrittweise, stufenweise
stock	Lager, Lagerbestand; Vorrat
▷ in stock	auf Lager
▷ stocks of goods/merchandise	Warenlager
▷ stock of finished goods	Fertigwarenlager, Vorrat an Fertigerzeugnissen
▷ stock of materials	Materiallager
▷ stock of raw materials	Rohstofflager; Vorrat an Rohstoffen
▷ stock on hand	Lagermaterial
▷ actual stock on hand	Ist-Bestand
▷ consigned stocks	Konsignationslager
▷ emergency stock	Mindestbestand
▷ to build up stocks	bevorraten
▷ to clear stocks	Lager räumen
▷ to cut, to liquidate stocks	Lager abbauen
▷ to keep stocks trim	Lagermengen niedrig halten
▷ to take stock	Inventur betreiben
▷ to replenish stocks	Lager wieder auffüllen
▷ stocks are depleted	Lagerbestände sind erschöpft
▷ stocks are running low (short)	Lagervorräte gehen zu Neige
to stock	lagern
stock accounting	Lagerbuchführung
stock analyst	Bestandsüberwacher
stock book	Lagerbuch
stockbuilding (activity)	Lagerdisposition
stock clerk	Lagerarbeiter, Lagerist
stock control	Bestandskontrolle
stock-in-trade	Betriebsmaterial
stock issue note/form	Materialausgabeschein
stockkeeper	Lagerarbeiter, Lagerist
stockkeeping	Lagerung
stock ledger	Lagerbuch
stock ledger card	Materialkarte
stockless production	lagerlose Fertigung
stock level	Lagergröße
stock location	Lagerort
stock movement	Lagerbewegung, Bestandsveränderungen
stock order	Lagerauftrag
stock ordering	Lagerdisposition
stockpile	Materialstapel
stockpiling	Bevorratung

stock policy

stock policy	Bestandspolitik
stock receipts register	Lagerzugangsliste
stock record card	Lagerkarte
stock reduction	Vorratssenkung, Lagerabbau
stock requisition	Entnahmeschein
stock status report	Lagerbestandsbericht
stockturn/stock turnover	Lagerumschlag
stockturn rate	Umschlaghäufigkeit
stoppage	Arbeitseinstellung
storage	(Ein-)Lagerung, Lager(raum)
▷ storage of goods	Warenlagerung
▷ storage of materials and supplies	Lagerung von Hilfs- und Betriebsstoffen
storage area	Lagerraum
storage bin/container	Lagerfach, Lagerbehälter
storage building	Lagerhaus, Lagergebäude, Lagerhalle
storage capacity	Lagerkapazität
storage charges	Lagergebüren, Lagerspesen, Lagergeld
storage container	Lagerbehälter
storage costs	Lagerhaltungskosten
storage expenses	Lagerungskosten
storage facilities	Lagereinrichtungen
storage insurance	Lagerversicherung
storage life	Lagerfähigkeit
storage quotas	Bevorratungsquoten
storage risk	Lagerrisiko
storage slot	Lagerfach
storage space	Lagerraum
▷ to provide storage space	Lagerraum bereitstellen
store	Vorrat, Bestände
to store	lagern
storehouse	Lagergebäude, Warenlager
storekeeper	Lagerist, Lagerarbeiter
stores department	Lagerhaltungsabteilung
stores materials requisition	Materialanforderung
stores requisition form	Entnahmeschein
storing	Bevorratung
▷ storing of goods	Warenlagerung

strap	Band, Riemen, Schlaufe
▷ strapping	Verpackung mit Riemen
to streamline	rationalisieren
▷ to streamline costs	Kosten rationalisieren
▷ to steamline production processes	Straffen des Produktionsablaufs
structure	Struktur, Gefüge
▷ the structure of a company	Unternehmensgefüge
study (on)	Untersuchung (über)
subcontract	Nachunternehmervertrag
to subcontract	Zulieferer verpflichten; Aufträge außer Haus geben
▷ to subcontract an entire business operation	einen gesamten Geschäftsvorgang außer Haus geben
subcontracted supplies and services	Fremdleistungen
subcontracting**	Fremdfertigung
subcontractor	Nachunternehmer
subject, to be subject to	Gültigkeit haben, Anwendung finden
▷ This order is subject to our purchasing terms and conditions overleaf	Für diesen Auftrag gelten unsere umseitigen Einkaufsbedingungen
to submit an offer	ein Angebot unterbreiten
subsidiary	Tochtergesellschaft
▷ wholly-owned subsidiary	hundertprozentige Tochtergesellschaft
subsistence economy	Bedarfsdeckungswirtschaft
substantial	beträchtlich, wesentlich; solid
▷ substantial costs	beträchtliche Kosten
to substitute	ersetzen
substitution	Ersatz
▷ in substitution	ersatzweise
subsupplier	Unterlieferant
success factors	Erfolgsfaktoren
▷ critical success factors	wichtige Erfolgsfaktoren
suitability	Eignung
superior	Vorgesetzter
to supersede	ersetzen
supervise, to	überwachen
supervision	Überwachung
supervisory board	Verwaltungsrat; *BRD:* Aufsichtsrat
supervisory staff	Überwachungspersonal
supplier	Zulieferer, Lieferant
▷ direct supplier	Direktzulieferer

supplier account

▷ established supplier	Stammlieferant
▷ key supplier	A-Lieferant; Stammlieferant
▷ main supplier	Hauptlieferant (quantitativ)
▷ low-cost supplier	preisgünstiger Zulieferer
▷ high-cost supplier	teurer Zulieferer
▷ regular supplier	Stammlieferant
▷ supplier to a plant	Zulieferer für ein Werk
supplier account	Lieferantenkonto
supplier analysis	Lieferantenanalyse
supplier assessment/evaluation	Lieferantenbewertung
supplier base	Zulieferstamm
▷ to reduce the supplier base	den Zulieferstamm reduzieren
supplier clustering	Zusammenfassen von Lieferanten
supplier reliability	Verlässlichkeit eines Lieferanten
supplier relationships	Lieferantenbeziehungen
supplier selection	Lieferantenauswahl
▷ supplier selection and development	Lieferantenauswahl und -entwicklung
supplier selection criteria	Lieferantenauswahlkriterien
supplies	Materialvorräte
▷ supplies are running low	Materialvorräte gehen zu Neige
supply	Lieferung, Versorgung, Bereitstellung; Angebot
▷ supply and demand	Nachfrage und Angebot
▷ supply and demand imbalance	Ungleichgewicht zwischen Nachfrage und Angebot
▷ supply of materials	Materialanlieferung, Materialbereitstellung
▷ supply-of-materials plan	Materialbereitstellungsplan
▷ supply of needs	Bedarfsdeckung
supply management	Versorgungswirtschaft
to supply	liefern, beliefern, bereitstellen; decken
▷ to supply demands/needs/requirements	Bedarf decken
▷ to supply a market	einen Markt beliefern
▷ to supply materials	Materialien liefern
▷ to supply a customer with goods	einen Kunden mit Waren beliefern
▷ supplied parts	Zulieferteile
supply chain	Versorgungskette
supply concepts	Versorgungskonzepte
supply contract	Liefervertrag
supply control	Lieferkontrolle
supply costs	Beschaffungskosten
supply goods	Beschaffungsgüter

supply industry weaknesses	Schwächen der Zulieferindustrie
supply management	Beschaffungsmanagement
supply market	Beschaffungsmarkt
supply network	Versorgungsnetz
supply problems	Zulieferschwierigkeiten, Versorgungsschwierigkeiten
supply procedures	Nachschubvorgänge
supply process	Zulieferprozeß
supply-sight economy	angebotsorientierte Wirtschaft
supply strategies	Versorgungsstrategien
support units	Versorgungseinheit
surplus	Überschuß, Überbestand
▷ surplus stock	überhöhter Bestand
▷ surplus delivery	Überlieferung
survey	Umfrage, Untersuchung
survey report	Schadensbericht, Havariezertifikat
to suspend	aussetzen, einstellen
▷ to suspend delivery	Lieferung einstellen
suspension of contract	Vertragssistierung
system	System, Verfahren
▷ system-oriented structure	Systemorganisation
▷ systems of production	Produktionssysteme
▷ turn-key system	schlüsselfertiges System
system development	Verfahrensentwicklung
system requirements	Pflichtenheft für Verfahren
systems design	Systemgestaltung, -programmierung
systems engineering	Systemplanung

T

tailor-made	maßgeschneidert
▷ tailor-made to meet customer requirements	auf die Bedürfnisse des Kunden zugeschnitten
to take	nehmen, aufnehmen
▷ to take delivery of goods	Warenlieferung annehmen
▷ to take inventory	Lager aufnehmen
▷ to take up production	Produktion aufnehmen
take-over	Firmenübernahme
target	Ziel
▷ target costing	Zielkostenbetrachtung

T — target-date

▷ target group | Zielgruppe
▷ main target group | Hauptzielgruppe
▷ target market | Zielgruppe
▷ target price | Preisvorgabe
▷ target standard costs | Kostenvorgaben
target-date, due date | Solltermin
target-performance comparison | Soll-Ist-Vergleich
target value | Sollwert
tariff | Frachttarif
task | Aufgabe
task force | Arbeitsgruppe
tax | Steuer
tax free | steuerfrei
tax year | Steuerjahr
technical | technisch
▷ technical progress | technischer Fortschritt
Technical Manager | Technischer Direktor
technician | technischer Assistent
temporary storage, interim stock | Zwischenlagerung
tender | Angebot, Ausschreibung
▷ to tender (for) | ein Angebot machen (für)
terms | Bedingungen, Konditionen
▷ general terms and conditions | Allgemeine Geschäftsbedingungen (AGB)
▷ terms of delivery | Lieferbedingungen
▷ terms of payment | Zahlungsbedingungen
to test | prüfen, testen
test equipment | Prüfmittel
test instructions | Prüfvorschriften
test order | Versuchsauftrag, Prüfauftrag
textile industry | Texilindustrie
tied capital | gebundenes Kapital
time | Zeit
▷ time of delivery | Lieferzeit
▷ scheduled time of delivery | geplante Lieferzeit
▷ time of performance | Leistungszeit
▷ time-phased order point (TPOP) | terminabhängiger Bestellpunkt
time fence | begrenzter Zeitraum
time network | Terminnetz
time phasing | Zusammenfassen von Bedarf, Lieferungen und Beständen in Zeitperioden

Training Manager

time sheet	Stundenzettel
time-to-market	Die zur Einführung eines neuen Produktes benötigte Zeit
to be working short time	Kurzarbeit fahren
ton(ne)	Tonne
▷ metric ton(ne)	1000 Kilogramm
▷ long ton(ne) (UK)	1016 Kilogramm
▷ short ton(ne) (USA)	907,18 Kilogramm
tool	Werkzeug
▷ tools of analysis	Analysewerkzeuge
tool allowance	Werkzeugwechselzeit
tool setting	Einrichten
top-of-the-range product	erstrangiges Produkt, Spitzenprodukt
total	Gesamt-, gesamt
▷ total cost	Gesamtkosten
▷ least total cost	kleinste Gesamtkosten
▷ total cost concept	Vollkostenansatz
▷ total input cost	Gesamtmaterialaufwand
▷ total profit	Gesamtprofit
▷ total revenue	Gesamteinkünfte, Gesamteinkommen
Total Acquisition Cost (TAC)	Gesamtbeschaffungskosten
Total Costs of Ownership**	Total Cost of Ownership**
Total Productive Maintenance (TPM)	reibungsloser Materialfluß
Total Quality Management (TQM)**	Total Quality Management**
tpa (tonnes per annum)	t/Jahr
tpd (tonnes per day)	t/Tag
trade	Handel
trade buyer	Einkäufer
trade discount	Händlerrabatt
trade fair	Messe, Handelsmesse, Leistungsschau
trademark	Handelsmarke
trade union	Gewerkschaft
trading enterprise	Handelsunternehmen
trading profits	Betriebsgewinn, Betriebsergebnis
trading year	Geschäftsjahr
training	Ausbildung, Weiterbildung
▷ trained staff	ausgebildetes Personal
▷ on the job training (OJT)	Ausbildung am Arbeitsplatz
Training Manager	Ausbildungsleiter

T transfer

transfer	Transport, Transfer
▷ transfer costs	Transportkosten
transport, transportation	Transport
▷ means of transport	Transportmittel
to transport	transportieren
▷ to transport by land, by air, by sea	auf dem Land-, Luft-, Seeweg befördern
transport(ation) facilities	Beförderungseinrichtungen
transportation inventory	Pipelinebestand
transport system	Verkehrsnetz
transshipment	Umschlag
▷ transshipment and transport of goods	Warenumschlag und Warentransport
treatment	Behandlung
trend	Trend, Tendenz
▷ to spot trends	Trends erkennen
trial order	Probeauftrag
turn-key	schlüsselfertig
turnover	Umsatz, Umschlag
turnover ratio/rate	Umschlaghäufigkeit
type and scope of production	Produktionsart und -umfang
type of costs	Kostenart

U

to understock	eine zu kleine Menge auf Lager haben; ein kleines Lager halten
unfounded complaint	unbegründete Beschwerde
to unify	vereinheitlichen
unit	Einheit
▷ unit of material	Materialeinheit
▷ unit of measure	Maßeinheit
▷ unit of work	Arbeitseinheit
▷ unit working costs	Betriebskosten pro Einheit
unit cost	Stückkosten
▷ least unit cost	geringste Stückkosten
unitized freight	vereinheitlichte Fracht
unskilled worker	ungelernter Arbeiter
to update	aktualisieren; auf den neuesten Stand bringen

warehousing

▷ updating of inventory | Lagerbestandsfortschreibung
updating procedure | Änderungsverfahren
user | Anwender
▷ user friendly | anwenderfreundlich, benutzerfreundlich

utilization | Gebrauch, Verbrauch
▷ utilization of materials | Materialverbrauch
▷ utilization of storage capacity | Lagerauslastung

V

vacency | Planstelle
valuation | Wertfestsetzung
value | Wert
▷ capitalized value | Ertragswert
value added tax (VAT) | Mehrwertsteuer
value analysis** | Wertanalyse
▷ total value analysis | Gesamtwertanalyse
value engineering** | Value Engineering**
value of raw materials and supplies | Wert der Roh- und Betriebsstoffe
variable | Variable, Kennzahl
▷ variable costs | variable Kosten
vendor | Verkäufer
vendor analysis | Verkäuferanalyse
vendor rating | Verkäuferbewertung
volume | Umfang, Volumen
▷ volume of output | Leistungsvolumen

W

wage | Lohn
warehouse | Lager, Lagergebäude, Lagerhaus
▷ market-positioned warehouse | günstig am Markt gelegenes Lager
warehouse charges | Lager(halt)ungskosten, Lagergeld
warehouse receipt/certificate | Lagerschein
warehousing | Lagerhaltung
▷ warehousing of goods | Warenlager

warehousing business

warehousing business	Lagergeschäft
warehousing contract	Lagervertrag
warrant, to	gewährleisten
warranty	Gewährleistung
warranty time	Gewährleistungszeit
▷ a warranty time of three years	eine Gewährleistungszeit von drei Jahren
wastage	Materialverschleiß, Materialschwund
waste	Abfall
to waste	verschwenden
▷ wasting of materials	Materialverschwendung
waste disposal	Entsorgung
waste material	Abfallmaterial
weak point	Schwachstelle
weak point analysis	Schwachstellenanalyse
wholesale	Großhandel
wholesale price	Großhandelspreis
wholesaler	Großhändler
to withdraw	sich zurückziehen, zurücktreten
▷ to withdraw from a contract	von einem Vertrag zurücktreten
withdrawal	Abzug, Entzug; Rückzug
▷ withdrawal from stock	Lagerentnahme
work	Arbeit
▷ work in process	auftragsbezogener Werkstattbestand
▷ work in progress	in Verarbeitung befindliches Material; auftragsbezogener Werkstattbestand
to work	arbeiten
▷ to work for one's own account	auf eigene Rechnung arbeiten
work break-down structure	Auftragsstrukturplan
work centre	Belastungseinheit
work clothing	Arbeitskleidung
worker	Arbeiter
▷ skilled worker	gelernter Arbeiter
▷ semi-skilled worker	angelernter Arbeiter
▷ unskilled worker	ungelernter Arbeiter
▷ qualified worker	qualifizierter Arbeiter
▷ certified worker	geprüfter Arbeiter
working assets	Umlaufvermögen
working capital	Betriebsmittel, Betriebskapital, Umlaufvermögen

▷ requiring a large amount of working capital | kapitalintensiv
working capital requirements | Betriebsmittelbedarf
working environment | Betriebsklima
working expense | Betriebsaufwand, Aufwendungen
work instructions | Arbeitsanweisungen
work load | Arbeitsauslastung
work permit | Arbeitserlaubnis
work place | Arbeitsplatz
work sampling | Stichprobenentnahme am Arbeitsplatz

works council | Betriebsrat
works regulation | Betriebsordnung
works standards | Werksnormen
to write | schreiben
▷ to write off | abschreiben
▷ to write off costs | Kosten abschreiben
▷ in writing | schriftlich
▷ written confirmation of an oral order | schriftliche Bestätigung eines mündlich erteilten Auftrages
write-off | Abschreibung
write-off, to | abschreiben

Y

yield | Ausbeute

A. Definitionen

Englische Fachbegriffe der Materialwirtschaft kurz definiert

Benchmarking
Die Ausarbeitung eines Kennzahlensystems auf der Grundlage eines Leistungsvergleiches hauptsächlich branchenführender Unternehmen mit dem Ziel, bei der Optimierung der eigenen Unternehmensleistungen Orientierungshilfe zu leisten.

Business Logistics
Begriff, der die Versorgung von Unternehmen mit Materialien, Gütern und Dienstleistungen im Bereich der zivilen Wirtschaft definiert und dem ursprünglich militärischen Terminus der Logistik gegenübergestellt.

Business Reengineering
Die Umstrukturierung interner Arbeitsabläufe und Strukturen eines Unternehmens zur Steigerung von Effizienz und Wettbewerbsfähigkeit.

Controlling
Die Beobachtung des betrieblichen Umfeldes, Schwachstellenanalysen sowie Leistungs- und Wirtschaftlichkeitsbeurteilungen sind die Instrumente des Controlling, die zur Erstellung eines umfangreichen Kennzahlensystems dienen; dies wiederum dient der Unternehmensleitung als wichtige Informationsquelle bei der Optimierung von Geschäftsprozessen, Kostensenkungen und der Verbesserung von Durchlaufzeiten und Serviceleistungen.

A. Definitions

A short definition of special terms in purchasing and materials management

Benchmarking
Benchmarking figures are worked out by thoroughly observing and comparing the performances of a sector´s leading companies and provide important management information for the evaluation and improvement of corporate performances.

Business Logistics
In accordance with the originally military definition of the term logistics, the term Business Logistics describes the process of supplying companies with the goods and services they require for their production and business activities.

Business Reengineering
Business Reengineering means the re-organisation of a company's internal structures and business processes in order to increase corporate efficiency and competitiveness.

Controlling
Controlling includes the monitoring of a company's business environment, the analysis of potential trouble spots as well as internal performance evaluations and efficiency ratings in order to elaborate a comprehensive system of key data and reference figures. These figures provide important management information in the process of optimizing business processes, reducing costs and improving lead times and services.

Direct Materials
Materialien, die bei der Herstellung unmittelbarer Bestandteil eines Produktes werden.

Direct Materials are materials which are to become a direct part of the manufactured product.

Design-to-Cost
Die Festlegung von Zielkosten für alle Einzelkomponenten einer Produktion bereits im frühen Stadium der Produktentwicklung und Konstruktion mit dem Ziel einer permanenten Kostensenkung.

When the Design-to-Cost concept is applied, target costs for all parts and materials required for the manufacturing of a product are fixed as early as in the stage of product development and construction in order to achieve permanent cost reductions.

Force Majeure
Höhere Gewalt: die Nichterfüllung eines Vertrages aufgrund von Umständen, auf die der Vertragspartner keinen Einfluß hat – wie z. B. Überschwemmungen, Feuer oder Krieg – und für die er deshalb bei Nichterfüllung nicht haftbar gemacht werden kann.

The term Force Majeure means that for reasons beyond a company's control – e.g. flooding, fire or war – it is impossible to fulfil the obligations of a contract; in case of Force Majeure the company in question cannot be held responsible for non-fulfilment of contract.

Indirect Materials
Materialien, die nicht unmittelbarer Bestandteil eines Produkts werden, aber für den Herstellungsprozeß benötigt werden, z. B. Hilfs- und Betriebsstoffe.

Indirect Materials are materials which are not a direct part of a product but enter the manufacturing process, e. g. auxiliaries.

Just-in-Time
Prinzip einer optimalen Zeitplanung zur Vermeidung von Leerlaufzeiten einerseits und unnötig hohen Lagerbeständen andererseits: Auftragserteilung und Anlieferung erfolgen so, daß die für die Produktion benötigten Komponenten möglichst genau zum Zeitpunkt des Bedarfs zur Verfügung stehen und der Lageraufwand möglichst gering ist.

The Just-in-Time principle focuses on optimal (procurement) timing in order to avoid idle production periods, on the one hand, and high inventory levels, on the other: The target is to have the goods required for production delivered "just in time", i.e. when they are needed for production.

Make or Buy

Die Entscheidung darüber, welche Teile in Eigenproduktion hergestellt und welche Teile zugekauft werden sollen, um optimale Kosten und Effizienz zu erzielen.

The decision that determines which parts and components are to be manufactured in a company's own plant and which ones are to be purchased from a supplier in order to achieve optimum costs.

Materials Management

Beschaffung und Umgang mit Materialien, die für die Produktion und Leistungserstellung in einem Unternehmen benötigt werden. Klassische materialwirtschaftliche Tätigkeiten sind Einkauf, Bevorratung, Bereitstellung sowie Recycling und Entsorgung.

Das Konzept der **integrierten Materialwirtschaft** propagiert eine stärkere Einbindung dieser klassisch materialwirtschaftlichen Tätigkeiten in die betriebliche Wertschöpfungskette, zum Beispiel durch engere Zusammenarbeit mit der Entwicklungs- und Konstruktionsabteilung, der Produktion und dem Vertrieb.

Materials Management includes all activities in connection with the purchase and handling of materials and parts required for production. Traditional materials functions are purchasing, storing, provisioning as well as recycling and waste disposal.

Integrated Materials Management focuses on a stronger integration of the materials functions into the corporate added value chain by increasing the cooperation between materials functions and the construction and development departments as well as production and distribution.

Operations Research

Betriebsanalyse – Die fortlaufende Analyse innerbetrieblicher Funktionen und Arbeitsabläufe mit dem Ziel der Betriebsoptimierung.

Operations Research focuses on evaluating the efficiency of all functions and business processes within a company in order to improve corporate performances.

Overengineering

Im Stadium der Produktentwicklung und Konstruktion werden häufig überteuerte Materialien und Komponenten in den späteren Produktionsprozeß eingeplant, ohne qualitativ hinreichende und doch preisgünstigere Alternativen zu bedenken; letztendlich führt Overengineering oft zu überteuerten Produkten.

In the stage of product development and construction, engineers often plan the use of expensive top-quality materials and components in production without considering alternative materials which are of satisfactory quality but less cost intensive; thus overengineering often results in all-too-expensive products.

Procurement

Der Begriff der Beschaffung geht über den des reinen Einkaufs von Waren und Dienstleistungen hinaus, da er weitreichendere Tätigkeiten, wie zum Beispiel Material-, Qualitäts- und Lagerbestandskontrollen sowie die Abnahme und Inspektion von zugelieferter Ware umfaßt.

The term procurement does not only include the purchasing of materials, goods and services but tasks such as materials management, inventory control, receiving and the inspection of incoming materials as well.

Purchasing

Der Einkauf von Materialien, Waren und Dienstleistungen in einer bestimmten Menge und Qualität zu einem bestimmten Preis und Zeitpunkt bei einer oder mehreren Beschaffungsquellen.

Purchasing includes the buying of a certain quality and quantity of materials and services at a certain price from a suitable source at a certain time.

Sourcing

Bezugsquellenforschung: Während sich der Einkäufer beim **Single Sourcing** auf die Erschließung und Entwicklung einer Zulieferquelle für eine Ware und beim **Dual Sourcing** auf zwei Zulieferquellen konzentriert, liegt der Schwerpunkt beim **Multiple Source Buying** und **Global Sourcing** durch den Bezug bei mehreren Zulieferern auf nationaler und internationaler Ebene auf der Entwicklung neuer Zulieferer und einer Verstärkung des Zulieferwettbewerbs.

Sourcing means that companies continuously try to find and develop suitable sources of supply for the goods and services they need. While some companies tend to rely on one main source of supply, i.e. on Single Sourcing, other companies prefer to have two sources, i.e. Dual Sourcing. However, many companies apply the concepts of Multiple Source Buying and Global Sourcing by purchasing from several suppliers at home and abroad so as to develop new suppliers and increase competition among suppliers.

Subcontracting

1. Geschäftsvorgänge ganz oder teilweise außer Haus geben;
2. Zulieferer verpflichten, die für die Produktion benötigten Teile und Halbfertigprodukte zu liefern, so daß diese nicht in Eigenproduktion hergestellt werden müssen.

1. Contracting other manufacturers who can carry out either parts of the production process or complete processes;
2. Contracting suppliers who can provide the parts and semi-finished products needed for production so that these parts do not have to be manufactured in the buying company's own plant.

Total Cost of Ownership

Gesamtkosten der Versorgung eines Unternehmens mit Waren und Dienstleistungen unter Berücksichtigung nicht nur der Beschaffungs- und Lagerhaltungskosten, sondern auch des Kostenaufwandes zum Beispiel für Mängelbehebung bei minderwertiger Ware, für Verwaltungsarbeiten, Recycling, Entsorgung etc.

Term for the total cost of providing a company with all the goods and services required for a company's production and business activities, including cost factors such as purchase prices, inventory costs, management and administrative expenses, costs caused by low quality and faulty materials as well as recycling and waste disposal costs.

Total Quality Management

Konzept eines umfassenden Qualitätsmanagement unter Berücksichtigung aller Einzelfaktoren der Qualitätssicherung.

Comprehensive concept of quality management and quality audits.

Value Analysis

Die Untersuchung von Materialien und Komponenten hinsichtlich ihrer Funktionalität und Effizienz unter Berücksichtigung ihres Beschaffungspreises mit dem Ziel, optimale Qualität zum niedrigst möglichen Preis zu erlangen. Gegenstände einer solchen Wertanalyse sind unter anderem Alternativmaterialien, verbesserte Fertigungsmethoden und die Leistungen spezialisierter Zulieferer.

Checking the performance of a material or a component regarding its function and unit price in order to achieve optimum quality at the lowest possible price. Value analysis tools are the evaluation of alternative materials, new production processes as well as the performances of specialized suppliers.

Value Engineering

Die Anwendung wertanalytischer Methoden als wesentliches Mittel zur Produktionskostensenkung bereits vom Stadium der Produktentwicklung und Konstruktion an.

The application of value analysis methods as early as in the stage of product development and construction in order to achieve optimum production costs.

B. Gesprochenes Englisch – Hilfestellung für den Geschäftsalltag

B. Spoken business German for everyday use

1. Am Telefon

Making a phone call

Good morning/afternoon, this is Mr./ Mrs. ... from XYZ GmbH. Could I speak to Mr. ..., please?

Hello, this is Mr. Braun speaking. Could I speak to Mr. Stuart, please?

I'd like the sales department, please.

Could you put me through to Mr. Gerrard/the purchasing manager/the person in charge of the marketing department?

Returning phone calls

I'm returning Mrs. Müller's call. She tried to ring me yesterday.

Answering phone calls

What's the name, please?

Could you repeat/spell the name, please?

Sorry, I did not understand. Could you repeat that, please?

Could you speak more slowly, please?

I'm sorry, but Mr. Schmidt is in a meeting/not in today/on a business trip.

Leaving a message

Could I leave a message for Mr. Smith, then?

Could you ask him to ring me back/call me back, please?

My telephone number/my direct telephone number/my fax number is ...

Making an appointment

I wish to make an appointment with Mrs...

1. On the phone

Guten Morgen/guten Tag, hier spricht Herr/Frau ... von der Firma XYZ GmbH. Ich würde gerne Herrn ... sprechen.

Guten Tag, Braun am Apparat. Könnte ich bitte mit Herrn Stuart sprechen?

Verbinden Sie mich bitte mit der Vertriebsabteilung.

Könnten Sie mich bitte mit Herrn Gerrard/dem Einkaufsleiter/dem Leiter der Marketingabteilung verbinden?

Frau Müller versuchte gestern, mich zu erreichen. Kann ich sie bitte sprechen?

Wie ist Ihr Name bitte?

Könnten Sie Ihren Namen bitte wiederholen/buchstabieren?

Ich habe das leider nicht verstanden. Könnten Sie es bitte wiederholen?

Könnten Sie bitte langsamer sprechen?

Es tut mir leid, aber Herr Schmidt ist in einer Sitzung/heute nicht im Hause/auf Geschäftsreise.

Könnte ich Herrn Smith dann vielleicht eine Nachricht hinterlassen?

Könnten Sie ihn bitten, mich zurückzurufen?

Meine Telefonnummer/Durchwahlnummer/ Faxnummer ist ...

Ich möchte einen Termin mit Frau ... vereinbaren.

Can you hold please, I'll look at his/her diary.	*Bleiben Sie bitte am Apparat, ich sehe in seinem/ihrem Terminkalender nach.*
Can you hold please, I'll see when he/she is free.	*Einen Augenblick bitte, ich sehe nach, wann er/sie Zeit hat.*
He is free at 2 p.m. on Tuesday, 8th December. Would that be suitable?	*Er hat am 8. Dezember um 14 Uhr Zeit. Paßt Ihnen das?*
This would be fine. Thank you very much.	*Das paßt mir gut. Vielen Dank.*
Could we arrange for an earlier date?	*Könnten wir vielleicht einen früheren Termin vereinbaren?*
Thank you, goodbye.	*Ich bedanke mich, auf Wiederhören.*

Establishing first contacts

I was given your number by Harald Thomas of Brown Consultants.	*Harald Thomas von der Firma Brown Consultants hat mir Ihre Nummer gegeben.*
Mrs. Sully advised me to contact you.	*Frau Sully riet mir, mich direkt an Sie zu wenden.*

Gathering information

I wonder whether you could give me some information on …	*Ich hätte gerne Näheres über … erfahren.*
We've received your sales letter and would like to get more detailed literature on your range of products.	*Wir haben Ihren Werbebrief erhalten und würden gerne ausführlicheres Informationsmaterial über Ihr Produktsortiment haben.*
Our company is looking for new suppliers in your area. I believe it would be mutually beneficial for us to meet.	*Unsere Firma sucht in Ihrer Region nach neuen Zulieferfirmen. Ich denke, ein Gespräch könnte für unsere beiden Unternehmen interessant sein.*
Could we meet to discuss this matter?	*Könnten wir uns treffen, um diese Angelegenheit zu besprechen?*

Arranging to meet somebody

Could we meet at … (place) at … (time) on … (date) to discuss this contract?	*Könnten wir uns am … (Datum) um … (Uhrzeit) in … (Ort) treffen, um diesen Vertrag auszuhandeln?*
The meeting will be about our future cooperation.	*Das Treffen hat unsere zukünftige Zusammenarbeit zum Thema.*
We will be meeting to discuss how to develop new suppliers.	*Bei dem Treffen werden wir Möglichkeiten der Lieferantenentwicklung besprechen.*

What would be the most suitable date and time?	An welchem Tag und um welche Uhrzeit paßt es Ihnen am besten?
Would you have any free time on …?	Hätten Sie am … Zeit?
When would be a suitable time to come and see you?	Wann wäre Ihnen mein Besuch recht?
Where do you suggest we meet?	Wo könnten wir uns treffen?
I have a pretty full diary for that date but I could meet you at … o'clock on …	Ich habe an diesem Tag leider keinen freien Termin, aber ich könnte Sie am … um … Uhr treffen.
Can I suggest that we meet at … o'clock on …?	Könnten wir uns am … um … Uhr treffen?
It would be best if we met at/in …	Es wäre vielleicht am besten, wenn wir uns in … treffen.
Shall we say in my office at 10 a.m. on 3th November?	Sagen wir also am 3. November um 10 Uhr in meinem Büro?

Special arrangements

Would you like to discuss it over lunch?	Würden Sie das gerne beim Mittagessen besprechen?
I will ask the head of our engineering department to be there as well.	Ich werde unseren technischen Leiter bitten, auch an dem Treffen teilzunehmen.
Shall I arrange for an interpreter to be at the meeting?	Möchten Sie, daß bei dem Treffen ein Dolmetscher anwesend ist?
I'll fax through a location map to help you find us.	Ich werde Ihnen eine Anfahrtsskizze zufaxen, damit Sie uns leichter finden können.

Confirming appointments

I'm calling to confirm my appointment with Mrs. …	Ich rufe an, um meinen Termin mit Frau … zu bestätigen.
I'm calling on behalf of Mr. … to confirm his meeting with Mr. … on May 6th.	Ich rufe im Auftrag von Herrn … an, um seinen Termin mit Herrn … am 6. Mai zu bestätigen.
I just wanted to confirm the date/the time of our meeting.	Ich wollte nur noch einmal Datum und Uhrzeit unseres Treffens bestätigen.
Can I just confirm the arrangements for …?	Kann ich kurz die Verabredungen für … bestätigen?
I would like to check the plans for …	Ich möchte gerne die Pläne für … kurz absprechen.
Can you confirm that the arrangements still stand?	Könnten Sie mir bitte bestätigen, daß das Treffen wie vereinbart stattfindet?

Is everything all right for our meeting on the 12th?

Cancelling appointments

I'd arranged to meet you at 3 p.m. on 6th June.

Mrs. ... is expecting me at 11 o'clock.

I expected to be in Munich on 6th June, but I'm afraid, I won't be free then.

Unfortunately, I'm going to have to cancel our appointment.

I'm sorry that I won't be able to keep our appointment.

Would it be possible to change the appointment to 5th January?

I wondered whether Mr./Mrs. ... would be free on 5th January instead of the 2nd?

Gilt unser Treffen am zwölften noch wie besprochen?

Wir hatten ein Treffen für den 6. Juni um 15 Uhr verabredet.

Frau ... erwartet mich um 11 Uhr.

Eigentlich sollte ich am 6. Juni in München sein, aber ich kann an diesem Tag leider nicht.

Ich muß unseren Termin leider absagen.

Es tut mir leid, daß ich unseren Termin leider nicht einhalten kann.

Wäre es möglich, den Termin auf den 5. Januar zu verschieben?

Wäre es für Herrn/Frau ... eventuell möglich, den Termin vom 2. auf den 5. Januar zu verschieben?

2. Konferenzen und Tagungen

Organizing meetings

I am phoning in connection with the conference we will have at your premisses on April 2nd.

We need a conference room for 30 people from 8.30 a.m. till 5 p.m.

Can you arrange the tables in a U shape/in a square?

We would like the chairs in rows.

Could you give us some paper for the flip chart please?

Could we have coffee for 30 people at 10.30, please?

What time is lunch arranged for?

We are expecting 35 people for lunch.

How long can we use the conference room?

2. Conferences and meetings

Ich rufe wegen der Tagung am 2. April in Ihrem Hause an.

Wir benötigen von 8.30 Uhr bis 17 Uhr einen Tagungsraum für 30 Personen.

Können Sie die Tische in Hufeisenform/in einem Viereck aufstellen?

Können Sie die Stühle bitte in Reihe aufstellen?

Könnten wir bitte Papier für das Flip-Chart haben?

Um 10.30 Uhr hätten wir gerne Kaffee für 30 Personen.

Für wann ist Mittagessen vorgesehen?

Wir rechnen mit 35 Personen zum Mittagessen.

Wie lange steht uns der Tagungsraum zur Verfügung?

Could we use your photocopying facilities if necessary?	*Steht uns gegebenenfalls ein Fotokopiergerät zur Verfügung?*
Is it possible to have a telephone extension/a fax machine/a VHS video player/an OHP in the conference room?	*Könnten wir im Tagungsraum bitte einen Telefonanschluß/ein Faxgerät/einen VHS-Videorekorder/einen Overheadprojektor haben?*

Arranging for accomodation

Can you arrange for hotel accomodation for 30 people?	*Können Sie bitte Hotelunterkünfte für 30 Personen buchen?*
We would like to book five single rooms with bath/shower and four double rooms with bath/shower from April 12th to April 16th. Could you please send us a confirmation of our booking as soon as possible?	*Wir würden gerne vom 12. bis 16. April fünf Einzelzimmer mit Bad/Dusche und vier Doppelzimmer mit Bad/Dusche reservieren. Könnten Sie uns bitte sobald wie möglich eine Buchungsbestätigung zusenden?*

2.2 Verhandeln und diskutieren / 2.2 Negotiating and discussing

Making a point

I'd like to point out that …	*Ich möchte darauf hinweisen, daß …*
I must point out that …	*Ich muß Sie darauf hinweisen, daß …*
I'd like to say that …	*Ich würde hierzu gerne sagen, daß …*
This is the situation at the moment.	*Das ist die aktuelle Lage.*
I'd like to ask Mrs. Taylor to …	*Ich möchte Frau Tailor bitten zu …*

Interrupting politely

Can I make a suggestion?	*Darf ich einen Vorschlag machen?*
Can I make a point here?/I'd like to make a point here …	*Darf ich hierzu etwas sagen?*
If I understand the situation correctly …	*Wenn ich die Situation richtig verstanden habe …*

Disagreement and doubt

I see the problem differently.	*Das Problem sehe ich anders.*
That's only partly true.	*Das ist nicht ganz richtig.*
I can't agree.	*Das sehe ich anders.*
Surely we should also consider …?	*Sollten wir nicht auch beachten, daß …?*
Our position is that we think the contract should include …	*Wir stehen auf dem Standpunkt, daß der Vertrag … beinhalten sollte.*

Considering other points of view

I appreciate your problem/your position.	Ich verstehe Ihr Problem/Ihre Lage.
I can see your point of view.	Ich verstehe Ihren Standpunkt.

Suggesting a compromise

Can you suggest a compromise?	Können Sie einen Kompromiß vorschlagen?
An alternative would be to …	Eine Alternative wäre …
Wouldn't it be possible for you to …	Wäre es Ihnen nicht möglich zu …?
We could agree to … if you were willing to …	Wir könnten … zustimmen, wenn Sie bereit wären zu …
Is there any way of changing/modifying …?	Gibt es eine Möglichkeit, …zu ändern/überarbeiten?
Well then, let me suggest that …	Darf ich dann vorschlagen, daß …
Are you prepared to accept …?	Wären Sie bereit, … zu akzeptieren?

Reaching an agreement

Can I take it that you agree?	Kann ich mit Ihrem Einverständnis rechnen?
I agree.	Ich bin einverstanden.
Yes, I think that we should …	Ja, ich denke, wir sollten …
I'll support that.	Ich bin auch dafür.
You're right.	Sie haben recht.
I think I can accept that.	Ich denke, das kann ich akzeptieren.
That seems to be the best solution.	Das scheint die beste Lösung zu sein.
Well, I think we have an agreement	Ich glaube, wir sind uns einig.
I think we've reached a compromise.	Ich glaube, wir haben einen Mittelweg gefunden.
I think that's fair to both sides.	Ich denke, das ist für alle Beteiligten eine annehmbare Lösung.

Summarizing the results of a meeting

We seem to have reached an agreement on the main points.	Ich glaube, wir sind uns in den wichtigsten Punkten einig.
So, can I just confirm that we've agreed to …	Darf ich also nochmals feststellen, daß wir uns einig sind, zu …
To sum up the main points in our discussion …	Wenn unsere Diskussion zusammenfassen darf …
Can I just check the points we have agreed on?	Darf ich kurz noch einmal die Punkte nennen, auf die wir uns geeignet haben?

I think it would be useful to meet again in order to work out the details of the contract.	*Ich denke, ein weiteres Treffen zur detaillierten Ausarbeitung des Vertrages wäre von Nutzen.*
I will have the contract amended.	*Ich werde den Vertrag abändern lassen.*
We will let you have the minutes of this meeting as soon as they have been worked out.	*Wir werden Ihnen das Tagungsprotokoll zuschicken sobald es ausgearbeitet ist.*

3. Lieferung und Transport

Arranging for delivery

3. *Delivery and transport*

When would you be able to deliver a load to our factory in Munich?	*Wann könnten Sie eine Ladung an unsere Fabrik in München liefern?*
How soon could you deliver?	*Wie schnell können Sie liefern?*
When do you expect to deliver the order?	*Wann denken Sie können Sie liefern?*
Can you deliver earlier/later?	*Könnten Sie früher/später liefern?*
Would you be able to collect the load on 4th May?	*Könnten Sie die Ladung am 4. Mai abholen?*
I want to arrange for delivery of a load to Frankfurt.	*Ich möchte veranlassen, daß eine Warenladung nach Frankfurt versandt wird.*
The load is on four pallets.	*Die Ladung besteht aus vier Paletten.*
The order will be ready for collection on 4th May.	*Die bestellte Ware wird am 4. Mai abholbereit sein.*
What are your rates?	*Können Sie mir Ihre Preise nennen?*
Can you pick up a load to Munich for delivery to London?	*Könnten Sie eine Warenladung von München nach London transportieren?*
I will fax you all the details today.	*Ich werde Ihnen heute alle näheren Angaben zufaxen.*
The documents will be ready when the driver calls on the load.	*Die Versanddokumente werden für den Fahrer bereitliegen, wenn er die Ladung abholt.*
The cost of transport will be paid by the customer.	*Die Transportkosten werden vom Kunden getragen.*

Carrier asks for details

Which address do you want the order delivered to?	*An welche Adresse soll die Lieferung gehen?*
The goods will be covered by insurance until they are delivered.	*Die Ware ist bis zur Anlieferung versichert.*

Do you have container handling facilities?	Haben Sie die nötige Ausstattung zur Handhabung von Containern?

Delivery problems

I'm afraid our lorry has been involved in an accident.	Unser Lkw ist leider in einen Unfall verwickelt worden.
There will be a delay in delivery because the lorry has broken down.	Die Lieferung der Ladung wird sich leider verzögern, da der Lkw eine Panne hat.
There will be a delay in delivery because there have been problems with the documents at customs.	Die Lieferung der Ladung wird sich leider verzögern, da es bei der Zollabfertigung Probleme mit den Papieren gibt.
There will be a delay in delivery because of the need to repack the goods.	Die Lieferung der Ladung wird sich leider verzögern, da die Waren umgepackt werden müssen.
There may be a delay in delivery because of heavy flooding in some parts of Germany.	Aufgrund der Überschwemmungen in einigen Teilen Deutschlands kann es eventuell zu Lieferverzögerungen kommen.

Complaining about deliveries

I'm ringing in connection with your latest delivery.	Ich rufe wegen Ihrer letzten Lieferung an.
I have a complaint about the recent delivery we had from you.	Leider war die Lieferung, die wir kürzlich von Ihnen erhalten haben, nicht einwandfrei.
We have a problem with order number 231/43.	Wir haben ein Problem mit Auftragsnummer 231/43.
We have only received part of the order.	Wir haben nur ein Teil der bestellten Ware erhalten.
There are some items missing from the order.	Es fehlen einige Posten der Bestellung.
The contents of some of the boxes has arrived damaged.	Der Inhalt einiger Kartons ist beschädigt.
We have been sent … in error.	Uns ist versehentlich … zugeschickt worden.
The color is wrong.	Es ist nicht die richtige Farbe.
The goods delivered do not match the samples you sent us.	Die Qualität der gelieferten Ware entspricht nicht den zugesandten Mustern.

Poor quality

We are very disappointed with the quality of the goods delivered.	Die Qualität der gelieferten Ware ist ganz und gar nicht zufriedenstellend.

We are very disappointed with the performance of the machines you sold us recently.	Wir sind sehr unzufrieden mit der Leistung der Geräte, die Sie uns kürzlich verkauft haben.

Delayed delivery

We are wondering why we have not yet received the goods we have ordered.	Können Sie mir sagen, warum wir die bestellte Ware noch nicht erhalten haben?
Do you think you can sort out the problem?	Glauben Sie, Sie können dieses Problem in den Griff bekommen?
How long will it take to sort out the problem?	Wie lange wird es wohl dauern, bis Sie dieses Problem in den Griff bekommen?

Cancelling orders

I am telephoning to cancel our order number 5543/1. I will fax a letter in confirmation.	Ich rufe an, um unsere Auftragsnummer 5543/1 zu stornieren. Ich werde Ihnen die Bestätigung zufaxen.

4. Einkäufer auf einer Messe | 4. Purchasing at trade fair

Information about trade fairs

Could we have some literature on the XYZ show in May 1997, please?	Könnten Sie uns bitte Informationsmaterial über die XYZ-Messe im Mai 1997 zukommen lassen?
Could you let's have a list of the exhibitors at last year's trade fair?	Könnten Sie uns bitte das Ausstellerverzeichnis der Vorjahresmesse zusenden?
When will catalogues be available?	Wann werden die Messekataloge erhältlich sein?
Can you tell me the dates of the … trade fair, please?	Könnten Sie mir bitte die Termine der … Handelsmesse nennen?
When is the trade day?	Wann ist Fachbesuchertag?

Establishing contacts

Could I have one of your brochures, please?	Könnte ich einen Ihrer Prospekte haben?
Could I have a look through your catalogue, please?	Dürfte ich einen Blick auf Ihren Katalog werfen?
Could you give me more details on your new product, please?	Könnten Sie mir bitte Näheres über Ihr neues Produkt sagen?
When are you going to demonstrate the new model, please?	Wann werden Sie das neue Modell vorführen?
Are you offering any discounts on orders placed during the exhibition?	Räumen Sie bei Messebestellungen Rabatte ein?

Could you let me have a quote and your general conditions of sale, please? I am the purchasing manager of … Here is my business card.	Könnten Sie mir bitte ein Angebot und Ihre allgemeinen Geschäftsbedingungen zukommen lassen? Ich bin Einkaufsleiter der Firma … Hier ist meine Visitenkarte.
I'm interested in learning more about your range of products. Could you arrange for a presentation on our premisses?	Ich würde gerne mehr über Ihr Produktsortiment erfahren. Könnten Sie eine Vorführung Ihrer Produkte in unserer Firma arrangieren?
Would it be possible to arrange for your local sales consultant to visit us?	Wäre es möglich, einen Besuch Ihres zuständigen Verkaufsvertreters zu arrangieren?

5. Betriebsbesichtigungen / 5. Visitors at your premises

Making the introductions

Good afternoon, ladies and gentlemen, and welcome at Schmidt GmbH.	Guten Tag, meine Damen und Herren, und herzlich willkommen bei der Schmidt GmbH.
My name is Sarah Parker. I am a manager with the company/I am responsible for public relations.	Ich bin Sarah Parker und eine der Führungskräfte unseres Hauses/zuständig für die Öffentlichkeitsarbeit.
I will be showing you our office complex/plant.	Ich werde Ihnen unseren Bürokomplex/unser Werk zeigen.
First of all, let me tell you a little about our company.	Erlauben Sie mir zunächst einmal, Ihnen einige Informationen über unsere Firma zu geben.
We are leading manufacturers of …/ leading suppliers of …	Wir sind führende Hersteller/Zulieferer von …
Let me give you a copy of this folder, which summarises our activities and corporate philosophy.	Darf ich Ihnen eine Kopie dieser Mappe mit Informationen über unsere Aktivitäten und unsere Unternehmensphilosophie geben.

A tour of the site

This is the main production area.	Das ist der Hauptproduktionsbereich.
Materials are stored here and finished products are stored in the warehouse over there.	Das Material wird hier gelagert, Fertigprodukte in der Lagerhalle dort drüben.
Raw materials/bought-out parts come in here and assembly takes place there.	Rohstoffe/Zulieferteile werde hier angeliefert, während die Montage dort drüben abläuft.

Finished goods are stored here and dispatched by lorry.	*Fertigwaren werden hier gelagert und dann per Lkw verschickt.*
Our quality circle meets weekly	*Unser Qualitätsteam trifft sich wöchentlich.*
Our purchasing, marketing and distribution departments cooperate closely.	*Unsere Einkaufs-, Marketing- und Vertriebsabteilungen arbeiten eng zusammen.*

C. Geschäftsbriefe

1. Anfragen

1.1

Dear Mr. Godart,

We acknowledge receipt of your brochure presenting the new items in your Weedolex range. We would be very grateful if you would let us have further details of your products and are looking forward to hearing from you soon.

Yours sincerely,

1.2

Dear Mr. Jones,

Having seen your range of products in your latest catalogue we have been particularly attracted by the fax machine, model X3/56 on page 56 of your catalogue.

Could you please let us know whether you are in a position to deliver 50 of these fax machines immediately?

Yours sincerely,

1.3

Dear Sirs,

Thank you for your letter of 8th March announcing the launching of your new hydraulic jacks.

Could you possibly send us the address of the distributor for our area?

Yours faithfully,

1.4

Dear Sirs,

Having seen your special range of hydraulic tools at the latest spring fair in Munich, we would be grateful if you would send us your current price list and let us know your conditions for delivery

C. Business letters

1. Enquiries

1.1

Sehr geehrter Herr Godart,

vielen Dank für die Zusendung Ihrer Broschüre, in der Sie die neuen Produkte Ihrer Weedolex-Serie vorstellen. Wir wären Ihnen sehr verbunden, wenn Sie uns weitere Informationen über Ihre Produkte zusenden könnten und verbleiben

mit freundlichen Grüßen,

1.2

Sehr geehrter Herr Jones,

bei der Durchsicht Ihres neuesten Kataloges ist uns in Ihrem Produktsortiment besonders das Faxgerät Modell X3/56 auf Seite 56 aufgefallen. Könnten Sie uns bitte mitteilen, ob Ihnen 50 dieser Geräte zur sofortigen Lieferung zur Verfügung stehen?

Mit freundlichen Grüßen,

1.3

Sehr geehrte Damen und Herren,

Ihr Schreiben vom 8. März, in dem Sie Ihre neuen hydraulischen Wagenheber vorstellen, haben wir mit Interesse gelesen. Könnten Sie uns bitte die Adresse Ihres Händlers mitteilen, der für unsere Region zuständig ist?

Mit freundlichen Grüßen,

1.4

Sehr geehrte Damen und Herren,

nachdem wir auf der letzten Frühjahrsmesse in München Gelegenheit hatten, Ihr Spezialsortiment an hydraulischem Werkzeug zu sehen, wären wir Ihnen sehr verbunden, wenn Sie uns Ihre aktuelle Preisliste sowie Ihre

overseas.
We are looking forward to hearing from you soon.
Yours faithfully,

1.5
Dear Sirs,

We are one of the world's leading companies in the computer sector and are looking for new suppliers in Eastern Europe.

Could you please provide detailed information on the types and quality of computer parts and components you have available, together with your current prices and general conditions of sale.

A visit of one of your sales representatives at our purchasing branch in Prague would be highly appreciated. If you are interested, please get in touch with Mr. Thomas at the address indicated above.

We are convinced that we could establish mutually favourable business relations and are looking forward to hearing from you soon.

Yours sincerely,

2. Anfragen beantworten
2.1
Dear Mrs. Jones,

Following your request dated 12th October, please find enclosed an illustrated catalogue presenting our Texfam range as well as our current price list and conditions of sale.

The reduced prices quoted are for bulk purchases.

Lieferbedingungen für den Überseehandel zusenden könnten.

In Erwartung Ihrer baldigen Antwort verbleiben wir mit freundlichen Grüßen,

1.5
Sehr geehrte Damen und Herren,

unsere Firma gehört zu den weltweit führenden Unternehmen im Bereich der Computertechnologie und ist zur Zeit auf der Suche nach neuen Zulieferbetrieben in Osteuropa.

Wir wären Ihnen daher sehr verbunden, wenn Sie uns detaillierte Informationen über die Art und Qualität der bei Ihnen erhältlichen Computerteile und Komponenten sowie Ihre aktuelle Preisliste und allgemeinen Geschäftsbedingungen zukommen lassen könnten.

Darüber hinaus würden wir ein persönliches Gespräch mit einem Ihrer Verkaufsleiter in unserer Einkaufsniederlassung in Prag sehr begrüßen. Bitte wenden Sie sich an unseren Herrn Thomas unter oben stehender Adresse, sollte Ihrerseits Interesse an einem solchen Gespräch bestehen.

Wir sind davon überzeugt, daß Geschäftsbeziehungen zwischen unseren beiden Firmen für beide Seiten vorteilhaft sein könnten und sehen Ihrer Antwort mit Interesse entgegen.

Mit freundlichen Grüßen,

2. Acknowledging enquiries
2.1
Sehr geehrte Frau Jones,

vielen Dank für Ihre Anfrage vom 12. Oktober. Wir übersenden Ihnen gerne einen illustrierten Katalog unserer Texfam Produktserie sowie unsere aktuelle Preisliste und allgemeinen Geschäftsbedingungen. Die reduzierten Preise gelten für Großbestellungen.

We are looking forward to receiving your order in the very near future.

Yours faithfully,

2.2

Dear Mrs. Tucker,

With reference to your letter of 25th January in which you requested details on our range of bottles, boxes and containers for the packing of food products and medicines, we have pleasure in sending you our latest catalogue and current price list.

Should you need any further information, please do not hesitate to contact us or our local representative, Mr. Thomas Harding, who will be pleased to help you select the products which suit your special requirements.

We are looking forward to hearing from you soon.

Yours sincerely,

3. Auftragserteilung

3.1

Dear Sirs,

Having examined your brochure presenting your water-cooled circular saws, we would like to place a trial order with you as follows:

100 circular saws, Reference No: 900 240, thickness 230 mm.

Please let us have a confirmation of our order, indicating the expected time of delivery. Hoping that this will mark the beginning of a continuing relationship between our two companies, we remain

Yours faithfully,

Wir würden uns freuen, in baldiger Zukunft einen Auftrag von Ihnen zu erhalten.

Mit freundlichen Grüßen,

2.2

Sehr geehrte Frau Tucker,

bezugnehmend auf Ihr Schreiben vom 25. Januar, in dem Sie Informationen über unser Sortiment an Flaschen, Schachteln und Behältern für die Verpackung von Nahrungsmitteln und Medikamenten erbitten, senden wir Ihnen gerne unseren neuesten Katalog sowie unsere aktuelle Preisliste.

Sollten Sie weitere Informationen benötigen, wenden Sie sich bitte an uns oder unseren für Ihre Region zuständigen Verkaufsvertreter, Herrn Thomas Harding, der Ihnen bei der Auswahl der für Ihre Bedürfnisse am besten geeigneten Produkte gerne behilflich sein wird.

Wir würden uns freuen, bald von Ihnen zu hören.

Mit freundlichen Grüßen,

3. Placing orders

3.1

Sehr geehrte Damen und Herren,

nach Durchsicht Ihrer Informationsbroschüre mit der Beschreibung Ihrer wassergekühlten Rundsägen haben wir uns entschlossen, Ihnen wie folgt einen ersten Probeauftrag zu erteilen:

100 Rundsägen, Bestellnummer 900 240; 230 mm starkes Sägeblatt.

Bitte senden Sie uns eine Auftragsbestätigung zu und teilen uns die voraussichtliche Lieferzeit mit. In der Hoffnung, daß dieser Auftrag den Anfang einer dauerhaften Geschäftsbeziehung zwischen unseren beiden Firmen darstellt, verbleiben wir

mit freundlichen Grüßen,

3.2

Dear Mrs. Simpson,

Following our telephone conversation of 10 March, we are ordering for immediate delivery:

150 safety valves – DN 10-250, series 8000.

Please send the goods by normal cargo service.

Hoping that you will execute the order with your usual care, I remain

Yours sincerely,

3.3

Dear Mr. Johnson,

Thank you for your quotation of 1st March as well as for the samples of textiles you sent us.

We have the pleasure of sending you enclosed our order No. 54/3. Please arrange for delivery by 24th March as the textiles are required to complete an urgent export order.

We are looking forward to receiving your advice of dispatch.

Yours faithfully,

4. Auftragsabwicklung

4.1

Dear Sirs,

Thank you for your letter of 4th November and for the accompanying Order No. 45/3.

We will let you know as soon as possible when we will be able to ship the goods and we have already contacted our local forwarder to arrange for delivery at your plant in Bochum. We shall do our utmost to have the goods delivered by 1st December, as requested.

Yours faithfully,

3.2

Sehr geehrte Frau Simpson,

bezugnehmend auf unser Telefonat vom 10. März bestellen wir zur sofortigen Lieferung:

150 Sicherheitsventile – DN 10-250, Modell 8000.

Bitte schicken Sie uns die Ware mit normaler Fracht. In der Hoffnung, daß Sie auch diesen Auftrag mit der üblichen Sorgfalt ausführen werden, verbleibe ich

mit freundlichen Grüßen,

3.3

Sehr geehrter Herr Johnson,

vielen Dank für Ihr Angebot vom 1. März und die Stoffmuster, die Sie uns zugeschickt haben.

Es freut uns sehr, Ihnen heute als Anlage unsere Auftragsnummer 54/3 übersenden zu können. Bitte veranlassen Sie, daß die bestellte Ware spätestens am 24. März geliefert wird, da die Stoffe für die Ausführung eines dringenden Exportauftrages benötigt werden.

In Erwartung Ihrer Versandanzeige verbleiben wir mit freundlichen Grüßen,

4. Dealing with orders

4.1

Sehr geehrte Damen und Herren,

vielen Dank für Ihr Schreiben vom 4. November und Ihre beigefügte Auftragsnummer 45/3.

Wir werden Sie sobald wie möglich darüber informieren, wann die Ware versandbereit sein wird. Wir haben bereits unser hiesiges Speditionsunternehmen mit dem Transport der Ware an Ihr Werk in Bochum beauftragt. Wir werden alles in unseren Kräften stehende tun, um die Ware wie gewünscht bis zum 1. Dezember zu liefern.

Mit freundlichen Grüßen,

4.2

Dear Sirs,

I have pleasure in acknowledging receipt of your order No. 5467/4 of the 15th of this month.

We are pleased to inform you that we have all requested articles in stock and that your orders should be ready for shipment next week. We have already contacted our forwarder to arrange for transport by lorry.

Yours faithfully,

5. Verpackung und Transport
5.1

Dear Sirs,

Following our order No. 234/5th of February, we would like to point out once more that the 20 grinding machines ordered are to be delivered to our branch in Hamburg.

On the other hand, the goods ordered on order form No. 356/5 are to be sent to our warehouse in Bremen.

Please make sure that the machines and all other items are carefully packed and that the boxes are marked with international signs.

Yours faithfully,

6. Lieferbestätigung
6.1

Dear Mr. Martin,

We have received our trial order No. 345 consisting of car parts and accessories which have arrived in perfect condition.

If, as we hope, your products prove to be suitable for our new line of production,

4.2

Sehr geehrte Damen und Herren,

wir bestätigen gerne den Erhalt Ihrer Auftragsnummer 5467/4 vom 15. dieses Monats und freuen uns, Ihnen mitteilen zu können, daß wir alle bestellten Artikel auf Lager haben und Ihre Bestellung in der nächsten Woche versandbereit sein wird. Wir haben unser Speditionsunternehmen bereits mit dem Transport per Lkw beauftragt.

Mit freundlichen Grüßen,

5. Packing and transport
5.1

Sehr geehrte Damen und Herren,

bezugnehmend auf unsere Auftragsnummer 234/5 vom 5. Februar möchten wir noch einmal darauf hinweisen, daß die 20 bestellten Schleifmaschinen an unsere Niederlassung in Hamburg geliefert werden sollen, während die in Auftragsnummer 356/5 bestellte Ware an unser Lager in Bremen gehen soll.

Bitte sorgen Sie dafür, daß sowohl die Maschinen als auch die anderen Artikel sorgfältig verpackt werden und die Versandkisten mit internationalen Zeichen versehen sind.

Mit freundlichen Grüßen,

6. Confirmation of delivery
6.1

Sehr geehrter Herr Martin,

wir haben die Autoteile und Zubehörteile entsprechend unserem Probeauftrag Nr. 345 in einwandfreiem Zustand erhalten.

Sollten sich, wie wir hoffen, Ihre Produkte für unsere neue Produktionsserie als geeignet er-

we shall be pleased to order larger volumes from you in future.
Yours faithfully,

6.2
Dear Sirs,

We woud like to thank you for your consignment of 23th March which arrived this morning within the required time and in good condition. Your invoice will be settled immediately.

We hope to be in a position to send you further orders soon. Thank you once more for the prompt execution of our order.

Yours faithfully,

7. Beschwerden
7.1
Dear Sirs,

We have just received the goods you sent us in accordance with our order No. 287 A.

Unfortunately, we have to inform you that the tools delivered do not match the quality of the tools you presented during the latest spring fair in London. The top quality of these tools was the main reason for our decision to place this order with you during the trade fair.

Moreover, the invoice attached does not include the early order discount agreed upon.

Could you please make the necessary arrangements for the replacement and delivery of tools which are up to the expected quality standard and send us an amended invoice.

In anticipation of your reply, we remain Yours faithfully,

---

weisen, werden wir Ihnen in Zukunft gerne größere Aufträge erteilen.
Mit freundlichen Grüßen,

6.2
Sehr geehrte Damen und Herren,

vielen Dank für Ihre Warensendung vom 23. März, die heute morgen rechtzeitig und in tadellosem Zustand bei uns eingetroffen ist. Ihre Rechnung werden wir umgehend begleichen.

Wir hoffen bald in der Lage zu sein, Ihnen weitere Aufträge zu erteilen. Nochmals vielen Dank für die schnelle Erledigung unseres Auftrags.

Mit freundlichen Grüßen,

7. Complaints
7.1
Sehr geehrte Damen und Herren,

wir haben soeben die Ware erhalten, die Sie uns in Ausführung unserer Auftragsnummer 287 A zugesandt haben.

Leider müssen wir Ihnen mitteilen, daß die gelieferten Werkzeuge nicht der Qualität der von Ihnen auf der letzten Frühjahrsmesse in London ausgestellten Werkzeuge entsprechen. Deren herausragende Qualität war der ausschlaggebende Grund dafür, daß wir Ihnen diesen Auftrag bereits auf der Messe erteilten.

Weiterhin berücksichtigt die von Ihnen ausgestellte Rechnung nicht den vereinbarten Frühdispositionsrabatt.

Bitte sorgen Sie für umgehenden Ersatz und die Zulieferung von Werkzeug, das der erwarteten Qualität entspricht, und schicken Sie uns eine berichtigte Rechnung.

In Erwartung Ihrer Antwort verbleiben wir mit freundlichen Grüßen,

7.2

Dear Sirs,

We regret to inform you that your consignment of computer equipment you sent us in execution of our order No. 23/349 was delivered at our plant in Bochum in a very bad state.

You can surely understand our disappointment.

We are now returning the damaged items and would be grateful if you would replace them immediately.

Yours faithfully,

7.3

Dear Sir,

The 20 bales of silk of our order No. 368 of 2nd April arrived today.

On examination we find them soiled at the edges because of torn outer wrappings. This is not the first time that we have had to make such a complaint about cloth received from you, and we must ask you to see the goods sent to us are more carefully packed.

The bales of silk are useable, but we feel that you should allow us a reduction of 20% on the price. The bales are available for inspection should you wish to appoint a representative.

Yours faithfully,

7.2

Sehr geehrte Damen und Herren,

wir bedauern Ihnen mitteilen zu müssen, daß die Computerteile, die Sie in Ausführung unserer Auftragsnummer 23/349 an unser Werk in Bochum geliefert haben, dort in sehr schlechtem Zustand eingetroffen sind.

Sie können unsere Enttäuschung darüber sicher verstehen.

Wir senden Ihnen hiermit die beschädigten Artikel zu unserer Entlastung zurück und wären Ihnen sehr verbunden, wenn Sie sie umgehend ersetzen könnten.

Mit freundlichen Grüßen,

7.3

Sehr geehrter Herr,

die 20 Ballen Seide, die wir am 2. April unter Auftragsnummer 386 bestellten, sind heute bei uns eingetroffen. Bei der Überprüfung der Ware mußten wir leider feststellen, daß die Ballen an den Rändern verschmutzt sind, da ihre äußere Verpackung aufgerissen war.

Dies ist nicht das erste Mal, daß wir bei Lieferungen Ihrer Firma Grund zu derartigen Beschwerden hatten und wir müssen Sie dringend bitten, in Zukunft darauf zu achten, daß die an uns gesandte Ware sorgfältiger verpackt ist.

Die Seidenballen sind brauchbar, aber wir halten einen Preisnachlaß von 20% für angemessen. Die Ballen können jederzeit von einem von Ihnen benannten Gutachter inspiziert werden.

Mit freundlichen Grüßen,

D. Incoterms und gängige Abkürzungen im Wirtschaftsenglischen
D. Incoterms and common abbreviations in business English

1. Abbreviations

Anno Domini	AD	im Jahre
ante meridiem, before noon	am	vormittags
appendix	app	Anhang
approximately	approx	ungefähr, etwa
arrival	arr	Ankunft
association	assoc	Verein, Verband
bill of exchange	B/E	Wechsel
bill of lading	B/L	Konnossement
cash on delivery	C.O.D	Barzahlung bei Lieferung
cash with order	C.W.O	Zahlung bei Auftragserteilung
delivery order	D/O	Lieferschein
exemplum gratia = for example	e.g.	z. B. = zum Beispiel
enlosure(s)	enc(s)	Anlage(n)
id est = that means	i.e.	d.h. = das heißt
without interest	ex interest	zinslos
gross	gr	brutto
gross weight	gr wt	Bruttogewicht
letter of credit	L/C	Akkreditiv
outstanding, out of stock	o/s	offenstehend, nicht auf Lager
paid	pd	bezahlt
registered	reg, regd	eingetragen
standing order	S/O	Dauerauftrag
value added tax	VAT	Mehrwertsteuer
by way of	via	via, über

2. INCOTERMS

ex works	EXW	ab Werk
free carrier	FCA	frei Frachtführer
free alongside ship	FAS	frei Längsseite Schiff
free on board	FOB	frei Schiff/frei an Bord
cost and freight	CFR	Kosten und Fracht
cost, insurance and freight	CIF	Kosten, Versicherung und Fracht
carriage paid to	CPT	Fracht frei
carriage and insurance paid to	CIP	frachtfrei und versichert
delivered at frontier	DAF	geliefert Grenze
delivered ex ship	DES	geliefert ab Schiff
delivered ex quay	DEQ	geliefert ab Kai
delivered duty unpaid	DDU	geliefert unverzollt
delivered duty paid	DDP	geliefert verzollt

E. Nationale und internationale Einkaufs- und Materialwirtschaftsverbände
E. National and international associations for purchasing and materials management

AACAM	Asociacion Argentina de compras y administracion de materiales	Secretariat: AACAM Mr. Noberto Villar Tucuman 141-6 Piso 1049 Buenos Aires, **Argentina**	Tel.: +54 1 311 8421
ABAM	Associacao Brasileira de Administracao de Material	Secretariat: ABAM Mr. Walter Pereira Avenida Nazareth 567 92030 Canoas Porto Alegre, **Brazil**	Tel.: +55 512 723245
ABCA	Association Belge des Chefs D´Approvisionnement	Secretariat: ABCA Mr. A. Dron Rue Ranci, 9 6860 Leglise, **Belgium**	Tel.: +32 63 433197 Fax: +32 41 751895
ADACI	Assoziazione Degli Aprovvigioatori e Compratori Italiani	Secretariat: ADACI Mr. Osvaldo Re Viale Ranzoni 17 20149 Milano, **Italy**	Tel.: +39 2 40072474 Fax: +39 240090246
AERCE	Asociacion Espanola de Responsables de Compras y de Existencias	Secretariat: AERCE Mr. J. M. Fernandez Fabrega c/o Rosselon 183 entlo.1a 08036 Barcelona, **Spain**	Tel.: +34 33 22 6984 Fax: +3433 22 6984
AGECOM	Associacion Gerentes de Materiales y Servicios; Costa Rica	Secretariat: AGECOM Mrs. Marielos Azofeifa Pieles Costarricenses P.O. Box 695 1000 San Jose; **Costa Rica**	Tel.: +506 41 23 10
AIPMM	Australian Institute of Purchasing and Materials Ltd.	Secretariat: AIPMM Mr. David Burrows P.O. Box 278 Burwoord 315 Victoria, **Australia**	Tel.:+61 3 808 0600
APCADEC	Associacao Portuguesa de Compras e Aprovisionamento	Secretariat: APCADEC Mr. Carlos Diniz de Torres 201 - 3 Dto 1700 Lisboa, **Portugal**	Tel.: +51 1 758 5340 Fax: +35 15 852707

ATUGA	Association Tunisienne de Gestion des Approvisionnements et des Achat	Secretariat: ATUGA Mr. Taoufik Ben Salah 78 Rue de Syrie 1002 Tunis, **Tunisia**	Tel.: +216 1 788 113
BME	Bundesverband Materialwirtschaft, Einkauf und Logistik e.V.	Secretariat: BME Dr. Ludwig Veltmann Bolongarostr. 82 65929 Frankfurt am Main, **Germany**	Tel.: +49 69 30838-100 Fax: +49 69 30838-199
CDAF	Compagnie des Dirigeants D´Apprivisionnement et Acheteurs de France	Secretariat: CDAF Mr. Michel Raffet 6, Rue Paul Czezanne 93364 Neuilly Plaisance Cedex, **France**	Tel.: +33 14 3082020 Fax: +33 14 3085389
CIPS	The Chartered Institute of Purchasing & Supply	Secretariat: CIPS Mr. Peter Thomson Easton House Easton on the Hill, Stamford Lincs PE9 3NZ, **Great Britain**	Tel.: +44 780 56 777 Fax: +44 1780 51610
CORPAC	Corporacion Nacional de Ejecutivos de Abastecimiento y Contratos	Secretariat: CORPAC Mr. Amador Auad Herezi Guardia Vieja 181 Apt. 1005 Santiago - Providencia, **Chile**	Tel.: +562 231 1392 / 2911
DILF	Dansk Indkobs - Og Logistikforum	Secretariat: DILF Mrs. Gudde Olsbro Charlottenlundvej 26 290 Hellerup, **Denmark**	Tel.: +45 31 622 401 Fax: +45 31 211566
HALPIM	Hungarian Association of Logistics, Purchasing and Inventory Management	Secretariat: HALPIM Ms. Anita Köhegyi Veres Palne u. 36 1053 Budapest, **Hungary**	Tel.: +36 1 1172 959 Fax: +36 134 20 500
HPI	Hellenic Purchasing Institute	Secretariat: HPI Mr. Kadoglou Antonis 36, Aristotelous Street 104.33 Athens, **Greece**	Tel.: +30 1 82 26 860 Fax: +30 18 226 204
IFPMM	**International Federation of Purchasing and Materials Management**	Secretariat: IFPMM Mr. Ferry J. de Kraaker Guurtjeslaan 18 Postbox 289 1860 AG, Bergen (NH), **Netherlands**	Tel.: +31 220 81 8748 Fax: +3170320 4940

IIMM	Indian Institute of Materials Management	Secretariat: IIMM Mr. K. R. Rama Ayyar 406, Kaliandas Udyog Bhavan Prabhadevi Bombay 400 025, **India**	Tel.: +91 22 437 2820
IIPMM	Irish Institute of Purchasing and Materials Management	Secretariat: IIPMM Mr. Owen O'Neill John Player House South Circular Road Dublin 8, **Ireland**	Tel.: +353 1 546 544 Fax: +353 1 4546544
IPMM	Institute of Purchasing and Materials Management; New Zealand	Secretariat: IPMM Mr. David Strutton 19, Moa Street Lower Hutt; **New Zealand**	Tel.: +64 4 569 6652
IPSA	The Institute of Purchasing South Africa	Secretariat: IPSA Dr. R. J. Stewart P.O. Box 82112 Southdale 2135, **South Africa**	Tel.: +27 11 726 3200
IPS HGK	Institute of Purchasing and Supply Hong Kong	Secretariat: IPS HGK Mr. Albert Au P.O. Box K 72241 Kowloon, **Hong Kong**	Tel.: +852 788 9146
IPSMA	Israeli Purchasing and Supply Managers Association	Secretariat: IPSMA Bilha Karmon Kaplan 12 Street P.O. Box 7128 61071 Tel Aviv, **Israel**	Tel.: +972 3 696 6944 Fax: +972 3 6919047
JMMA	Japan Materials Management Association	Secretariat: JMMA Mr. T. Miyazawa Ginza TS Sankei Bldg. 7F 14-5 Ginza 6-Chome Chuo Ku Tokyo 104, **Japan**	Tel.: +81 3 3545 6131
KPMA	Korea Purchasing & Materials Association	Secretariat: KPMA Mr. Ph. D. Jin-Hyung, Jin 151-10, Ssanglim-Dong Chungku, Seoul (2 F, Ssangsu Building), **Korea**	Tel.: +82 2277 2784

MIPMM	Malaysian Institute of Purchasing and Materials Management	Secretariat: MIPMM Mr. Peter C. O. Lee 5, Jalan Hargreaves 116 00 Penang, **Malaysia**	Tel.: +60 4 88 2771
NAPM	National Association of Purchasing Management	Secretariat: NAPM Mr. R. Jerry Baker - CPM 2055 E Centennical Circle P.O. Box 22160 Tempe, AZ 85285-2160, **USA**	Tel.: +1 602 752 6276/3009
NEVI	Nederlandse Vereniging Voor Inkoop Management	Secretariat: NEVI Mr. E. J. F. Bosman P.O. Box 409 2260 AK Leidschendam, **Netherlands**	Tel.: +31 70 320 9291 Fax: +31 70 320 4940
NIGP	National Institute of Governmental Purchasing Inc., USA	Secretariat: NIGP Mr. J. E. Brinkamm, CPPO 11800 Sunrise Valley Drive Suite 1050 Reston, VA 22091, **USA**	Tel.: +1 703 715 9400
NIMA	Norwegian Association of Purchasing and Logistics	Secretariat: NIMA Mr. Karl-Erik Bastiansen P.O. Box 6703 Rodeloka 0503 Oslo, **Norway**	Tel.: +47 22 379 710 Fax: +47 22 385 323
ÖPWZ	Arbeitsgemeinschaft Einkauf — Forum für Beschaffung, Materialwirtschaft und Logistik in ÖPWZ, Österreich	Secretariat: ÖPWZ Mr. Heinz Pechek Postfach 131 Rockhgasse 6 1010 Wien, **Austria**	Tel.: +431533 863656 Fax: +431533 863672
PSLZ		**Poland**	Fax: +48 22 391 400
SILF	Swedish National Association of Purchasing and Logistics	Secretariat: SILF Mr. Seth Jonsson Box 1278 164 28 Kista, **Sweden**	Tel.: +46 8 752 0470 Fax: +46 8 750 6410
SIMM	Singapore Institute of Materials Management	Secretariat: SIMM Dr. Peter Law Level 5, Pico Creative Centre 20 Kallang Avenue **Singapore** 1233	Tel.: +65 295 4427
SIPMM	Singapore Institute of Purchasing and Materials Management	Secretariat: SIPMM Mr. Patrick Poh NPB Building # 14-02 2 Bukik Merah Central **Singapore** 0315	Tel.: +65 273 4172

SMTY	Suomen Materiaalitaloudellinen Yhdistys	Secretariat: SMTY Mr. Tytti Arimo Kumpulantie 3A 00520 Helsinki, **Finland**	Tel.: +358 0 1461 767 Fax: +358 0 177 675
SVME	Schweizerischer Verband für Materialwirtschaft und Einkauf	Secretariat: SVME Mr. Arnold Bachofner Postfach 5001 Aarau, **Switzerland**	Tel.: +41 6424 7131 Fax: +41 628246045
TPC	The Thai Purchasing Club	Secretariat: TPC Mr. Cheocharn Ratanamahatana 940/98 Soi Challiang 7 Banga - Trad Road, Banga - Prakannong Bankog 10260, **Thailand**	
VIB	Vereiniging Voor Inkoop En Bedrijfslogistiek; Belgium	Secretariat: VIB Mr. Roger Gnat Frankrijklei 40 bus 2 2000 Antwerpen, **Belgium**	Tel.: +32 3 233 0329 Fax: +32 3 286 8098

NOTIZEN/NOTES

NOTIZEN/NOTES

NOTIZEN/NOTES

NOTIZEN/NOTES

NOTIZEN/NOTES

NOTIZEN/NOTES

NOTIZEN/NOTES

NOTIZEN/NOTES

NOTIZEN/NOTES

Zur Autorin

Seit einigen Jahren ist Alexandra Lüders mit ihrem Sprachendienst P & L Translations europaweit tätig. Schon während ihrer Sprachstudien im In- und Ausland entwickelte sie durch ihre Tätigkeit für den Bundesverband Einkauf, Materialwirtschaft und Einkauf e.v. (BME), Frankfurt, den Tätigkeitsschwerpunkt Einkauf und Materialwirtschaft. Neben klassischen Übersetzungs- und Dolmetscherarbeiten, zu denen auch die Ausarbeitung der monatlich in der Fachzeitschrift Beschaffung aktuell erscheinenden Kolumne „Außenansichten" gehört, ist sie zur Zeit hauptsächlich als Tutorin bei firmeninternen Sprachtrainingsmaßnahmen „Englisch für den internationalen Einkauf", die in Kooperation mit der BME-AKADEMIE angeboten werden, tätig.

The author

Alexandra Lüders is the author of the present dictionary as well as the owner and managing director of the international language service P&L Translations. During her language studies in Germany and other European countries she started working for the German Association of Materials Management, Purchasing and Logistics (BME), thus developing a special interest in the field of purchasing and materials management. Apart from her work as a translator and interpreter she publishes articles and press reviews on new developments in international purchasing and logistics in the German magazin "Beschaffung aktuell". Moreover, she is in charge of the special in-house language workshops "English for International Purchasing" P&L Translations offers, partly in cooperation with the BME-AKADEMIE, in Germany, Switzerland and UK.

Zum Verlag

Die Konradin Verlagsgruppe, Leinfelden, verlegt auf dem hier angesprochenen Themengebiet die Fachzeitschrift ‚BA Beschaffung aktuell', meinungsbildendes Magazin für Einkauf und Beschaffung und gleichzeitig offizielles Organ des Bundesverbandes Materialwirtschaft, Einkauf und Logistik e.V. (BME).

Themenspektrum: Fach- und Marktinformationen aus der Einkaufspraxis, aus Wirtschaft, Wissenschaft und Technik, für das unternehmerisch handelnde Einkaufsmanagement.

Herausgeber: Konrad Kohlhammer
Chefredaktion: Heinz K. Kruse
Anzeigen: Klaus Paletta
46. Jahrgang
Erscheint monatlich, plus 1 Special (BeschaffungsMARKT)
Bezugspreis: Jahresabonnement Inland DM 191,10/Jahresabonnement Ausland DM 202,80 (Studentenpreise auf Anfrage)
Probeheft: Konradin Verlag, Leserservice BA, 70765 Leinfelden-Echterdingen, Fax 0711 7594-221, Tel. 0711 7594-229

The publishing house

The Konradin Group, Leinfelden/Germany, publishes the technical magazin BA Beschaffung aktuell, a specialist publication in the field of purchasing and materials management which is widely known among experts in Germany. Moreover, BA Beschaffung aktuell is the official publication of the German Association of Materials Management, Purchasing and Logistics (BME). The magazine provides purchasing managers with up-to-date information about general economic issues, technical innovations and market developments as well as new specialist and scientific theories and findings in the field of purchasing, logistics and material management.

Publisher: Konrad Kohlhammer
Editor-in-chief: Heinz K. Kruse
Advertising Manager: Klaus Paletta
46th year of publishing.
BA Beschaffung aktuell is published once a month. Once a year, there is a special edition called BeschaffungsMARKT.
Subscription fees: Annual subscription/Germany: DM 191.10, Annual subscription/abroad: DM 202.80
Should you be interested in a free sample please contact: Konradin Verlag, Leserservice BA, 70765 Leinfelden-Echterdingen, Germany, Fax 0711 7594-221, Tel. 0711 7594-229

Wörterbuch der Materialwirtschaft
Deutsch-Englisch/ Englisch-Deutsch
Kurzeinführung PC-Version

Dictionary of Materials Management
German-English/ English-German
Short Introduction in the Computer Programme

Die Computerversion des Wörterbuchs der Materialwirtschaft ermöglicht einen leichten Zugriff auf eine Vielzahl wichtiger Begriffe in Einkauf und Materialwirtschaft. Um einen größtmöglichen Bedienkomfort zu gewährleisten, existieren folgende Features:

- ▷ Alle Aktionen sind mittels Tastatur erreichbar.
- ▷ Kontext-sensitive Hilfe ist jederzeit über die Taste F1 zu erreichen.
- ▷ Zwei Suchmethoden erleichtern das Auffinden von Begriffen, außerdem besteht die zusätzliche Möglichkeit der Pattern-matching-Suche (Sternchen-Suche).
- ▷ Erweiterbarkeit des „Wörterbuches der Materialwirtschaft" um persönliche Vokabelverzeichnisse.
- ▷ Transparente Einbindung der selbst erstellten Vokabelverzeichnisse in die Programmumgebung.
- ▷ Importmöglichkeit von externen Vokabalverzeichnissen.
- ▷ Einfaches Kopieren von Daten zu anderen Windows-Anwendungen über die Zwischenablage.
- ▷ Historylisten geben einen Überblick über die zuletzt gesuchten Begriffe.
- ▷ Automatische Speicherung der Historylisten für den nächsten Programmaufruf.
- ▷ Schnelles Blättern in den Wörterbuch-Dateien erleichtert Suche nach Begriffen.
- ▷ Freie Fontwahl für das Ansichtsfenster des „Wörterbuches der Materialwirtschaft".

The computer version of the "Dictionary of Materials Management" gives you easy access to a large number of important terms and expressions used in purchasing and materials management. The following features make the use of the "Dictionary of Materials Management" extremely easy and comfortable:

- ▷ *You can use your keyboard to work with the Dictionary of "Materials Management".*
- ▷ *You can open a context-sensitive Help File any time by simply pressing F1.*
- ▷ *You have two standard search options which make the search for special terms and expressions easy and efficient and the additional option of a pattern matching search (Search for stars).*
- ▷ *You can extend the "Dictionary of Materials Management" by including your own terms and expressions.*
- ▷ *You can make your own terms and expressions visibly distinguishable from the original "Dictionary of Materials Management".*
- ▷ *You can import external vocabulary files to be integrated into the "Dictionary of Materials Management".*
- ▷ *You can easily copy data from the "Dictionary of Materials Management" to be used in other Microsoft Windows Applications by using the clipboard.*
- ▷ *You can easily look up the most recently used terms and expressions in your History List.*
- ▷ *You can save the History List for later use.*
- ▷ *You can scroll through the files of the "Dictionary of Materials Management".*

▷ Größenanpassung der Programmoberfläche an die Windows-Einstellung.
▷ Geringer Speicherverbrauch: nur aktuelle Begriffe werden im Speicher gehalten.

Das Programm ist in fünf verschiedene Komponenten eingeteilt, die über ein Register erreicht werden können. Jede Komponente behandelt ein eigenes Themengebiet. Die Zugriffsart auf die Informationen hängt von den jeweiligen Datenstrukturen ab und ist eingehend in der Hilfedatei der PC-Version des „Wörterbuches der Materialwirtschaft" erklärt.

▷ *You can choose the fonts in your view of the "Dictionary of Materials Management".*
▷ *You can adjust the size of the view of the "Dictionary of Materials Management" to your other Microsoft Windows applications.*
▷ *The programme is highly economical: only the most recently used terms and expressions are saved specially, thus taking up little storage capacity on your hard disk.*

The programme consists of five different chapters which can be selected from a register in the "Dictionary of Materials Management". Each chapter is dedicated to a special subject. Access to the information depends on the data structure of the different chapters. For details please refer to the Help Files of the computer version of the "Dictionary of Materials Management".

Wörterbuch der Materialwirtschaft

Deutsch-Englisch/ Englisch-Deutsch

Kurzanleitung PC-Version

Inhalt
1. Systemanforderungen
2. Installation
3. De-Installation
4. Benutzung
5. Bemerkung zur Gewährleistung

1. Systemanforderungen

Das Programm ist für Windows entwickelt worden und läuft sowohl unter Windows 3.x als auch Windows 95. Für die Installation werden ca. 1.8 MB freier Speicher auf der Festplatte benötigt.

2. Installation

Die Installation erfolgt unter Windows durch das Programm ‚Install.exe', daß sich auf der Diskette befindet. Hierzu kann das Installationsprogramm unter Windows 3.x aus dem Dateimanager heraus aufgerufen werden und unter Windows 95 aus dem Explorer heraus.

Nach Angabe des gewünschten Zielverzeichnisses durch direkte Angabe oder über den Verzeichnisdialog erfolgt die Installation auf die Festplatte durch Betätigen des Installations-Buttons. Während der Installation wird auf Wunsch eine Programmgruppe oder ein Icon in einer bestehenden Programmgruppe erzeugt.

WICHTIG: Es ist stets nur eine installierte Version des Programms möglich. Um eine erneute Installation durchzuführen MUSS das Programm zuvor mit dem Programm ‚Install.exe' deinstalliert werden, da sonst KEINE Lizenzfreischaltung erfolgt. Das Wör-

Dictionary of Materials Management

German-English/ English-German

Important Information about the Computer Programme

Contents
1. *Hardware requirements*
2. *Installation*
3. *Deinstallation*
4. *How to use the computer version of the "Dictionary of Materials Management"*
5. *Warrenty*

1. Hardware requirements

The present programme has been developed as a Microsoft Windows Application and can be installed under both Windows 3.1 and Windows 95. Approx. 1.8 MB free memory on your hard disk are required for the installation of the programme ion your personal computer.

2. Installation

You can install the programme of the "Dictionary of Materials Management" by using the installation programme INSTALL.EXE on the installation disk. Open the standard installation programme, e.g., via your file manager in Windows 3.1 or the programme Explorer in Windows 95.

Insert the installation disk and tell the programme in which directory on your hard disk you want the programme to be saved by using your keyboard or the directory dialogue shown. You can start the installation process by selecting the Installations button in the dialogue. During the installation process you can choose whether you want a separate directory to be created for the programme or an icon in an existing directory.

Note:

This is not free software. Only one installation per programme is possible and allowed as the licence for this programme is limited to one user only.

terbuch-Programm DARF also NICHT einfach von der Festplatte gelöscht werden.

3. De-Installation

Die De-Installation erfolgt unter Windows durch das Programm ‚Install.exe' (Aufruf: siehe Installation). Nachdem der Pfad des installierten Wörterbuchprogramms angegeben und die Lizenzrechte überprüft wurden, erfolgt die De-Installation.

Falls eigene Erweiterungen für die Wörterbücher existieren, sollten diese zuvor gesichert werden, damit diese Daten verloren gehen (s. Verzeichnis ‚Konradin/private').

Nach erfolgreich erfolgter De-Installation ist die Lizenz für eine erneute Installation wieder freigeschaltet.

4. Benutzung

Die Benutzung des Programms kann der beiliegenden Hilfedatei entnommen werden. Diese kann aus dem Programm heraus über den Menüpunkt ‚Hilfe/Inhalt' aufgerufen werden. Außerdem ist jederzeit die kontextsensitive Hilfe über die Taste ‚F1' zu erreichen.

5. Lizenzvereinbarung

Diese Software darf nur durch Beschaffung Aktuell (Konradin Verlag), Stuttgart/Deutschland vertrieben werden.

6. Bemerkung zur Gewährleistung

Dieses Programm wurde sorgfältig entwickelt und auf mehreren Systemen unterschiedlicher Konfigurationen getestet. Weder der Autor dieses Programms noch eine der anderen an der Produktion und dem Vertrieb dieser Software beteiligten Parteien, ist für direkten, indirekten, resultierenden oder zufälligen Schaden haftbar, der aus der Benutzung oder nicht möglichen Benutzung dieses Produktes hervorgehen sollte. Dies schließt Schäden für den Verlust von Geschäftsgewinnen, die Unterbrechung von Geschäften und den Verlust von Informationen usw. ein.

Should you wish to install the programme on another personal computer, you will have to deinstall it first off the personal computer on which you installed it in the first place. In order to achieve this you will have to start the installation programme which you will find on your installation disk and start the deinstallation process. If you fail to do this and simply delete the programme from your hard disk, you will not be able to install it again.

3. Deinstallation

For the deinstallation you will need to start the programme "Install.exe" in Windows and indicate the directory in which you have saved the programme on your hard disk. Then press the Deinstallation button. After having checked the installation and your licence number, the programme will deinstall the "Dictionary of Materials Management" off your hard disk. Your personal vocabulary files will be backed up automatically in the process. After the deinstallation process has been successfully completed, you can install the programme on another personal computer.

4. How to use the computer version of the "Dictionary of Materials Management"

All details on the use of the present computer programme can be found in the Help File included in the programme. You can get to the Help File by selecting the option Help/Contents from the main menu of the programme. Moreover, you can get context-sensitive help any time by simply pressing the F1 key on your keyboard.

5. Licence terms

This software may only be distributed by Beschaffung aktuell (Konradin Verlag), Stuttgart, Germany.

6. Warranty

This software and the accompanying files are sold "as is" and without warranties as to the performance or merchantability or any other warranties whether expressed or implied. No warranty of fitness for a particular purpose is offered. No warranty on any form of performance of this software is offered. Neither the author of the printed "Dictionary of Materials Management" nor the author

7. Copyright
Alle Copyrights liegen ausschließlich bei Alex Lueders, P&L Translations, Frankfurt/Deutschland.

of the computer version of the "Dictionary of Materials Management" are liable for any damages caused by use or failure of this software, including but not limited to loss of data, damage to hardware, or virus infection.

7. Copyrights
All copyrights are held exclusively by Alex Lüders, of P&L Translations, Frankfurt/Germany.